HELL OR HIGH WATER
New Zealand Merchant Seafarers Remember the War

Notes: Page 42 Hauraki group capture.
Re mv HAURAKI " 52 Ref: Sailing under N.Z. Articles of Agreement

Also in this series:

'A Unique Sort of Battle': New Zealanders Remember Crete
Inside Stories: New Zealand Prisoners of War Remember
A Fair Sort of Battering: New Zealanders Remember the Italian Campaign
The Desert Road: New Zealanders Remember the North African Campaign

HELL OR HIGH WATER
New Zealand Merchant Seafarers Remember the War

Edited by Neill Atkinson

Foreword by the Right Honourable Helen Clark

HarperCollins*Publishers*

in association with
the Ministry for Culture and Heritage

National Library of New Zealand Cataloguing-in-Publication Data

Hell or high water : New Zealand merchant seafarers remember
the war / edited by Neill Atkinson.
Includes index.
ISBN 1-86950-519-0
1. World War, 1939-1945—Personal narratives, New Zealand.
2. World War, 1939-1945—Naval operations. 3. Merchant
marine. I. Atkinson, Neill.
940.545092323—dc 22

First published 2005
HarperCollins*Publishers (New Zealand) Limited*
P.O. Box 1, Auckland

Crown copyright © 2005

All rights reserved. No part of this publication may be reproduced, stored in a retrieval system or transmitted in any form or by any means, electronic, mechanical, photocopying, recording or otherwise, without the prior written permission of the publishers.

ISBN 1 86950 519 0

Set in Bembo

Cover design by Darren Holt, HarperCollins Design Studio
Book design by Dexter Fry
Typeset by Janine Brougham
Printed by Everbest Printing, China

Main cover photo: *Ships glide through surface fog in the Arctic Sea.* Royal New Zealand Navy Museum
Inset photo: *Seamen on the Union Company freighter* Kaiwarra, *photographed in Auckland in December 1940 while loading RNZAF aircraft for delivery to Fiji.* Museum of Wellington City & Sea

This book is dedicated to all the merchant seafarers who lost their lives during the Second World War.

Foreword

I am very pleased to welcome this book of personal accounts from New Zealanders who served in the Merchant Navy during the Second World War.

Hell or High Water continues a series of books based on oral histories of veterans from the 1939–45 conflict. This volume is a little different from its predecessors, because the veterans whose stories appear in the following pages were neither soldiers, airmen nor naval sailors. Instead, they belonged to what was sometimes called the 'fourth service'—the Merchant Navy, whose ships delivered troops, military equipment and essential cargoes of food, fuel and raw materials across the world's oceans.

An island nation half a world away from its main trading partner, New Zealand was overwhelmingly dependent on sea transport for its prosperity and security. We relied on merchant ships and seafarers to deliver our farm produce to Britain and to Allied forces in the Pacific, and to return with manufactured goods, oil and war supplies. Merchant ships carried New Zealand troops to the battlefields of the Middle East, Europe and the Pacific, brought home the wounded, evacuated civilians from Singapore and elsewhere, and performed dozens of other tasks. Smaller vessels maintained essential services across the Tasman, in the South Pacific and around the New Zealand coast.

The seafarers who manned these ships were essentially civilian volunteers going about their ordinary jobs in extraordinary times. They ranged in age from 14 to at least 75, and most did not wear uniforms. Civilian status counted for little during wartime, as German and Japanese forces targeted Allied shipping across the globe—even in the Tasman Sea and New Zealand coastal waters. Yet the Merchant Navy has seldom featured prominently in this country's war history. Many veterans have felt that the efforts and sacrifices of their comrades have not received the recognition they deserve.

Although it is impossible for those who were not there to know what it was like to serve in the wartime Merchant Navy, oral histories give us a glimpse of what veterans went through. The reminiscences in this book vividly capture the constant fear of torpedo attack, the confusion of abandoning a sinking ship, the anxiety of days adrift in lifeboats, as well as the day-to-day realities of rough seas, hard work, cramped accommodation and often awful food. These stories illustrate the self-reliance, determination, modesty, humour and loyalty to mates that are the hallmarks of New Zealanders at war, and have helped shape our nation's identity.

I thank the veterans who have generously shared their stories with us. I congratulate Neill Atkinson and the highly professional team in the Ministry for Culture and Heritage for producing this book. I urge New Zealanders to read *Hell or High Water* and learn more about this fascinating chapter in our country's war history.

Helen Clark
Prime Minister

Contents

Preface	11
Glossary	15
Introduction: New Zealand Merchant Seafarers at War, 1939–45 Neill Atkinson	21
Further Reading	53
'You Knew You Were on the Bull's-eye' Lionel Hodgson	55
'The Old *Aquitania*' John Montgomery	71
'Caught by the Japanese' Bill Hall	87
'Five Hundred Ships' Pat O'Shea	101
'The Santa Marija Convoy' John Gregson	113
'Four Days of Hell' Les Watson	129
'It Seemed Like an Eternity' Darcy Hoffman	143

'I Don't Like the Look of Tonight' 155
    Allan Wyllie

'Loch Ewe to Murmansk' 165
    Dan Bashall

'It Was the Most Astounding Thing' 179
    Dewi Browne

'We Had to Feed the Troops' 195
    Cliff Turner

'I Put My Age Up' 205
    Lou Barron

'A Pierhead Jump' 221
    Thor Larsen

'Up the Red Sea' 233
    Steve Carey

'Real True Adventures' 249
    Jim Blundell

Index 266

PREFACE

Preface

This book presents the personal stories of 15 New Zealand seafarers who sailed on merchant ships during the Second World War. Unlike most histories of war, which focus on those serving in uniform in the armed forces, the men whose stories appear here, and the thousands like them who served in the wartime Merchant Navy, were essentially civilian workers. As we shall see, however, civilian status was no guarantee of safe passage during wartime, when the world's merchant fleets and their crews found themselves thrust into the front lines of the war at sea.

Those who appear in this book served in a variety of roles at sea: as able seamen and firemen, mates and engineers, apprentices and deck boys, stewards, even a baker. They sailed on ships of all shapes and sizes, from grand ocean liners through modern refrigerated cargo ships and oil tankers to the humblest tramp steamers and coasters. We see the Second World War as a truly global conflict, ranging from the Arctic Circle to the Red Sea, from the Caribbean to the Caroline Islands, from Cook Strait to the River Plate. Most of those interviewed were born or raised in New Zealand. Reflecting the powerful British influence on the New Zealand shipping industry, both during and after the war, two British seamen are included. Both settled here soon after the war: one, like many hundreds of his countrymen, 'jumped ship' in a New Zealand port; the other spent many years as an officer and master in the coastal trade.

The introduction is intended to provide readers with a sense of the wider context in which these individual experiences took place. It begins with a discussion of New Zealand's close economic and maritime links with Britain, and the sea war's long reach into the South Pacific. This is followed by an overview of the central campaign at sea, the Battle of the Atlantic, and an assessment of New Zealand's Merchant Navy casualties. The introduction concludes by drawing on the personal memories of the interviewees to explore some of the key themes in the experience of merchant seafarers in the Second World War. A glossary is included to assist readers who are unfamiliar with the many nautical and military terms used in the interviews.

Previous page: *Wellington's Aotea Quay in 1942, lined with United States transport ships and military stores; dozens of other vessels ride at anchor in the harbour. From that year until the end of the war American military transports and merchant ships were frequent visitors to New Zealand ports.* Alexander Turnbull Library, F-61343-1/2

As with the other oral history projects undertaken by the Ministry for Culture and Heritage, the recordings of the interviews and supporting material will be archived in the Oral History Centre at the Alexander Turnbull Library, Wellington, where they will be available to future researchers subject to any conditions placed on them by the interviewees. While I have attempted to preserve the informal language of the interviews so that readers might 'hear' the way the interviewees spoke, the text has been edited for brevity and clarity.

Many people and institutions have assisted me during the course of this project. My greatest debt is to the Merchant Navy veterans who agreed to share their experiences with me, loaned me photographs and other memorabilia and, with their families, welcomed me into their homes. I am grateful to the Prime Minister, Right Honourable Helen Clark, for her continued support for the Ministry's series of oral histories and for contributing the foreword. Ray Grover, then a member of the History Group's Advisory Committee, was instrumental in getting the project under way and organised my first interview in Wanganui. Ian Dymock and Stan Kirkpatrick, of the Wellington and Otago Merchant Navy Associations respectively, were generous in their support and put me in touch with many of the veterans who appear in the following pages. As well as sharing his experiences and research material, and driving me around Dunedin, Stan recorded the interview with the late Steve Carey as part of his own valuable oral history project in 1993–94. I am grateful to the Carey family, the Otago Maritime Society and the Turnbull Library's Oral History Centre for allowing me to include an edited version of this interview. I would also like to thank Earle Crutchley, Phillip O'Shea, Terry Hall, John Middleton, Howard Anderson, Murray Henderson, Alan Jenkins, Norm Lamont, Trevor Bell and Billy McGee for introducing me to veterans, talking about their own experiences or providing other information.

As always, I must thank the staffs of libraries and museums: the National Library and Alexander Turnbull Library, especially Turnbull Library Pictures, the Photographic Archive and the Oral History Centre; Archives New Zealand; Wendy Adlam at the Museum of Wellington City & Sea; the Royal New Zealand Navy Museum, Devonport, especially Paul Restall; the Kippenberger Military Archive and Research Library at the Army Museum, Waiouru; Auckland City Libraries (Central Library); the Australian War Memorial, Canberra; and the Imperial War Museum, London. Thanks also to Tracey Wogan and the team at HarperCollins, and to my colleagues at the Ministry for Culture and Heritage: Megan Hutching, who generously shared her oral history expertise and experience; Bronwyn Dalley,

Gavin McLean and Ian McGibbon, who commented on the introduction; David Green, who copy-edited the manuscript; Gwen Calnon and Claire Taggart, who arranged travel and helped order photographs; Alison Parr, Jamie Mackay, Fran McGowan and Redmer Yska. Finally, I am grateful to my family and friends, especially Lauren Perry, for all their support and encouragement.

Neill Atkinson
January 2005

Glossary

2NZEF	Second New Zealand Expeditionary Force
AB	able seaman, a deckhand able to perform all the duties of a seaman aboard ship
aft, after	at or towards the stern
Aldis lamp	electric lamp with shutters for sending signals at sea
apprentice	indentured trainee officer
Armed Guard	navy gun crew on United States merchant ships
articles	ship's papers detailing the crew's conditions of employment
Asdic	sonar, underwater sound-ranging apparatus used to locate submarines (originally from Allied Submarine Detection Investigation Committee)
AWOL	absence without leave
ballast	additional weight carried in a ship to provide stability, especially when a cargo vessel is sailing empty (or 'light-ship')
bilges	lowest internal part of a ship's hull
bosun	boatswain, the leading hand or foreman of the deck crew
bow	foremost end of the ship, the opposite of stern
boy	lowest rank in a ship's crew (often deck boy, galley boy, bridge boy, etc.)
bridge	elevated platform above upper deck from which master and officers direct operations
bulkhead	vertical partition dividing a ship's hull into compartments
bunkering	replenishing the bunkers
bunkers	internal compartments holding the ship's fuel supply of coal or oil
cable	measure of distance at sea equivalent to 200 yards (183 metres)
captain's tiger	master's personal steward
chippie	carpenter
cleaner	low-ranking engine-room hand whose job involved cleaning the boilers
clinker	stony residue or slag from burnt coal
coaming	raised lip around a hatch

The Conference Lines' big refrigerated cargo-liners, or Home boats, were familiar sights in New Zealand ports, where they routinely spent five or six weeks emptying their holds of general cargo and refilling them with meat and dairy products. Although they engaged their crews in Britain, Home boats regularly recruited New Zealand seamen during these visits, usually as replacements for men who had jumped ship (deserted) or fallen ill. Such jobs were keenly sought after, especially by youngsters looking for a career at sea, adventure or a passage 'Home'. As well as those serving on locally owned ships (see below), at least a thousand New Zealanders were to sail on British and other overseas vessels during the war years.

At the outbreak of war all British merchant ships came under the control of the Ministry of Shipping, which was incorporated into the Ministry of War Transport in 1941. New Zealand had no control over the Home boats' movements, but as they were specially designed for the refrigerated trade most initially remained on their usual routes. By 1943, however, diversions to the shorter Atlantic trades and spiralling shipping losses had halved the number and tonnage of British vessels arriving in New Zealand. Under the direction of a government Shipping Controller, exporters sought to make more efficient use of cargo space by boning and 'telescoping' meat carcasses and centralising cargo-handling at the main ports, reducing the average time Home boats spent on the New Zealand coast from 36 days in 1939 to 18 in 1942. Later in the war, shipping shortages were eased by the growing fleet of American Liberty ships, which visited in large numbers in 1943–44.

Despite the vulnerability of the 12,000-mile ocean lifeline between the two countries, war strengthened rather than weakened the economic ties between New Zealand and Britain. In 1939 the New Zealand government offered its entire exportable surpluses of meat, butter, cheese, wool, tallow, flax and other agricultural products to its British counterpart. Over the next six years almost two million tons of meat (76 million carcasses), 1.3 million tons of butter and cheese, and four million bales of wool were shipped to the United Kingdom; even during the dark days of 1942, the Dominion's farms provided 80 per cent of Britain's butter imports and 40 per cent of its cheese. In the last four years of the war an additional 190,000 tons of meat and 137,000 tons of vegetables were shipped to United States forces in the Pacific. As well as farm produce, New Zealand's wartime exports included 250 million rounds of small-arms' ammunition, five million hand grenades and almost three million pairs of boots. But production was one thing—delivering these cargoes halfway around the world in wartime was another matter. As the Minister of Marketing, Ben Roberts, acknowledged in 1945, 'This has only been accomplished at great

degaussing	system devised to protect steel ships against magnetic mines, in which an electrical current is passed through a wire around the hull to neutralise the vessel's magnetic field
DEMS	Defensively Equipped Merchant Ship
dhobiing	washing clothes
doodlebug	German V-1 rocket
engineer	executive officer in the engine department, divided into chief, second, third, etc., to indicate seniority
Eyeties	Italians
fiddley	grating above the engine and boiler rooms to let hot air and fumes escape
fireman	engine-room hand on a steamship (especially a coal-burner) whose job was to feed the furnaces with fuel; in naval service, a 'stoker'
fo'c'sle	forecastle, in the bows of the ship; traditionally the location of crew accommodation
for'ard	forward, towards the bow
galley	ship's kitchen
gharry	Indian horse-drawn carriage
gig	small ship's boat
glory hole	fo'c'sle, crew's quarters
gob hat	American sailor's hat
greaser	engine-room hand whose job involved monitoring and lubricating machinery
HMAS	His/Her Majesty's Australian Ship
HMNZS	His/Her Majesty's New Zealand Ship
HMS	His/Her Majesty's Ship
hull down	description of a ship so far away that only its masts or funnels are visible
Jerries	Germans
job-and-finish	system that requires workers to complete a specific task rather than work set hours, and allows them time off once the job is done
Liberty ships	mass-produced, prefabricated cargo ships with all-welded hulls built in United States shipyards during the Second World War

Glossary

light-ship	*see* ballast
lighter	flat-bottomed barge used to load and unload ships in port
Limey	American nickname for the English
liner	vessel belonging to a shipping company (or line) that carries passengers on scheduled routes. A cargo-liner is a cargo-carrying vessel with accommodation for a few passengers
logging	docking a crew member's pay for misconduct, such punishment being recorded in the ship's official log
Luftwaffe	German air force
Manpower	system for directing workers into essential occupations in wartime New Zealand
master	captain, commanding officer of a merchant ship
mate	executive deck officer, ranked just below the master. Divided into first (or chief), second, third, etc., to indicate seniority
merchantman	a merchant ship
monkey island	small open bridge above the main bridge of a ship
MP	Military Police
MTB	Motor Torpedo Boat
MV	prefix denoting that a ship is a motor (diesel) vessel
Oerlikon	anti-aircraft gun of Swiss design
old man	seamen's name for their ship's master, regardless of his age
OS	ordinary seaman, a deckhand who has not qualified for the rank of AB
palliasse	straw mattress
paravanes	bow-mounted towing devices designed to deflect contact mines away from the ship's hull and sever their mooring lines
peggy	messroom hand
pierhead jump	joining a ship at the last possible moment before sailing, usually to fill an unexpected vacancy
Pom(mie)	English(man)
Pool	Merchant Navy Reserve Pool, a register of merchant seafarers established in Britain in 1941 to allocate crews to ships. Pools later also operated in Montreal and New York

poop	raised deck in after part of ship
port	left-hand side of ship, looking forward
POW	prisoner of war
purser	officer who keeps the ship's accounts
quartermaster	senior helmsman
Red Cap	military policeman
red duster	red ensign, flag of the British Merchant Navy
RMS	Royal Mail Ship, prefix denoting that a ship is licensed to carry the Royal Mails
R(NZ)AF	Royal (New Zealand) Air Force
RSA	Returned Services' Association
scow	in New Zealand, a flat-bottomed sailing or powered vessel used for carrying bulk cargoes around the coast
SS	prefix indicating that a vessel is a merchant steamship (originally Screw Steamship, as opposed to PS, Paddle Steamship)
starboard	right-hand side of ship, looking forward
stern	after end of ship, the opposite of bow
steward	member of ship's catering (or providore) department, whose job is to look after officers and/or passengers
tramp	general cargo ship that does not run on regular routes to a fixed schedule, but sails from port to port picking up cargo wherever it is available
trimmer	low-ranking engine-room hand whose main task was to supply coal from the bunkers to the firemen
turn to	start working
'tween decks	space between any continuous decks below the main deck
U-boat	German submarine, from *Unterseeboot*
VAD	Volunteer Aid Detachment nurse
VE Day	Victory in Europe Day
VJ Day	Victory over Japan Day
WAAF	(member of the) Women's Auxiliary Air Force
watch	(1) four-hour period of duty; (2) the corresponding organisation of the ship's officers and crew to provide for periods of work and rest within each 24-hour day

wiper	low-ranking engine-room hand
wolf pack	group of U-boats operating together to attack convoys
Yank(ee)	American

Note on Measurements

There are several different ways of expressing shipping tonnages. The figures in this book refer to gross registered tonnage (GRT), which measures volume, not weight, and is given in tons (1 ton = 100 cubic feet). Distances at sea are given in nautical miles, which remain the standard measure today. Equivalent to 1852 metres, the nautical mile differs substantially from the standard mile on land (1609 metres).

INTRODUCTION

NEW ZEALAND MERCHANT SEAFARERS AT WAR, 1939–45

Neill Atkinson

As THE SS *PORT HUNTER* sliced through the Atlantic swells off West Africa on the night of 11 July 1942, lookouts anxiously scanned the darkness for signs of danger. Ten days out of Liverpool, the 8437-ton British cargo-liner had earlier left the relative safety of convoy OS33 to sail alone for Durban and ultimately Auckland. Suddenly, just before midnight, a torpedo fired by the German submarine *U-582* tore through the ship's hull and exploded in a hold packed with munitions. The *Port Hunter* rolled over and sank within two minutes. Three crew members were rescued after six hours afloat in a slick of oil and debris, but the other 89 on board—including at least seven New Zealanders—went down with their ship. Among the victims were Thomas Burke and Edward Walls from Moera, Lower Hutt, who had joined the vessel as deck boys during its previous visit to New Zealand. They were both 15 years old.

The loss of the *Port Hunter* provides a glimpse of a largely forgotten chapter in New Zealand's war history. Burke, Walls and their shipmates were among several thousand New Zealanders who sailed as crew in cargo ships, passenger liners (often converted to troop or hospital ships), oil tankers and other merchant vessels during the Second World War. These ships and the seafarers who manned them were known variously as the merchant or mercantile marine, merchant service or, especially in wartime, the Merchant Navy—a symbolic title adopted in Britain in the 1920s in recognition of the shipping industry's

Previous page: *An Atlantic convoy seen from the deck of the* Port Hunter *in 1940. Two years later this Port Line freighter was torpedoed off the West African coast with the loss of 89 lives, including at least seven New Zealand seafarers—two of them just 15 years old.* Alexander Turnbull Library, J. Sutherland Collection, PAColl-0566-02

efforts during the First World War, when the British Empire lost 2500 merchant ships and 15,000 seafarers. While the scale of those losses was unprecedented, the involvement of merchant seafarers in warfare was nothing new. For centuries governments had regarded the ships and men of their countries' merchant and fishing fleets as a military reserve, ready for 'impressment' in times of crisis.

The strategic importance of sea transport was again underlined during the total war of 1939–45, which demanded the mobilisation of not just nations' armies but their entire economies. So essential was the Merchant Navy to the war effort of Britain and its allies that it was effectively regarded as an arm of the state, a 'fourth service' alongside the army, navy and air force. But although ships' cargoes, destinations and routes came under government or naval control, the Merchant Navy was neither a military force nor even a single, coherent body. It remained, as before, a diverse collection of private companies and ships crewed by civilian volunteers who ranged in age from 14 to at least 75. Aside from officers, and cooks and stewards, merchant seafarers wore no uniforms; ashore, they were identified only by a silver lapel badge bearing the letters 'MN'.

The Merchant Navy badge, which was distributed to seamen on British ships from January 1940 and to those on New Zealand ships from July 1941. Phillip O'Shea collection

Regardless of their civilian status, merchant seafarers of all nations soon found themselves in the front lines of the war at sea. The *Port Hunter* was one of at least 64 ships trading between New Zealand and Britain to be sunk by enemy action, at a cost of over a thousand lives. This was only a fraction of total merchant shipping casualties: between 1939 and 1945 almost 4800 Allied and neutral merchant vessels (over 21 million tons worth) were sunk and around 60,000 seafarers killed—more than half of them while sailing under the 'red duster' (red ensign) of the British Empire and Dominions. Indeed, Britain's Merchant Navy suffered proportionately higher casualties than any of that country's armed forces. Allied seafarers were not the only ones at risk: Germany and Italy, whose merchantmen were largely

The Union Steam Ship Company's Awatea *(13,482 tons) in Sydney in 1940. One of the finest passenger liners of its size in the world at the outbreak of the war, the* Awatea *was soon pressed into service as a fast troopship—a role that ultimately led to its destruction in the Mediterranean in November 1942.* Phillip O'Shea collection

confined to northern European and Mediterranean waters, also lost many ships, while by 1945 the large merchant fleet of Japan—like Britain an island nation heavily dependent on overseas imports—had been almost completely destroyed by American submarines and aircraft.

In the Atlantic, a determined German campaign to cut Britain's ocean lifelines ultimately ended in failure. Despite heavy losses, tens of thousands of Allied merchant ships successfully evaded Germany's submarines (or U-boats), warships, bombers and mines to reach their destinations and unload their essential cargoes. Without the hundreds of millions of tons of food, fuel, raw materials and munitions, the many thousands of tanks, vehicles and aircraft, and the millions of soldiers and other personnel they delivered across the world's oceans, the Allies could not have won the Second World War. For all their efforts and sacrifices, however, some Merchant Navy veterans feel that theirs was not so much a 'fourth' as a 'forgotten' service.

Introduction

This book presents the personal stories of 15 men (the seafaring workforce was almost exclusively male and became more so during wartime)[1] who took part in this global struggle. Their experiences are as diverse as the industry and ships in which they worked. They served on deck as mate, bosun, ordinary or able seaman, apprentice or deck boy; down in the engine room as engineer, fireman or trimmer; and in the catering department as steward, pantryman or baker. Like most merchant seafarers, they tended to move from ship to ship rather than spend their careers on only one or two vessels. John Montgomery, for example, left a 100-ton Wellington scow for a job in the engine room of one of the world's largest and most famous passenger liners, the 45,647-ton *Aquitania*—in drab wartime grey and carting soldiers rather than socialites—and later sailed on a British cargo-liner and an American oil tanker.

Many of the other ships that appear in these pages were household names in 1940s New Zealand: the Union Steam Ship Company's *Awatea* and *Maunganui*, the Canadian-Australasian Royal Mail liners *Niagara* and *Aorangi*, and the New Zealand Shipping Company's *Rangitane*, *Rangitata* and *Rangitiki*. Far less glamorous were the grimy, hard-working tramp steamers and coasters that made up the bulk of the world's merchant fleets, creaking veterans salvaged from 'Rotten Row' for the war effort, and the prosaic 'Liberty' ships churned out in their thousands by American shipyards. As well as the red ensign, those interviewed sailed under the flags of the United States, Panama, Norway and Poland, alongside shipmates of many nationalities; their ports of call circled the globe, from Auckland to Abadan, Fremantle to Freetown, Montevideo to Murmansk.

THE RED DUSTER AND THE SOUTHERN CROSS

NEW ZEALAND IN THE MID-20th century was, as today, overwhelmingly dependent on sea transport to carry its international trade. In the era before scheduled air services, everything and everyone leaving or entering these islands did so in a ship. Reflecting the Dominion's economic dependence on the United Kingdom—the destination in 1939 of 84 per cent of its exports and source of 48 per cent of its imports—the long-distance or blue-water shipping routes between the two countries were largely in British hands. The 'Home' trade, as it was called in New Zealand, was dominated by four British companies, collectively known as the Conference Lines: Shaw Savill & Albion, the New Zealand Shipping Company (and its affiliated Federal Line), the Port Line, and the Blue Star Line.

A waterside worker loading frozen beef onto the Rangitiki *at Wellington in 1945. Despite shipping shortages, New Zealand exported 76 million meat carcasses to Britain during the war years.* Alexander Turnbull Library, John Pascoe Collection, F-1870-1/4

hazard and with the loss of many lives and many ships . . . It is no exaggeration to say that the Merchant Navy has been the axis round which the war effort of the United Nations has revolved.'[2]

New Zealand's domestic shipping industry also played a vital role. A small tributary of the vast British shipping empire, it was largely confined to 'short-sea' trades: trans-Tasman, South Pacific and coastal. The Union Steam Ship Company, itself controlled since 1917 by the British giant P & O, dominated the main Tasman, Pacific island and coastal routes, and also traded to India and North America. The smaller fleets of the Northern, Holm, Richardson, Anchor, Canterbury and other companies bustled between coastal ports. In December 1939 the New Zealand registry listed 186 vessels (excluding some of the larger Union Company ships, registered in London for insurance purposes) which provided jobs for nearly 3000 seafarers. By 1945 the figures had fallen to 136 and 2200 respectively, reflecting the transfer of some vessels to naval service, the rationalisation of coastal trades, and the departure of seafarers into overseas ships, the armed forces or industry ashore.[3]

Probably the most unusual outcome of wartime shipping shortages was New Zealand's use of the four-masted barque *Pamir*, which was seized in prize from its Finnish owners in Wellington in August 1941. Managed by the Union Company and crewed almost entirely by New Zealanders, the big square-rigger was to make ten successful (if not always profitable) voyages under the New Zealand ensign, mostly carrying wool and tallow to San Francisco and Vancouver. Despite suggestions that it be retained as a sail training vessel for the New Zealand Merchant Navy, the *Pamir* was eventually handed back to the Finns in November 1948.

If the *Pamir* was a throwback to an earlier age, the rest of the Union Company's large, relatively modern fleet of steamers and motor ships was one of New Zealand's most valuable war assets. Several vessels were requisitioned by the government for military use. The 10,852-ton liner *Monowai* was immediately taken over by the New Zealand Division of the Royal Navy and converted into an armed merchant cruiser manned by a combination of naval regulars, reservists and merchant seamen engaged under temporary naval articles. The old *Maunganui* (7527 tons) was converted to a hospital ship, primarily to serve the needs of 2NZEF in the Middle East, and was to carry 5677 patients during wartime. The flagship of the Union fleet, the fast trans-Tasman liner *Awatea* (13,482 tons) completed a number of troop-carrying and evacuation voyages before being sunk during Operation Torch, the Allied invasion of Vichy French North Africa in November 1942. The *Rangatira*, *Wahine* and *Matua* periodically ferried troops around the Pacific, while the 17,491-ton *Aorangi* (flying the Canadian-Australasian Line flag but under Union management) also gave outstanding service as a troopship. By the end of 1945 the Union fleet had carried over 874,000 troops and airmen and repatriated 18,000 prisoners of war and refugees.[4]

Introduction

RAIDERS OF THE SOUTH PACIFIC

IN THE EARLY HOURS of 19 June 1940 the Second World War arrived in New Zealand with a bang, shattering any illusions that isolation alone would protect these islands from enemy attack. The 13,415-ton trans-Pacific liner *Niagara* had just left Auckland on its regular run to Suva and Vancouver. While everyone on board knew there was a war on, they could rest easy in the knowledge it was happening somewhere else, half a world away from the peaceful South Pacific. They were wrong. At 3.40 a.m., as the liner passed Northland's Bream Head, a violent explosion tumbled passengers out of their bunks. The *Niagara* had slammed into two contact mines, part of a 228-mine barrage secretly sown across the northern and eastern approaches to the Hauraki Gulf several days earlier by the German 'auxiliary cruiser' *Orion*, a heavily armed raider disguised as a neutral merchantman. Fortunately, all 349 passengers and crew got away safely in the liner's 18 lifeboats, the only casualty being the ship's cat, Aussie. Of greater concern to the New Zealand government was the loss of the *Niagara*'s secret cargo of gold ingots worth £2.5 million—almost all later recovered in an epic salvage job—and half of the Dominion's stock of small-arms' ammunition, destined for Britain to replenish losses suffered in France.

Survivors from the Niagara *about to be rescued on the morning of 19 June 1940. Although all 146 passengers and 203 crew (most of whom were Australian) were saved, the loss of the liner in a German minefield off the Northland coast came as a severe shock to the New Zealand authorities and public.* S.D. Waters, German Raiders in the Pacific (1949)

Over the following six months the *Orion* and another raider, the *Komet*, were to claim a further 11 victims in the Pacific. In August, the New Zealand Shipping Company freighter *Turakina* went down fighting with 36 of its British crew in the Tasman Sea's first gun battle. In late November, after dispatching the little *Holmwood* off the Chatham Islands, the raiders snared their greatest prize, the 16,712-ton liner *Rangitane*, 300 miles off East Cape. A hail of German shells killed 15 passengers and crew, and around 300 survivors joined those already aboard the raiders and their supply ship, the *Kulmerland*. In early December, another five merchantmen succumbed to the raiders' guns off the strategic phosphate island of Nauru, including the Union Company's *Komata,* two of whose officers were killed. Just before Christmas, the Germans landed some 500 of their captives, including 58 women and six children, at Emirau Island in the Bismarck Archipelago, near New Guinea, from where they were repatriated in January 1941. The remaining 150 (including several New Zealand merchant seamen) were eventually interned in Germany.[5]

Although the raiders' intrusion exposed the inadequacy of New Zealand's naval and air defences, the Merchant Navy was not totally unprepared for war. As elsewhere, on the outbreak of hostilities naval authorities altered merchant ships' usual peacetime routes to frustrate enemy raiders. Merchant ships were painted grey and progressively fitted with defensive armament and additional lifesaving equipment. They were also ordered to maintain strict radio silence (unless attacked) and night-time blackouts, although prior to the *Niagara*'s loss these were unevenly implemented in local waters. Thereafter, coastal navigation lights were extinguished or dimmed, details of shipping movements censored, and the public warned that 'loose lips might sink ships'. Over the following years harbour defences were bolstered by searchlights, patrol boats, anti-submarine booms and defensive minefields.

Attacks by German raiders intensified fears that Nazi spies were operating in New Zealand, peering around wharf sheds and eavesdropping in waterfront pubs. Although a subsequent government inquiry found no evidence that the enemy had prior knowledge of shipping movements, posters like this one reminded the public that careless talk could cost lives. Alexander Turnbull Library, Eph-D-WAR-WII-1941-02

One of the most important

Introduction

Seen here at Vava'u, Tonga, during a troop-carrying voyage, the Union Company's MV Matua *was fitted with a 4-inch stern gun in September 1939. Its DEMS armament was later bolstered by the addition of a 12-pounder, 20-mm Oerlikons, machine-guns and depth charges.* Museum of Wellington City & Sea

preparations for war, which began months before September 1939, was a state-funded programme to convert larger vessels into Defensively Equipped Merchant Ships (DEMS). A typical upgrade involved fitting an antiquated 4- or 4.7-inch gun on a specially strengthened stern deck, a couple of machine-guns for anti-aircraft defence, and extra protection around the bridge and wireless room. Later in the war, as the favoured 20-millimetre Oerlikon became more widely available, anti-aircraft batteries were considerably enhanced. Many ships were also fitted with paravanes to deflect contact mines and 'degaussed' to neutralise the magnetism of their hulls and thus counteract magnetic mines. Some were equipped with PAC (parachute-and-cable) rockets, grenade throwers and other experimental weapons. By January 1941 New Zealand had armed 28 ships, fitted paravanes to 11 and degaussed 21. Eventually, more than 170 New Zealand, British and Norwegian ships were armed or modified in local ports. DEMS were usually supplied with a small squad of naval or army gunners, but many merchant seafarers, especially deckhands, were also trained to operate these weapons.[6]

Although of limited use against submarines or warships, DEMS armament at least provided merchant seafarers with some means of defending themselves, an important capability for an occupational group that prized self-sufficiency. Indeed, many merchant ships resisted bravely when attacked, including the *Turakina*, whose solitary 4.7-inch gun proved no match for the six 155-millimetre (5.9-inch) weapons of the *Orion*. Others had more luck: in March 1942 the Union Company's *Narbada* foiled an attacking Japanese submarine off Western Australia through evasive action and accurate gunnery, while in November that year the little Dutch tanker *Ondina* sank the Japanese armed merchant cruiser *Hokuku Maru*.

As well as the big ships of the Union Company, the New Zealand government requisitioned dozens of small coasters, trawlers and private launches for conversion into minesweepers, patrol boats and harbour examination vessels, causing considerable disruption to coastal services. Often their crews went with them, and by 1942 several hundred merchant officers and seamen were serving in the Royal New Zealand Naval Reserve or under temporary naval articles. Minesweeping could be hazardous work: in May 1941 HMS *Puriri*, a former Anchor Company coaster, became the second victim of the *Orion*'s minefield, along with five officers and ratings—all of them ex-merchant seamen. Other reservists served further afield, including John Holm, who swapped commands from a New Zealand coaster to a Royal Navy corvette in the Battle of the Atlantic.[7] From 1942 coastal shipping resources were further stretched by the need to supply American forces with auxiliary craft for use in the Pacific.

When the German raiders quit the South Pacific in mid-1941, the immediate danger to New Zealand shipping receded. Japan's entry into the war in December that year threatened far greater disruption, but the Imperial Japanese Navy lacked the Germans' enthusiasm for commerce raiding and its advanced, long-range submarines (or I-boats) seldom ventured into New Zealand waters. In 1942–43 up to ten I-boats operated at times off Australia's east coast, where they sank 18 Allied merchant ships, including the Union Company's *Kalingo* and *Limerick*. Meanwhile, submarines and surface raiders—both German and Japanese—stalked the vast Indian Ocean, threatening New Zealand's supply lines to the Middle East. It was here that the Union freighter *Hauraki* was captured by two Japanese armed merchant cruisers in July 1942, condemning its crew, including engineer Bill Hall, to three years of 'starvation labour'.

From mid-1943, as the Americans advanced in the Solomon Islands and the central Pacific, Japan's

I-boats withdrew from the Tasman to harass invading forces or run supplies to beleaguered island garrisons. If New Zealand waters were thereafter calm, the struggle for control of the world's sea lanes was far from over. Throughout the war the greatest threat to New Zealand's shipping links lay not in home waters but in the distant North Atlantic, which the Home boats and thousands of other merchant ships had to cross. It was here that many New Zealand merchant seafarers took part in one of the most decisive and dramatic campaigns of the Second World War.

THE BATTLE OF THE ATLANTIC

ALTHOUGH IT WAS WAGED half a world away, few military campaigns were as vital to New Zealand's interests as the Battle of the Atlantic. A German victory, which would have severed the Dominion's links with Britain, was one of the gravest threats this country has ever faced. Yet the Atlantic struggle has seldom featured prominently in our war history, probably in part because it did not involve distinctive New Zealand units. While the *Awatea* and some other locally owned ships spent time in the Atlantic, almost all the New Zealand merchant seafarers who took part in this campaign served under the British flag—as did their many compatriots in the ships and squadrons of the Royal Navy, Fleet Air Arm and RAF Coastal Command.

Germany's Atlantic strategy was simple: to starve Britain into submission by destroying merchant ships and their essential cargoes of food and raw materials faster than they could be replaced. Although mines, bombers and surface ships would claim many victims, the deadliest threat was the U-boat. The Allies' defence against and eventual victory over the U-boats in the Battle of the Atlantic was based on three main factors. The first and most important was the convoy system, in which merchant ships were herded across the North Atlantic and elsewhere in vast formations of up to 60 ships, protected where possible by air patrols and naval escorts armed with Asdic (sonar) and depth charges. The second ingredient, the painstaking, secret work of Allied signals intelligence, was a mystery to those at sea. By using high-frequency direction-finding to trace the location of U-boats through their radio signals and, most famously, breaking the sophisticated Enigma code the U-boats used to communicate with their headquarters, the naval authorities were able to redirect convoys away from danger. Finally, the deployment

Safety in numbers: the convoy system was the linchpin of the Allies' long and hard-fought victory in the Battle of the Atlantic. Royal New Zealand Navy Museum

from 1943 of more powerful escort forces, longer-range aircraft and improved anti-submarine weapons and tactics enabled the Allies to contain and ultimately defeat the U-boat menace.

The Atlantic campaign began on 3 September 1939, within hours of Britain's (and New Zealand's) declaration of war, when the liner *Athenia* was torpedoed off Ireland with the loss of 112 lives—the first British casualties of the war. Mindful of the costly lessons of the First World War, Britain immediately introduced a convoy system and evasive routeing of merchant ships. But as the Royal Navy lacked escort vessels, convoys only operated within a few hundred miles of Britain or Canada, and many ships still sailed alone. Fortunately, Germany's submarine force was scarcely better prepared. Its commander, Karl Dönitz, had calculated that 300 U-boats were needed to win the 'tonnage war' against Britain. In September 1939 he had 57, and less than half of these were suitable for Atlantic operations.

The first nine months of the Atlantic campaign were inconclusive. Hunting mainly in the North Sea and the Western Approaches to Britain, U-boats sank over a hundred ships, mostly outside of convoys. Air attacks and mines also claimed numerous victims around the British coast. Among them was the tanker *Inverlane*, mined in the North Sea in December 1939, whose assistant cook, 24-year-old Leslie Yates from Hawke's Bay, was probably the first New Zealand merchant seaman killed in action. Further out in the Atlantic, German surface ships made sporadic strikes on the shipping lanes, while raiders like

Introduction

An American oil tanker burns fiercely after a torpedo attack. In the first half of 1942 German U-boats wreaked massive destruction among tankers operating out of the oil ports of the Gulf of Mexico and Caribbean. The crews of these vessels lived with the knowledge that they were sailing in floating bombs. Imperial War Museum, OEM6477

the *Orion* and *Komet* began hunting in more distant oceans. By the end of April 1940 German forces had sunk over 800,000 tons of Allied shipping, but 23 U-boats had been lost, as well as the *Admiral Graf Spee*, scuttled in the River Plate in South America.

A more deadly phase of the battle began in June 1940, following Germany's stunning conquests in

Western Europe. Operating from a string of bases between Norway and Bordeaux, Dönitz's 'grey wolves' could now strike deep into the Atlantic sea lanes, often guided to their prey by long-range Focke-Wulf Kondor aircraft. At the same time, Italy's entry into the war closed the Mediterranean to through traffic and added 10,000 miles to the supply lines between Britain and Egypt. Moreover, as U-boat production surged in early 1941, Dönitz was able to implement new tactics: submarines now converged to attack convoys in groups ('wolf packs'), typically on the surface at night. Between June 1940 and June 1941 U-boats destroyed over three million tons of shipping. Britain's shipping resources, however, were bolstered by a flood of exiled merchant ships and seafarers from occupied countries, especially Norway, whose pre-war fleet was the world's fourth largest. The convoy system was extended right across the North Atlantic and air patrols were increased where possible. Aided by the ULTRA intelligence derived from Enigma code-breaking, and the death or capture of several leading U-boat 'aces', the number of sinkings fell sharply in the second half of 1941.

America's entry into the war in December that year, however, reinvigorated the German campaign. A small group of U-boats was immediately dispatched to attack the huge concentration of shipping along the eastern seaboard of the United States. Preoccupied by the Japanese threat in the Pacific and reluctant to follow British advice, the US Navy allowed merchant ships to sail alone and unescorted along brightly lit coasts. In six months almost 400 ships were sunk—including dozens of precious oil tankers operating out of the Gulf of Mexico—and thousands of seafarers perished. When a convoy system was finally established in American and Caribbean waters in mid-1942, the U-boats returned to the mid-Atlantic, concentrating in the Greenland air gap (or 'black pit') beyond the reach of Allied air cover. While a new version of Enigma deprived the Allies of ULTRA intelligence for ten months in 1942, Germany's own code-breakers were highly successful in detecting convoy movements. Shipping losses soared. In the last six months of the year 480 merchant ships totalling 2.6 million tons were sunk in the North Atlantic alone—close to the monthly average Dönitz calculated was needed to win the tonnage war. With many large ships diverted to the Operation Torch invasion in November, Allied shipping resources were stretched close to breaking point.

Adding to the carnage of 1942 were the terrible losses suffered by convoys bound for two special destinations: the Russian Arctic ports of Murmansk, Archangel and Molotovsk, through which Britain and the United States were shipping vital war supplies to their Soviet ally, and the besieged Mediterranean island of Malta. In these narrow seaways, merchant ships faced the dangers of enemy submarines, mines,

Operation Pedestal, August 1942: merchant ships struggle towards Malta under intense attack from German and Italian bombers. The two vessels in the centre of this photograph, Shaw Savill's Empire Hope *and* Waimarama, *were among nine merchantmen sunk in the following days.* Frank Bowen, The Flag of the Southern Cross (1947)

bombers, warships and motor torpedo boats—often all at the same time. The greatest disaster occurred in July 1942, as convoy PQ17 steamed towards Archangel. Convinced (wrongly) that the battleship *Tirpitz* was poised to attack, the Admiralty ordered the convoy to scatter, leaving the merchantmen to be slaughtered by U-boats and bombers; 24 out of 37 were sunk. The following month in the Mediterranean, nine out of 14 fast merchant ships were lost during Operation Pedestal, the most decisive of the many costly supply convoys to Malta.

Several of those interviewed for this book had first-hand experience of these perilous campaigns. Among those who took part in Operation Pedestal was 18-year-old John Gregson, who lost his ship and was decorated for bravery. The following year, Dan Bashall sailed in a convoy to Murmansk, during which Royal Navy forces sank the marauding battlecruiser *Scharnhorst*. The near 24-hour midwinter darkness afforded some protection, but brought sub-zero temperatures and violent gales. When he and his fellow firemen came off watch, Dan recalls, 'We often used to go right along the propeller shaft [tunnel] and up the rungs that way, because if you got on the open deck you'd get blown away.'

The most decisive phase of the Battle of the Atlantic was fought between March and August 1943. After a relatively quiet midwinter period when atrocious weather helped reduce Atlantic losses, a renewed wolf pack offensive threatened to overwhelm the Allies' convoy system. Among several convoys mauled in early March was SC121, which, as Les Watson recalls, lost 12 ships during 'four nights and four days of

Hell or High Water

A German U-boat, caught on the surface in the Bay of Biscay, is attacked by a Sunderland flying boat of RAF Coastal Command. In 1943 Allied aircraft destroyed dozens of U-boats in these waters.
Coastal Command (1944)

hell' in the air gap. Then, between 16 and 19 March, during an agonising nine-day ULTRA blackout, three wolf packs of over 40 U-boats converged on the 90 merchant ships of SC122 and HX229. In the greatest convoy battle of the war, 22 merchantmen were sunk and 360 seamen lost, at a cost of one U-boat destroyed and a dozen damaged. Among the many New Zealanders involved was Darcy Hoffman, an AB on the ill-fated *Canadian Star*, who was rescued after what 'seemed like an eternity' clinging to a raft in freezing seas. North Atlantic losses for March totalled 82 ships (476,000 tons); of even greater concern to the Allies, two-thirds of them had been sailing in convoy.

Despite these stunning successes, the U-boat onslaught quickly faltered. At the beginning of the year British and American leaders had agreed to make the Battle of the Atlantic their top priority. Long-range Liberator bombers began to close the mid-Atlantic air gap, and convoys were soon sailing with more numerous, better-equipped escorts that often included small aircraft carriers. Enigma was cracked again in late March, further strengthening the Allies' position. As merchant sinkings fell, U-boat losses soared. After 41 were sunk in May, Dönitz withdrew his battered wolf packs from the North Atlantic. The Allies' victory was confirmed in July and August, when a further 62 U-boats were destroyed, many by air attacks, shattering German hopes of regaining the initiative.

Even so, the Battle of the Atlantic was far from over. U-boats continued to prey on merchant ships until 7 May 1945, the day Germany capitulated. Some found new hunting grounds in the South Atlantic and the Mozambique Channel, and a 'Monsoon' wolf pack operated out of Japanese-held Malaya from 1943 to 1945. But overwhelming Allied naval and air power and a steady flow of ULTRA intelligence ensured the security of the transatlantic lifeline for the rest of the war. So too did shipbuilding, especially in the United States, where a staggering 13 million tons was launched in 1943 alone. The wolf packs returned to the North Atlantic in September that year armed with acoustic homing torpedoes and improved anti-aircraft defences, but lost another 40 boats in four months. Later developments such as the *Schnorkel* breathing apparatus, which allowed U-boats to submerge for longer periods, failed to turn the tide. By the end of the war Germany had lost over 750 U-boats and nearly 30,000—more than 70 per cent—of its submariners.

Victory in the Battle of the Atlantic allowed the Allies to go onto the offensive in Western and Southern Europe. Again, merchant seafarers had a vital role to play, manning troop, supply and hospital ships during the great amphibious landings on Sicily and at Salerno and Anzio in 1943–44, in Normandy in June 1944 and in the South of France that August. The D-Day invasion was 'the most astounding thing,' recalls AB Dewi Browne. 'On the way over I had two thoughts uppermost: goodness me, there's not that many ships in the whole world; and the other thing, all these planes going over by the hundreds, all going the same way. I thought, they're all ours, and I thought, I know who's winning the war now.' Within a month, 1.7 million troops, 370,000 vehicles and more than two million tons of supplies had been landed in France, with another 10,000 soldiers and 15,000 tons of equipment pouring in every day. Thereafter, each cargo of men and matériel unloaded at European ports and beachheads pushed Germany closer to defeat.

The Battle of the Atlantic was the longest and one of the most decisive campaigns of the Second World War. It was, as Winston Churchill recognised, the 'dominating factor' on which all other aspects of the Allies' war effort depended. Had Germany succeeded in severing the transatlantic lifeline, Britain would soon have been faced with a choice between starvation and surrender. Without fuel, the RAF could not have withstood the *Luftwaffe*; nor could Britain have later become the 'unsinkable aircraft carrier' from which Allied air power could strike deep into Germany. The vast industrial resources of the United States could not have been mobilised in support of their British and Soviet allies. Without the ceaseless flow of troops, equipment and fuel across the Atlantic, Western Europe could not have been liberated.

THE SEA'S TOLL

AT LEAST 120 New Zealand merchant seafarers are known to have lost their lives during the Second World War. The true total is probably higher, as the reporting of Merchant Navy casualties was less thorough than for members of the armed forces, and it is likely that some New Zealanders were counted among general British losses. Five died in Japanese prison camps and several were killed during air raids while in port, but most have 'no grave but the sea'. The great majority were lost while sailing on British vessels, with around 90 perishing in the Atlantic or Mediterranean. The loss of seven New

Survivors of ships sunk by the German raiders Orion *and* Komet *on board the SS* Nellore, *which rescued them from Emirau Island in the Bismarck Archipelago. The evacuees, who reached Townsville on New Year's Day 1941, included about 70 New Zealand merchant seamen, 170 Chinese and Pacific Islanders, 58 women and six children.* S.D. Waters, German Raiders in the Pacific (1949)

Zealand-owned or -operated ships to enemy action fortunately produced only 11 fatalities. At least seven New Zealanders died aboard American or Panamanian-flagged ships (including a purser on the *Donerail*, which was sunk by a Japanese submarine the day after the attack on Pearl Harbor), while others were lost on Australian, Dutch, Greek, Indian and Swedish vessels. In addition, an unknown number succumbed to accidents or illness, including two *Awatea* crew members who died of smallpox in 1942.[8]

The age of some of the victims is striking. As a civilian industry, the Merchant Navy naturally contained employees who were younger or older than those in the armed forces. For centuries, seafarers had embarked on their careers when barely into their teens, typically as deck, galley or cabin 'boys', or as apprentices (trainee officers). In 1941 a quarter of the seamen on British ships were aged 21 or under, and during the war many hundreds of teenagers lost their lives at sea. Among them were at least 15 New Zealanders, including the two 15-year-olds on the *Port Hunter*—almost certainly the youngest New Zealanders killed in combat during the 20th century—and a 16-year-old on the same company's *Port Victor*. Labour shortages also encouraged older seafarers to stay at sea or come out of retirement to help the war effort. Possibly the oldest of all New Zealand's war dead was the 65-year-old greaser James McKenna, who was lost when the *Tuscan Star* was torpedoed in the Atlantic in 1942.

In addition, at least 128 New Zealand merchant seafarers were taken prisoner during the Second World War. The first large group of New Zealanders to be captured were seamen and passengers from the *Holmwood, Komata, Rangitane* and other ships sunk by German raiders in late 1940. About 70 New Zealand seamen from these ships were subsequently released on Emirau Island, after signing an oath not to 'bear arms' against Germany for the remainder of the war. Others, mostly captured in the Atlantic, were interned in a special Merchant Navy camp, Milag Nord, at Westertimke, near Bremen. Among them was Jack Fowke, plucked out of the freezing Arctic by a German destroyer after the *Empire Ranger* was sunk during convoy PQ13, and radio officer Jack Holt, taken aboard *U-160* after his Norwegian tanker, the *Havsten*, was torpedoed in August 1942.

One seaman who never got as far as Milag Nord was AB Bernard Cooper, one of the first New Zealanders to escape from German captivity. Taken prisoner when the *Port Hobart* was sunk by the *Admiral Scheer* off Bermuda in November 1940, he spent three months at sea on several German vessels before being landed at Bordeaux. In April 1941, Cooper and another seaman jumped from the train taking them to Germany, crossed into Vichy territory and eventually reached the Spanish border, where they were nabbed by local police. After several months in the notorious Miranda de Ebro concentration camp, Cooper was released in January 1942 and made his way to Gibraltar. He got back to New Zealand in June.[9]

For Allied servicemen and civilians alike, captivity in the Far East was generally more gruelling than it was in Europe. The *Hauraki*'s 56 officers and crew were the largest group of New Zealand personnel to fall into Japanese hands. Five died in captivity, while the ship's Australian master never recovered from his ordeal and succumbed in 1947.[10] Unlike the Germans, who separated merchant seafarers from military prisoners and generally treated them well, Japan's handling of this category of captives was unpredictable and often brutal. Lou Barron and his *Gloucester Castle* shipmates, who were landed in Singapore from a German raider in 1942, were put to work alongside military prisoners, as were Bill Hall and other members of the *Hauraki*'s engine-room staff, who were sent to Japan as forced labourers. In contrast, the remainder of the *Hauraki*'s crew were interned with civilians in Singapore's Changi prison and later Sime Road camp. None, however, escaped the inadequate diet, primitive living conditions and random beatings that characterised the experience of captives of the Japanese.

Remembering the Merchant Seafarers' War

'I CAN'T REMEMBER whether we expected it or not. But the point is, a chap's a seaman and you just keep going, war or no war, that's your job.' Dewi Browne's response when asked about his reaction to the news that war had broken out in 1939 reflects one of the key differences between the wartime experiences of merchant seafarers and military personnel. Rather than describing the creation of a citizen army like the New Zealand 'Div', this story is as much about continuity—the persistence of pre-war patterns of work and behaviour—as it is about the dramatic changes brought by war. Despite new demands and dangers, the body of laws, rules and customs that had shaped shipboard life and work for centuries continued to exert a powerful influence, while the colourful 'crew culture' of seafarers helped indoctrinate the flood of young recruits who (like the majority of those interviewed for this book) first entered the industry during wartime.

Six decades on, mortality ensures that those who feature in the following pages were all young men during the war years; the eldest, Bill Hall, turned 34 in 1945. Eight of those interviewed were at sea

Seamen on the Union Company freighter Kaiwarra, *photographed in Auckland in December 1940 while loading RNZAF aircraft for delivery to Fiji.* Museum of Wellington City & Sea

by the time they were 17, the main exception being marine engineers, who were required to serve an apprenticeship on shore. English-born Lou Barron shipped out at 14 (while claiming to be 16) and had been a captive of both the Germans and Japanese by his 17th birthday; Cliff Turner went to sea at 15, Thor Larsen and John Gregson at 16. Some, like John Montgomery, joined the Merchant Navy precisely because it would accept them at a younger age than the armed forces. After an unsuccessful attempt to enlist in the army by faking his age, John went to sea at 17 and spent four eventful years on overseas ships. Like most of those interviewed, he came ashore soon after the war, but others remained at sea for decades; several enjoyed long careers as masters, chief engineers or chief stewards.

As is typical of war histories, the most dramatic memories in the following chapters concern moments of action: recollections of attack by submarines, aircraft or warships, of narrow escapes from sinking ships, of days spent in lifeboats or terrifying hours clinging to liferafts. Even in quieter moments, the fear of

One of 18 Allied ships sunk by Japanese submarines in the Tasman Sea, the Kalingo *(2047 tons) was torpedoed by I-21 about 60 miles east of Sydney on 18 January 1943. Two firemen, one of them a New Zealander, went down with the ship, but the other 30 crew members got away in a lifeboat. When the submarine surfaced and attempted to machine-gun the boat, its occupants were saved by a sudden rain squall. They were rescued after rowing and sailing towards Sydney for three days.*
Alexander Turnbull Library, F-18185-1/2

submarine attack, of an unseen enemy striking without warning, was ever-present—and not just in the North Atlantic, as Allan Wyllie discovered off New South Wales in April 1943. 'All through the war at sea you knew you were a target', explains John Gregson. 'You knew you could be torpedoed any time, day or night, because you couldn't see the submarines.' Many slept in their clothes and even their lifejackets, especially in the Atlantic, with a 'getaway' or 'panic' bag handy in case of emergency. For those working down below—'on the bull's-eye amidships', as Lionel Hodgson puts it—the sense of vulnerability was all the more acute: 'No one ever said a word about it, but I'm sure everyone thought about it. Because, oh well, if they hit the engine room you wouldn't have to worry about it, would you?'

Even if they managed to escape their sinking ships, seafarers were far from safe, especially in the freezing waters of the North Atlantic or the shark-infested tropics. Many survivors swallowed seawater or oil, while tanker crews in particular risked terrible burns. Those sailing in convoy stood a better chance of quick rescue, although any vessel stopping to assist exposed itself to danger. Survivors of ships attacked while sailing alone faced the prospect of days or weeks adrift in lifeboats or rafts awaiting a rescue that might never come. Many suffered from dehydration, severe sunburn, hypothermia or 'trench foot' from constant immersion in water. They were also more likely to experience close encounters with U-boats, which frequently approached to finish off damaged ships and sometimes took masters or chief engineers as prisoners. Contrary to legend and British wartime propaganda, there was only one proven case of a German U-boat commander firing on survivors in lifeboats; more often, they offered food, water, sailing directions and condolences to their victims. The same cannot be said, however, of encounters with Japanese submarines, many (although not all) of whose commanders machine-gunned lifeboats and executed survivors. While the crew of the *Kalingo* were saved from this fate by a sudden Tasman squall, others were not so fortunate. After sinking the British freighter *Fort Mumford* in the Indian Ocean in 1943, *I-27* killed all but one of the 51 crew (including five New Zealanders) by machine-gun fire.

Enemy attacks were not the only hazard: wartime blackouts and radio silence complicated routine navigation, while sailing in convoy greatly increased the risk of collision; the *Awatea* alone was involved in three collisions in 1941–42. Seafarers, however, seldom dwelled on the risks they faced. After all, theirs had always been a dangerous occupation, carried out in an immensely challenging physical environment. If some were sunk more than once (the record probably belongs to a Canadian who was torpedoed on nine occasions, twice being the sole survivor), others crossed the North Atlantic dozens of times without incident. Like soldiers and others confronted with the terrible randomness of war, many of those interviewed attribute their own survival to luck or fate. 'My whole life at sea was a lucky one', muses Dewi Browne. 'I had ships next to me hit, two ships away hit, a straggler hit, but I survived . . . It's just your luck I suppose.'

As the following interviews remind us, moments of adrenaline-charged action were by no means the sole defining features of seafarers' wartime experiences. Like soldiers, airmen and naval sailors, much of their time was occupied with the more mundane activities of everyday life: sleeping, eating, washing and so on. Daily routine was especially important to merchant seafarers, who were after all civilian workers employed to carry out essential shipboard tasks, whether operating the engines, shovelling coal, navigating, taking their 'trick' at the wheel, keeping lookout, cooking, cleaning or serving meals. Despite the heightened hazards and special demands of wartime voyaging (sealed orders, blackouts, keeping station in convoy), the daily lives of most seafaring workers were largely unchanged, governed as before by the bells of the 24-hour watch system and the rigid hierarchies of shipboard society.

To be sure, the war transformed the organisation of the shipping industry: cargoes, destinations and routes all came under the control of government and naval authorities. These changes brought some welcome and long-overdue improvements to seafarers' pay and terms of engagement, especially for those employed by the traditionally tight-fisted British shipping companies. War-risk bonuses, essentially funded by government, closed the gap between seafarers' wages and those paid in most industries ashore. Seamen on New Zealand ships, who were generally better paid than their British counterparts, also received bonuses that depended on the location of their service, as did those in the United States merchant marine (which, like that country's armed forces and industries, paid considerably higher wages than those of its allies).

At the same time, seafarers' terms of engagement were transformed by the British government's Essential Work Order (EWO) of May 1941, which introduced continuity of employment and paid leave for the first time. For centuries most seafaring workers had been employed on a casual basis, usually for the duration of a particular round trip, after which they were 'paid off' and had to find a new ship. Shipping companies offered permanent employment only to masters and officers (and, during the Depression of the 1930s, sometimes not at all). The EWO also removed a major source of grievance in the early years of the war: the termination of seafarers' pay the moment their ship was sunk—paid off 'at sea', as the terse entries in their discharge books put it. To ensure a steady supply of crews to ships, Merchant Navy Reserve Pools were established in British ports and later Montreal and New York. On completing a

Accommodation on merchant ships varied greatly with the age, size and type of vessel, and the rank of its occupants. This image shows the seamen's quarters of an American merchant ship that visited New Zealand before the war. Alexander Turnbull Library, New Zealand Seamen's Union Collection, PAColl-6249-1-03

voyage, a seaman was granted leave and told when and where to report back for his next trip. There was no formal pool system in New Zealand, where engagement was controlled by the Marine Department, companies and unions, but shipping was recognised as an essential industry and seafarers were exempted from military conscription—as long as they stayed at sea. Depending on the length and location of their service, they were also eligible for the same war benefits as service personnel, including pensions and post-war rehabilitation assistance.

On the other hand, many fundamental aspects of the industry—shipboard accommodation, the provision of food and drink, discipline, training and promotion—were left largely undisturbed. Living conditions at sea varied enormously with the size, age and trade of the ship, and the status of officers and crew. The most uncomfortable accommodation was usually found on old British liners and tramp steamers, where seamen frequently slept in tiered bunks in dank communal fo'c'sles, sometimes on a 'donkey's breakfast' (straw mattress) as their predecessors had done for centuries. Dan Bashall's description of the 'pokey' quarters on the ancient *Themistocles*, and Thor Larsen's memories of the *Carola*'s fo'c'sle—'with

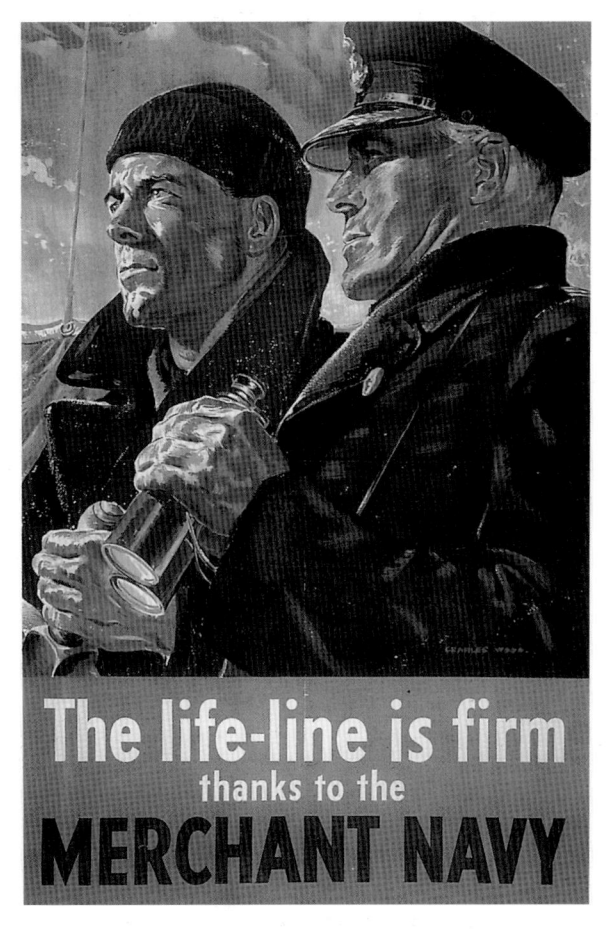

British wartime propaganda typically portrayed Merchant Navy men as quiet heroes, cheerfully braving submarine-infested seas to maintain their nation's vital ocean lifeline. After the war, however, many merchant seafarers felt that they were treated as a 'forgotten' rather than a 'fourth' service. Kirkpatrick collection

14 or 16 men in there, all farting and belching and snoring and swearing'—recall 19th-century portrayals of sea life. For those used to New Zealand ships, the spartan facilities aboard British tramps could come as a rude shock, as Dewi Browne discovered when he left Wellington on the *Cornish City* in 1942. In general, accommodation was far superior on the wartime standard ships, which typically provided two-berth cabins, messrooms, showers and toilets amidships or aft. Even on large, modern liners, however, the crew's quarters were sometimes cramped and uncomfortable, as Allan Wyllie's description of the stewards' 'glory hole' on the *Awatea* reveals.

Perhaps the most important of seafarers' daily concerns was food, a perennial source of grievance at sea since the bad old days of salted meat, hard-tack biscuits and lime juice. While New Zealand, American and Scandinavian ships generally had a good reputation for food, the same could not be said of many British vessels. The notorious Board of Trade scale of provisions was improved during the war, but if the quantity of food was usually adequate, its quality—and the competence of those cooking it—still varied widely from ship to ship. As Les Watson, a steward on Shaw Savill's *Raranga*, recalls, many wartime cooks were 'pretty hopeless' and 'some terrible food went to the crew. I'd be in the captain's cabin when crew were bringing up their food to him, and they were saying, "Captain, how could you eat this stuff?"'

Although wartime propaganda emphasised merchant seafarers' quiet stoicism, exchanges of this kind illustrate the persistence of pre-war patterns of industrial conflict at sea. Apart from a handful of hold-ups on West Coast colliers, there were few serious disturbances on New Zealand ships, probably in part because of Seamen's Union President F.P. Walsh's close relationship with Peter Fraser's Labour government. Strikes on British ships were equally rare (except in the case of some Indian and Chinese seamen, who refused duty to protest at the huge gap between their own wages and those of Europeans). On the other hand, British seafarers continued to jump ship in large numbers—more than 3000 cases were reported in 1942–43, a third of them in New Zealand and Australian ports. Many more (including a number of those in this book) were fined and imprisoned for less dramatic offences, especially absence without leave.[11]

Predictably, disciplinary offences occurred most often in port, where the greatest temptations lay and where seafarers' traditional behaviour was again largely undisturbed by war. At sea much time was spent yarning about the last 'run ashore' or dreaming of the next one. Seafarers' fondness for drinking, fighting and whoring in port has often been exaggerated, reflecting the fact that it was inevitably condensed into short, intense bursts between voyages; many steered clear of such activities altogether. Nevertheless, sudden release from shipboard discipline and wartime tensions could produce volatile results, especially where large groups of seafarers and servicemen congregated. Local merchant seamen, for example, were central protagonists in Wellington's infamous 'Battle of Manners Street' with American servicemen in 1943. Similarly, the use of prostitutes by seafarers, like soldiers, was not uncommon during wartime; after all, the availability of commercial sex had been a feature of waterfront 'sailortowns' for centuries.

This 'disreputable' behaviour did not mean that seafarers were especially lawless or disloyal. Rather, it was the product of an occupational culture that tolerated or even encouraged certain acts—jumping ship, heavy drinking, fighting—while condemning others, especially letting down or stealing from a shipmate. 'You never thieved on a ship because you're all in close quarters and the whole ship would condemn you,' explains Les Watson. 'I felt there was a character to them, merchant seamen, and yet they were classed as the scum of the world. But they had a great code of ethics—their own code, but it was an honesty code.'

Most of those interviewed for this book look back on their seafaring careers in overwhelmingly positive terms, in large part because of the camaraderie they found at sea. As Thor Larsen explains, your shipmates 'looked after you like a long-lost brother, no matter who you were . . . The unwritten law was that no matter what happened, everyone stuck together.' Even in the infernal stokehold of an old coal-burner, seafarers could find satisfaction in their work: 'Sometimes there were fights and a little blood about,' Bill Hall recalls, 'but there was also singing and laughter.' In the end, despite all the hard work, poor food, rough seas and moments of danger, it was this sense of community that made their experience in the Merchant Navy one they would not have missed.

Historians have often scoured New Zealand's war history for evidence of an emerging national identity. That a distinctive New Zealand character is less easily discernible in this story is in part a reflection of the international nature of the shipping industry and the fact that many New Zealanders served as individuals or in small groups within a larger British service—an experience shared by thousands of their compatriots in the RAF and Royal Navy. Certainly, those who appear in this book displayed many of the qualities typically associated with New Zealanders at war: self-sufficiency, modesty, teamwork, egalitarianism, irreverence and an easy-going pragmatism. Steve Carey's comments on the all-round skills of the *Maunganui*'s engineering staff, which impressed Scottish shipyard engineers, fit this pattern, as do John Montgomery's remarks about class distinctions on British ships. Ultimately, however, seafarers' wartime experiences were shaped less by parochial concerns than by their powerful occupational culture, which transcended national boundaries.

Whether maintaining New Zealand's perilous 12,000-mile ocean lifeline to Britain, carrying troops and supplies across other seas, or shipping goods around the coast, merchant seafarers played a vital role in the Allied war effort. No other group of New Zealand civilians faced such risks during wartime. Like most participants in the events of 1939–45, the majority of seafarers had little concern for the politics and grand strategies of war beyond a simple faith in the justice of the Allies' cause. Typically, they were motivated by more limited aims: a determination to 'keep going, war or no war', because that was their job, even if it sometimes thrust them into the front lines. For them, victory lay in the restoration of the routines and rhythms of peacetime voyaging, the moment in 1945 when after six years of darkness the lights of their ships went back on.

NOTES

[1] In the late 1930s around 30–40 New Zealand women were employed as stewardesses on passenger liners and ferries. Most lost their jobs as passenger traffic fell away and liners were requisitioned for trooping duties, although some continued working on the coast throughout the war.

[2] The quote is from *Appendix to the Journals of the House of Representatives* (*AJHR*), 1945, H-30, p. 40. See also ibid., p. 15; J.V.T. Baker, *The New Zealand People at War: War Economy*, Department of Internal Affairs, Wellington, 1965, pp. 375, 623; and 'Notes on New Zealand's War Effort', pp. 25–7, Prime Minister's Department, 22/3/5, Archives New Zealand (ANZ).

[3] *AJHR*, 1948, H-19B, p. 21.

[4] Sydney Waters, *Union Line: A Short History of the Union Steam Ship Company of New Zealand 1875–1951*, Coulls Somerville Wilkie, Wellington, 1952, p. 96.

[5] See Sydney Waters, *German Raiders in the Pacific*, Department of Internal Affairs, Wellington, 1949; A.K. Muggenthaler, *German Raiders of World War II*, Prentice-Hall, New Jersey, 1977; and Fred Abernethy's description of the loss of the *Holmwood* in Anna Rogers (ed.), *The War Years*, Platform, Wellington, 1989. The *Rangitane* victims included two (British) stewardesses and four female passengers. Most accounts understate the number of deaths, probably because several victims died of their wounds aboard the raiders (a 16th victim died in German captivity four months later); I am grateful to Trevor Bell for the correct figures.

[6] For a detailed account of the DEMS programme, see Peter Cooke, *Defending New Zealand: Ramparts on the Sea*, Defence of New Zealand Study Group, Wellington, 2000, vol. I, pp. 428–55.

[7] See John Holm, *No Place to Linger: Saga of a Wartime Atlantic Kiwi*, Holmwork, Wellington, 1985.

[8] These casualty figures (which do not include DEMS gunners serving aboard merchant ships or ex-merchant seamen in naval service) have been compiled from 'War – Notification of Casualties to New Zealand Personnel', Marine Department (M), 1/25/2744, ANZ; and the Commonwealth War Graves Commission database, www.cwgc.org

[9] 'War Risk – Compensation to Seamen', M 1/25/875B, ANZ; Wynne Mason, *Prisoners of War*, Department of Internal Affairs, Wellington, 1954, pp. 37–8.

[10] At least 37 of the *Hauraki*'s officers and crew were New Zealanders; most of the others (including Captain Creese) were Australian. As the vessel was sailing under New Zealand articles of agreement, they were officially regarded as New Zealand prisoners. See M 1/25/2744 and 1/25/2744/1, ANZ.

[11] See Tony Lane, *The Merchant Seamen's War*, Manchester University Press, Manchester, 1990, especially pp. 110–17.

Further Reading

There are few published sources on New Zealand merchant seafarers at war. Although the *Official History of New Zealand in the Second World War* series eventually comprised 48 volumes and 24 shorter studies, none deal with the Merchant Navy in any detail. The most useful are Sydney Waters' volume on the *Royal New Zealand Navy* (1956) and his shorter account of *German Raiders in the Pacific* (1949). In 1946 John Daysh-Davey published a slim, non-official booklet entitled *They Also Served: The Merchant Navy and its Contribution to Allied Victory*. John Crawford's *Atlantic Kiwis* (1993) provides an overview of New Zealanders' involvement in the Battle of the Atlantic. The Union Company's war effort is discussed in *Union Line* (1952), also by Waters, while Jack Churchouse, *The Pamir Under the New Zealand Ensign* (1978), and W.A. Laxon, *Davey and the Awatea* (1997), focus on individual ships. *A Merchant Navy Man's Story* (1998), by David Hodgson, traces the wartime career of his father Lionel, who also appears in this book. Other personal accounts include Walter Caldwell's *Kiwi in a Crow's Nest* (1978), and the chapters on Stan Kirkpatrick and Johnny Cawley in Roy Sinclair's *Journeying with Seafarers in New Zealand* (1999).

In contrast, numerous books about the Merchant Navy at war have been published in Britain. Several of the companies engaged in the New Zealand trade produced their own war histories, including Shaw Savill & Albion (Frank Bowen, *The Flag of the Southern Cross, 1939–45*, 1947), the New Zealand Shipping Company (Sydney Waters, *Ordeal by Sea*, 1949), and Blue Star (Taprell Dorling, *Blue Star Line at War*, 1973). In general, see Martin Middlebrook, *Convoy: The Battle for Convoys SC.122 and HX.229* (1976); Tony Lane, *The Merchant Seamen's War* (1990); John Slader, *The Fourth Service* (1995); and, by Richard Woodman, *Arctic Convoys, 1941–1945* (1995), *Malta Convoys, 1940–1943* (2000), and *The Real Cruel Sea* (2004). Also recommended is Mike Parker's *Running the Gauntlet: An Oral History of Canadian Merchant Seamen in World War II* (1994).

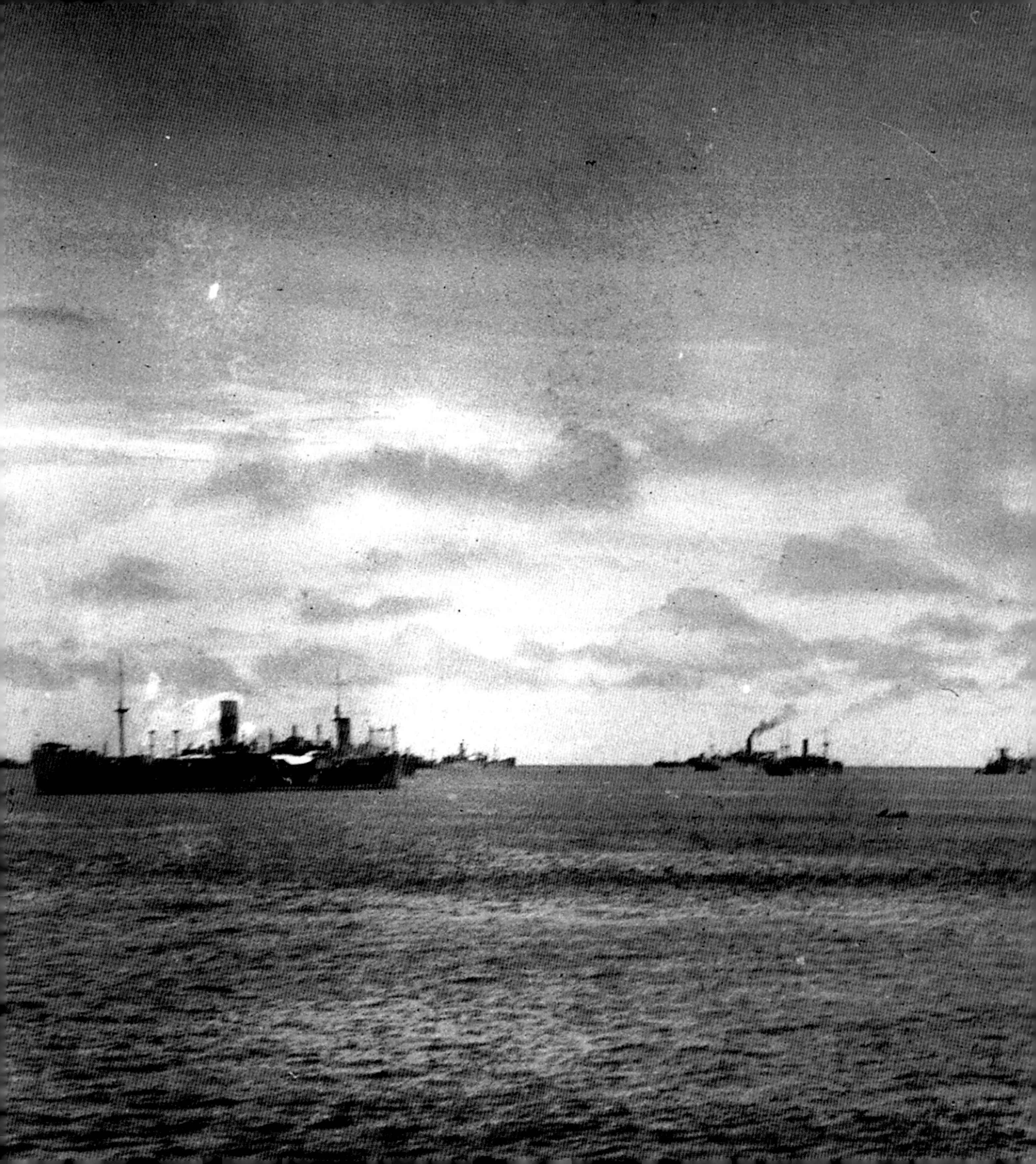

'YOU KNEW YOU WERE ON THE BULL'S-EYE'

LIONEL HODGSON, Engineer Officer

Lionel Hodgson, the son of a former marine engineer who worked at the local meatworks, was born in March 1918 at Ngauranga, Wellington. After short spells in Islington (Christchurch) and Kaiapoi, the family settled in Picton. Lionel had a couple of years at Marlborough College before starting an apprenticeship as a fitter and turner at Islington freezing works.

I FINISHED MY APPRENTICESHIP in 1938, about August, and I went to sea. My father had been a Londoner and he'd come to New Zealand when he finished his apprenticeship. He sailed around the coast for a year or two and then joined the New Zealand Shipping Company. So he knew one or two chief engineers in that company and one of them arranged for the *Ruahine*, when it came to New Zealand in 1938 on one voyage, to come out one short of its two refrigerating engineers. And that place was for me.

So I did the remainder of that trip as second refrigerating engineer and when we got to London and discharged the cargo I was appointed seventh engineer. They had seven engineers on the main engines. I was on the bottom rung there. We went right round the UK and then left for New Zealand again. At the end of that trip they laid up the ship in Falmouth in Cornwall, and I joined a ship called the *Kent*. New Zealand Shipping Company ships had Maori names and the Federal Steam Navigation Company—which was really the same company, you were interchangeable—had English county names.

We went from London to Hamburg in Germany and we may have been there for a week. That was 1939, about three months before the war. We went down the Elbe. It was quite nice there. The British Merchant Seaman's Institute there took us for a picnic, and I took a photograph, not realising, of a village street—and there was a flagpole there with a swastika on it. They gave us a pep talk on the way over to behave ourselves when we got there. I always took a camera ashore with me, quite openly, in case there was any objection to it, but there never was.

Previous page: *Calm before the storm: merchant ships at Freetown, Sierra Leone, waiting to form a convoy for Britain shortly after the outbreak of war in September 1939.* Hodgson collection
Above: *Lionel Hodgson, engineer officer, New Zealand Shipping Company.* Hodgson collection

Then we went out to Australia, around the Cape [of Good Hope]. We worked our way right round Australia till we got to Cairns and then came back again—discharged all the way round, then loaded all the way back. Between Melbourne and Adelaide, I came on watch at 12 o'clock (12 to 4 in the morning) and the first thing they told me was war had been declared with Germany. You had a pretty good idea of what happened with ships during the First World War. Anyway, we carried on and went round the Cape and up to Freetown in Sierra Leone, and we waited there for a few days until there were enough ships to form a convoy. It was quite interesting in convoy, keeping position—it would be a couple of revs up, a couple of revs down, you had to be on your toes.

The *Kent* was a steam turbine and it's a bit monotonous down there on turbines, so I asked if I could go back on the open-engine, crankcase-like steam engines. So I went to the *Remuera*, which was docked

Lionel photographed this charming village on the Elbe River—complete with fluttering swastika—during the Kent's visit to Hamburg in May 1939. Hodgson collection

in London, and I did two voyages to New Zealand. Each time we went out we'd go in convoy for three or four days and then they'd let you loose and you'd go on your own. We went to New Zealand through Panama, loaded round the coast, and then back through Panama to the UK. On the way we called at Pitcairn, and the islanders came out with their longboats and we got fresh oranges and things.

The Panama Canal was very interesting too, to see exactly how it worked on the way through the locks. The electric mules held you in position in the locks and guided you through to the canal. When we left Panama we went up the American coast to Halifax in Nova Scotia, and we lay there for a few days until they built up enough ships for a convoy across the North Atlantic.

Bound for Britain with a cargo of frozen meat from New Zealand, in August 1940 the Remuera *(11,445 tons) crossed the North Atlantic as part of convoy HX65.*

When we were a couple of days from the UK on the Western Approaches we got pulled out of our bunks in the middle of the night. There'd been a tanker torpedoed on the after end of the convoy, and I didn't know it at the time but there were two other ships torpedoed too. The next night about midnight—we were in the middle at the head of the convoy, there were about five abreast and 12 at least in line behind us—they sunk the ships either side of us, both of them. Of course, you go down below in the engine room and you're really on the bull's-eye down there. There were depth charges going off, and when you're down there it shakes you up a bit. What you didn't know was whether it was the ship next door being torpedoed or a depth charge, so it was pretty harrowing.

They ordered the convoy to disperse, so it was full steam ahead, not the convoy speed of about seven or eight knots. We could do about 14 to 15 knots, so we got a ring down, 'Full ahead', and then a few minutes after that we got another ring down on the phone to tell us that we were smoking that badly on the funnel they couldn't see where they were going. We'd put her full speed ahead and put the oil up on the boilers but we'd forgotten to open the fan up for the air, so we cured the smoke very quickly when we gave the fan the right air pressure.

In the morning the convoy formed again. Then I think half the convoy went down the Irish Sea, probably to Liverpool or the Bristol Channel, and the section we were in went round the north of Scotland, between the Orkneys and the mainland—Pentland Firth. We went through there and down the North Sea and we got about three-quarters of the way across the Moray Firth by about eight in the

'You Knew You Were on the Bull's-eye'

Two New Zealand engineers, Hodgson (left) and Daly, on the deck of the Remuera *off the north-east coast of Scotland on 26 August 1940. The helmets and lifejackets were put on for the camera, but seven hours after the photograph was taken the ship was sunk by a German torpedo bomber.* Hodgson collection

evening. Well, I came off watch at eight o'clock. I went and had a bit of a bath, such as it was, and I was there washing myself in the bath and I heard a whistle—the first time I'd ever heard a bomb whistle, I didn't know what it was then. They missed, but it didn't take me long to get out of there and get dressed! It must have been for'ard of us where the bomb dropped because when I got out on deck you could see a big circle, about 60 foot in diameter.

I got to the entrance to the engine room and I saw a plane approaching. It was only about 100 feet above the water, about 30 degrees off the port bow, and I could see flashing lights. I thought it must be a German plane and the flashing lights machine-guns, so I thought I'd better get down where there's armour between me and the bullets. Just as I went to go into the entrance I saw them drop something in the sea and I thought, that's a funny place to drop a bomb, but of course I knew afterwards. I'd just got to the top of the engine room and the torpedo struck between [Nos] 4 and 5 holds. We had three holds for'ard of the passenger accommodation and two aft, and it struck on the bulkhead between the two. If it had hit the hold without destroying the bulkhead, I don't think she would have sunk.

They gave the 'Abandon Ship' signal, which was a series of short blasts. The alarm was one long blast, but you knew what to do when you got short blasts. So I went to the boat deck. I didn't go back to the accommodation to pick up anything because the torpedo had gone in under our accommodation and if it had blown a hole in the deck and it was dark, well, I wasn't going back. So we all got off, and there were no passengers on that trip. We just drifted away from the ship and lay there and watched as she slowly went down. The air raid had finished by that time. She slowly filled up from the stern and the last I saw of her, from the bridge up she was vertical and she just slowly went down. In those days at least, the ship was your home, and I'll never forget the feeling of seeing my home disappear under the waves.

There was another ship torpedoed in the same convoy. When we saw our ship go down—it took about an hour—the convoy slowly went past. Then a naval sloop came along and the mate, who was in charge of this lifeboat, said, 'I think we'll go to the sloop, we'll be under the guns then if there's any more attacks.' So that's what we did. Its name was *Egret*. They gave us a blanket each and we just slept on the wooden deck, under cover of course.

The *Egret* stayed with the other ship that had been torpedoed. It had come from Canada and it had a big load of logs on deck. They sent for a tug, which came out, and they put a line aboard, but unfortunately the line got tangled around the tug's propeller. The ship was slowly going down, dead level all the way, so they had to cut the tug adrift because they could see it was going down and it was big enough to take the tug with it. So we just waited there and it just slowly went down and about midday or one o'clock it disappeared below the waves, dead level the whole way. A few minutes after it had gone down there was a loud explosion, just like a gun going off. The logs that were on the deck had had chains over them, and the buoyancy of the logs was too much for the chains under those circumstances

Lionel (left) with the Remuera's *third engineer, Maurice Hendry, wearing their tropical white uniforms in the latter's cabin. The settee covers and curtains were made by Hendry's wife. He was lost at sea in 1943.* Hodgson collection

and the bang was the sound when the chains went. After that, mountains of logs came up, a great big pile. It was quite spectacular, you'd see the pile go shuddering and then one would come up through the middle of it. I'll never forget that.

After it had gone down they took us to a port on the coast called Peterhead. The next day we went to Aberdeen by bus, and took the night train to London. My father was a Londoner and he had a sister who lived in Guildford, just out of London. You see, even in Peterhead, you didn't get a night's sleep—there were air raids. When we got to London we didn't get a night's sleep there—air raids. My aunt said she was quite pleased to look after me, so I went to Guildford.

Were you given survivor's leave?
Yes, well you stayed with the shipping company, you see. Engineers were officers of the ship just the same as the deck officers and radio officers, so you were kept on and they just sent you your pay each week. Actually, I signed off the *Remuera* in Guildford, in the post office—a very unusual place to sign off a voyage. So I was there for a month, and had a lovely time.

When I went to sea I wanted to get marine qualifications, and you had to have 18 months' sea-time, on articles, to sit for a second-class steam certificate. If the *Remuera* had got in and I'd had everything,

The Federal Steam Navigation Company's SS Westmoreland *(8967 tons) in Wellington before the war.* Alexander Turnbull Library, F-16742-1/2

I'd have had the time. I lost all the documents, so I went to the Board of Trade and explained the whole position to them, and they said no, they wouldn't accept it. So I had no option but to make another voyage. They sent me to join the *Rimutaka*. It was in Cardiff and it was a passenger ship too, but it was about 16 to 17,000 tons, turbine. So I joined the *Rimutaka* and it was backwards and forwards to New Zealand. And I made sure my documents were with me everywhere I went. I thought if I go down to Davy Jones's locker they'll be with me there too.

So, when we went back to Liverpool and were discharged I went ashore there for three or four months. I went to school to brush up on everything that was required for my examination. This was between February and May 1941. I was just about ready to go for the examination when Liverpool got the heaviest blasting that it had during the war. They blew up the Board of Trade building where I would have sat the exam, they blew up a house next to where I was staying, and the house I was in was made uninhabitable.

Were you in an air-raid shelter when the bombs hit?
Well, that night I'd decided that I would go to the air-raid shelter. I never had before. I got the urge to go to the shelter, so I went down the stairs and another chap from the school was there, and the landlady and her husband. They said, 'We're coming with you.' I just got to the door of the lounge—there was a hall out the back and the staircase upstairs—and a bomb landed. You couldn't see from here to there for dust. I was the first one under the staircase, everyone piled on top of me. So I never did get to the air-raid shelter.

The school got blown up too, so they sent me to sit the exam in a church in Birkenhead. I think it was three days, or two-and-a-half days; the two days was written and the third day was drawing. Anyway, I passed the exam all right. I let the company know—they had an office in Liverpool—and they sent me to the *Westmoreland*.

Lionel joined the Westmoreland *in August 1941 as fifth engineer. After delivering munitions from the United States to New Zealand, the ship loaded supplies for 2NZEF in the Middle East.*

We left Auckland and about the time we got to Fremantle, that's when Pearl Harbor occurred. So we knew that the Americans had come in, that we were at war with Japan as well. A few days out from Fremantle in the middle of the day we saw a very bright object in the sky. Was it a Japanese balloon or something? So [the gunners] loaded up the 12-pounder up for'ard, elevated it, and then suddenly discovered it was Venus. They were a wee bit crestfallen when we found out!

The next port was Colombo. We went from there to Aden and laid out at buoys and bunkered. Then we went up the Red Sea to Tewfik, through the Suez Canal to Port Said, and lay there for about three weeks while we slowly discharged. Then we went up to Haifa to finish discharging.

After the Japanese came in, the Australians called some of their troops home. So we loaded up with one half of an ambulance unit—we had all their vehicles in the hold, some of them on deck—and we took them from Port Said back to Adelaide. They brought a little dog aboard with them. It was about 18 inches long. When I came off watch (I was on the 4 to 8, twice a day) this little dog always used to waylay me and grab hold of my boiler-suit leg so I'd drag it along. When we got back to Australia, they were very strict about bringing in animals, but the captain assured them that the dog would stay on the ship. So they didn't destroy it, which they would have done otherwise.

After loading around the New Zealand coast, the Westmoreland *left Wellington for Britain on 26 April 1942 with a cargo of 20,820 lamb and mutton carcasses, 7400 pork carcasses, 3235 tons of butter, 20,450 crates of cheese and 9554 bales of wool.*

We went through Panama and from there we were to go to Halifax to join a convoy. We must have gone pretty well out into the Atlantic. Prior to Pearl Harbor most German U-boats operated close to Europe, but after Pearl Harbor of course they were thick as you like on the American coast. When we left Panama the radio operator used to give us a happy thought every day, telling us there were a couple of ships sunk off the American coast. They were sinking two or three off the coast every day at that period.

One night, about a week after we left Panama, we had the old long blow—the alarm. They'd seen lights, over on the starboard side, I think. Now, what were the lights? Could have been a decoy, could have been crews in a lifeboat trying to attract our attention. Well, the only safe thing to do was carry on. The fourth engineer [Olly Olsen] in the cabin next to me—he was a New Zealander, and Plymouth Brethren—had a verse of the Bible to look at every day. The 91st Psalm is really a psalm of protection. So I took the Bible in to Olly and said, 'How about reading the 91st Psalm to me?' So he read it. Well, when you get down a bit it talks about not being afraid, and one verse goes, 'Thou shall not be afraid

This fuzzy photograph of Lionel and another engineer on watch captures something of the gloominess and vibration of the steamship's engine room.
Hodgson collection

of the terror by night.' Well, it stuck out like a sore toe to me, this 'terror by night'. And you know what I thought when I heard that?—I haven't got an enemy. I don't remember anything else he read, but just 'terror by night' and 'no enemy'.

The following night, in the early hours of 1 June, the Westmoreland *was torpedoed by U-566 about 240 miles north of Bermuda. Three crew members lost their lives.*

There's this big explosion and I rush out on deck. Some of them used to sleep in their clothes, but I always slept with my pyjamas on. I didn't waste any time to get dressed, though, and went up. Of course, I had the old lifejacket on. Olly said, 'What was that bang? Something must have come adrift.' Well, when I went to secondary school, at the end of the year we used to fire .303s at the firing range—it's an unmistakable smell, cordite. The same smell there. So I said, 'No, Olly, that was a torpedo, that one.'

They lowered the lifeboat and she was rolling a wee bit. They'd put welded metal guards over where the sewage ports were in the side, and when she rolled and went against those guards you could hear the old lifeboat creak. And I thought to myself, gee, I hope she doesn't crack. Well, one of them did, on the other side, broke up on the way down. They picked the crew out of the sea and the next day it turned out that there were two lifeboats with the normal amount in and one with double the number in.

We got the oars out and pulled away. Gee, those lifeboat oars, they were very long and very cumbersome. So, we pulled away a bit and waited. She wasn't going to sink. The torpedo went into No. 3 hold, just for'ard of the bridge, and it was full of cheese—and we could have picked a few crates out as we were drifting away, but no one thought of that.

We were about quarter to half a mile off and then the U-boat opened fire on the ship. It probably saw that it wasn't going to sink. You could see the tracer shells arcing across, hitting the ship. We waited till the morning, and when daylight came the ship was just hull up, more or less, and the U-boat was about a quarter-mile away. They were running their engines, charging their batteries. There was no aggro as far as they were concerned.

About midday the U-boat took off. We assembled and distributed the crew amongst the three boats. We had 24 men in a 24-foot lifeboat, so we just sat up each side. We decided we couldn't miss the American continent if we went west, so we took off [under sail]. Before we left the *Westmoreland* the little dog came up and hopped in the lifeboat I was in. The first night in the lifeboat—the weather wasn't that cold but the little dog must have felt it needed company—it snuggled up with me. There were lots of oars in the lifeboat and they put them fore-and-aft on the thwarts. But by morning you knew where every oar had been because you'd feel it, laying there all night.

The next day there were only two lifeboats there. Well, the other one could have sailed a slightly different angle and be over the horizon. A very high-flying aircraft went overhead, but it was too high [to see us]. Then part-way through the day a Catalina flying boat came out on lookout for U-boats. They couldn't land; they couldn't get us all aboard anyway. So they dropped us a bag with a loaf of bread in and a note. There were 12 slices in the loaf so we had half a slice each. On the note they said they'd scout around to see if they could get another ship and direct them, and if they couldn't they'd come back before dark and drop a smoke float, and that would be the direction to the nearest land. Well, they duly did that—they couldn't get another ship, so just before dark they flew over us and dropped the smoke float.

The third morning, when daylight came we were on our own; the other lifeboat must have been on a slightly different course. About half past five in the morning, on the port side about a mile away, there was a ship, going in the same direction as us. We cheered a bit—they couldn't hear that, of course—but then to our disappointment it turned at right angles and went away from us. But what happened was they'd sailed up between the two lifeboats and they ran into the other lifeboat, picked them up, and they said there's another lifeboat around. So they came back.

The occupants of the Westmoreland's *third boat were rescued three days later by another ship.*

I'll always remember clambering up the side of that ship, up the old Jacob's ladder. They were going between Canada and the West Indies and they had lots of sugar and rum aboard. They had a black crew, and on the hatch when I came up over the side there was a black chap there with a five-gallon jar full of coffee, ringed with pint mugs. I downed two. On the lifeboat, you see, you got about two egg-cups full of water a day. Well, we didn't know how long we were going to be out there. So then they paired us off: we went with the engineers, and the deck officers and the others went to their respective quarters. The engineer I was with was one of these chaps that slept with his clothes on, so he slept on a settee. So the three days it took us to get to Halifax I slept in his bunk.

We were in Halifax for about ten days. It was quite nice, too, to get ashore and sleep in a bed and wander around. While we were there the sailors took care of the dog. And then the dog wandered off. There's a main street in Halifax called Barrington Street, and it had trams running up it. One day I was out there and saw the little dog in the middle of the tram track, doing its business. A tram came up and was clanging its bells to try to get this dog off the track, which it eventually did. So that's the last time I saw the little dog, but I've always hoped that someone found it and took it as a pet.

Did you ever have cats or dogs on other ships?
Later, on the *Rangitiki* we had a cat, and one time when we left Gibraltar to go to the UK in convoy, lots of little birds about the size of sparrows came and perched on the bulwarks. Well, this cat couldn't help itself, it jumped and it went clean over right into the sea. I went right down the after end and the last I saw, it was a couple of hundred yards astern. So that was the end of that cat.

On the *Orari* we had a cat, too. It used to jump up on the hatch at sea, and they used to bring it stuff to eat there. At one port in Australia, when they took the hatch covers off, that cat jumped up and of course it went 60 foot down into the bottom of the hold and that was the end of that cat. It's rather sad when you think of things like that.

After returning to Britain, Lionel spent several months in Glasgow studying for his first-class marine engineer's certificate—and got engaged to a young Scottish woman.

I decided that I wanted to go in motor ships—and I had enough steam-time to get the first-class but not enough sea-time. So I wrote to head office, and they sent me to Cardiff and I joined the *Rangitiki* as fifth engineer. On the first voyage [in November 1942] we went to North Africa through the Straits of Gibraltar—it was called Operation Torch, when they landed the troops there. We had about 3000 Americans aboard, and there were another six or eight other ships bigger than us in the convoy. There was another big convoy that went in about a week ahead of us, and the Tasman Sea 'greyhound', the *Awatea*, was sunk coming out, after she'd discharged everyone.

We went through the Straits of Gibraltar under darkness. I imagined there'd be lots of people either side looking to see who went through. We landed in a place called Mers El Kébir, the port for Oran, and we were there four or five days. We discharged the Americans and the equipment we had for them, and we came out and went back through the Straits again.

The 16,698-ton MV Rangitiki *in wartime grey at Wellington, with extra liferafts, gun nests and paravane booms visible on the foredeck.* Alexander Turnbull Library, W.H. Raine Collection, G-20746-1/4

After I got married [in May 1943], the *Rangitiki* went to South America. We went out to Freetown and from there to Montevideo, then up the River Plate to Buenos Aires—it's about 120 miles, I think. When we left Montevideo the ship took a list, and, of course, if it takes a list they ring down from the bridge and you transfer oil from one side tank to the other. We started to transfer oil and it didn't make the slightest bit of difference. If you went aft and looked over the stern it was like chocolate coming out—we were sitting on the bottom and it was sloping. The engines went twice the distance that the ship did! So, we got to Buenos Aires and I believe they said we were the biggest ship that ever got in there, because the *Rangitiki* was about 17,000 tons.

For the next two voyages we went to New York and back again. We loaded up with American troops, and we would have taken frozen meat or canned stuff back to the UK. After that I had enough sea-time to sit for my first-class steam and first-class motor certificate. It was quite nice having this spell ashore again in Glasgow. When I got the certificates I wrote to head office again and they sent me to the *Orari*, which was the last ship I sailed on, as third engineer.

When you were ashore, in civilian clothes, did you ever get any negative reaction from people who thought you should have been in the armed forces?
Only once. When I left Glasgow, before I joined the *Rangitiki*, they sent me to Falmouth. On the way down I went to the restaurant on one station, and there were naturally a lot of soldiers journeying. I got to the counter and there was a soldier behind me, and the woman there said to me, 'We've got to serve the soldiers first, you know.' So I just let it go. You see, that soldier would probably have never seen a shot fired in anger. I'd been torpedoed twice, bombed out once, sailed the ocean, never knowing how many had been fired at you and missed. All you knew when you were in the engine room was you were on the bull's-eye amidships.

How did you cope with that feeling when you went down below?
No one ever said a word about it, but I'm sure everyone thought about it. Because, oh well, if they hit the engine room you wouldn't have to worry about it, would you? But you knew exactly what you had to do. If they'd hit the hold next door and the bulkhead had got fractured or something, and you got a lot of water in, you knew what you had to do. You had circulating water for your condensers on the steamers, circulating water to keep the engines cool on the motor ships, and on the suction side of that pump you had what they called a bilge injection. Now, you could open that, shut the valve to let the sea water in, and that would have pumped a huge lot of water out through your condenser. And if you kept the water down enough with that, you would have kept the ship afloat. You knew if you got smacked somewhere else, you took the way out of the ship by putting the engines astern. That made it easier for lowering lifeboats, when they got in the water and that sort of thing. There wasn't really any schooling, but you knew what you had to do.

In 1945 the Orari *delivered supplies to United States forces in the south-west Pacific before returning to Britain in August. Lionel did one more round trip to New Zealand and then resigned from the New Zealand Shipping Company. He was repatriated aboard his old ship, the* Rangitiki, *arriving home in July 1946. After six months in Picton, he settled in Christchurch and worked as an engineer at the Islington freezing works until his retirement in 1979.*

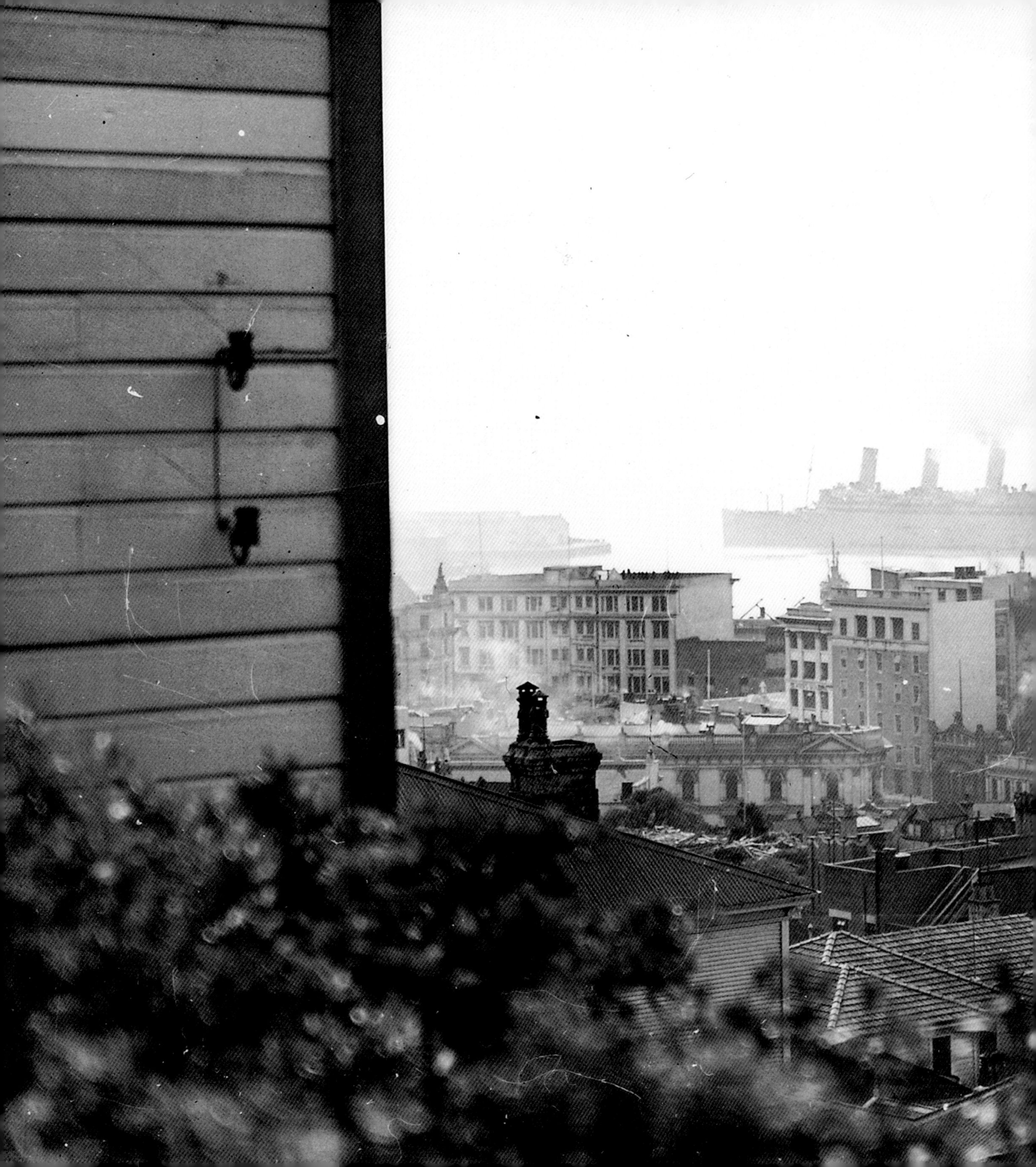

'THE OLD AQUITANIA'

JOHN MONTGOMERY, Cleaner, Fireman

John Montgomery was born in Wellington in December 1923, two years after his parents arrived in New Zealand from Scotland. After leaving Island Bay School in 1937, he worked on a dairy farm in Happy Valley, in a hosiery factory and at the Wellington markets. In 1940 he got a job in a butcher's shop.

I HAD TRIED TO JOIN the army when I was 16. I put my age up, but my father got [my application] cancelled. I'd been working in a butcher's shop after the war had started, for Jock Cardno. And when Italy came into the war [in June 1940] he lost most of his customers because they thought he was an Italian. I was going to join the navy—I'd got my father to sign me up to 12 years in the navy. They would take you at 17 or 18. I was telling one of the customers and he said, 'Oh, the navy, they've got all that discipline. We've got a friend of ours, he's got a scow and he can never get a boy. He's looking for a boy now.' So I went down and saw Tom Sawyer on the *Te Aroha*, a scow on Wellington Harbour.

I was 17 when I joined the *Te Aroha*, which allowed me to join the Seamen's Union, because it was a closed union at the time. So then I went down to what they called 'The Corner'—the shipping office—and I was down there for months and months. It turned out people in the know got jobs. Anyway, the *Aquitania* came in to take troops away. I said to my parents, 'If I can get a job on the *Aquitania*, can I go?', so they agreed that I could. It was 1941 by this time, September 1941.

This fellow called Titch Campbell—he was a bit younger than I was, he'd been at sea on the coast for a while before—both of us were in the same boat, trying to get a job on a ship. So we went down to the shipping office and everybody was crowded in, and the shipping master got up on the bench and said, 'You'll all have to get out. This is not the way it's done. All out, clear the place.' As they were putting everybody out, Titch said, 'Come on, we'll get behind the door.' So we got behind the door,

Previous page: *The Aquitania (45,647 tons) in Wellington Harbour in 1940. At the time the Cunard White Star liner was the largest merchant ship to have visited New Zealand.* Alexander Turnbull Library, Evening Post Collection, G-49250-1/4

Above: *John Montgomery, fireman, photographed in the United States during the war.* Montgomery collection

'The Old Aquitania'

The little Wellington scow Te Aroha, *in which John sailed before joining the* Aquitania *in 1941.* Alexander Turnbull Library, F-8535-1/2

and when the shipping master said, 'Who's first?', of course him and I walked out first and signed on. Titch signed on as a bridge boy and I signed on as a cleaner. I said, 'What's a cleaner do?' 'We'll find out when we get on board.' I found out the cleaners are down on the boilers, keeping the boilers clean, and you had to run messages and one thing and another.

We left Wellington on 15 September. One of the soldiers was an uncle of mine, my Uncle Sam. My first port of call was Colombo, which was a big change from Island Bay. Everything you bought, you had to argue with the person selling it. This uncle of mine bought a little ebony ashtray, and I got two maps of Ceylon for the same price that he paid. So he wrote to my mother to tell her I could look after myself.

We finally got the troops up to Port Tewfik. At night-time we had to leave Port Tewfik and go down the Red Sea just in case, because of the risk of the Germans coming over and sinking us. The *Aquitania* was a very lucky ship. It was in the First World War as a hospital ship, went right through the Second World War and finished up as scrap.

Built in 1913, the Cunard White Star Line's RMS Aquitania *(45,647 tons) was still one of the biggest ships in the world.*

It was the fourth largest, I think. The scow *Te Aroha* was 100 tons and the *Aquitania* was nearly 50,000! There were over 500 crew on it. A lot of them had come from Britain, of course. We were just [replacements for] the ones who had got sick and been sent home and the ones who had got off without paying off. There were quite a few Australians on there when I got on.

The Aquitania *eases away from the Wellington wharves in May 1940, carrying part of the Second Echelon of 2NZEF to the Middle East.* Alexander Turnbull Library, F-21894-1/2

Anyway, we finally left Port Tewfik with a load of Eyetie prisoners, about 500 of them. We took them to Bombay. I actually saw the 'Gateway to India' while I was there, when I got ashore one day. Crikey dick, the smell of the place was terrible. Even in Colombo everything seemed to stink like hang. Then we went to Singapore, which was another interesting place. We went into the dock at the navy yard there because it was big enough to hold the *Aquitania*, to scrape the bottom. While we were there they had air-raid drills, because of the possibility of the Japanese coming into the war. That was November '41, and they told us we'd have to get out because there were two battleships coming in, the *Prince of Wales* and *Repulse*, and they both got sunk [on 10 December].

Then when we came out of Singapore and were coming down the west coast of Australia a lookout reported an object in the sea, and it was 26 Germans off the *Kormoran*, the raider that sunk the *Sydney*. They both sunk each other. We took them round to Sydney. I didn't actually see them, I was asleep at the time that we picked them up (I was off watch), but I did see their uniforms and that. They reckoned they'd been in the liferafts for some time. We were sworn to secrecy, of course.

In November 1941 the German raider Kormoran *and the Australian cruiser HMAS* Sydney *were both sunk following an engagement in the Indian Ocean. None of the* Sydney's *645 crew survived.*

A couple of days later we were over in the Macquarie Hotel, and of course I used to drink in those days too—I got a lifetime habit from when I went to sea. They had barmaids in Sydney, which was rather strange to us. [At that time New Zealand did not allow women to work in bars.] They'd say, 'Now, now, sonny, you'd better stop that swearing or I'll ask you to leave.' You were relying on them to serve you, so you behaved yourself.

When we were in Sydney the Japanese bombed Pearl Harbor, and Singapore and Hong Kong, and it was all on. We took the first load of Australian militia to go overseas to Port Moresby in December '41; New Guinea was under the protection of Australia at the time. When we got to Port Moresby we tied up next to a ship called *Westralia*, which was from the Huddart Parker Line. Anyway, we got a message to get out of Port Moresby as quickly as possible, and it was all hang to pay. They threw the lines over from this ship. There were blokes from the *Aquitania* over there visiting mates and they sang out, 'Look after my gear for me,' because they pulled off that quickly they didn't even have time to get aboard.

So we got out. They told us the Japanese were bombing Rabaul at the time, which was not very far from Port Moresby. We set off at full speed, as fast as the old *Aquitania* could go, which was something like 24 knots, an amazing speed in those days, and we were in a ten-knot current coming down the Coral Sea. We were doing well over 30 knots as far as the land was concerned. The watch I was on, No. 4, was the control stokehold. There was big competition to see which watch got the most steam. With the steam turbines, of course, the more steam you got the faster the ship went.

Then we went from Sydney round to Fremantle with the AIF [Australian Imperial Force]. We took the troops up through the Sunda Straits to a cove called Oosthaven and transferred them onto Dutch ferries. They got to Singapore just as it fell. They never fired a shot. Then we came back through the Sunda Straits. Of course, the *Aquitania* must have been at risk all the time, really. We never got any news or whatever about what was going on at all.

We got back to Sydney and a joker from the shore told me we were going to Honolulu. I said, 'Well, we don't know till we get three miles out, they don't tell us at all.' There was nothing on board to tell you where we were going or anything. He said, 'I'm telling you, you're going to Honolulu.' Crikey dick, we got three miles outside of Sydney and they opened up the directions and sure enough we went to Honolulu. That was our secret! We were to help in the evacuation of people from Honolulu, women and children. We took them to San Francisco, and when we got there they took all the wooden bunks out and put steel bunks in. They got 25 per cent more troops on board.

Then the English crew paid off; they'd been away from England for about two years by then. They paid them off and got a crew down from Montreal. They had a [Reserve] Pool up there. We said, 'What about us?' The Aussies started to get a bit upset, about the crew getting paid off and not us. They said they wanted $100 [about £25] to take the troops to Honolulu, because American seamen were getting a bonus for taking troops. The actual wages on the *Aquitania* weren't a hang of a lot, about £15 a month or something. That was with the war-risk bonus. And you got half-a-day a month leave and half-a-day a month holiday pay as well. All the conditions on British ships were under the British Board of Trade, even the food and that. One time we went and complained about the food, and the joker said, 'Has anybody got a knife and fork?' He tasted it and said, 'I can't see what you people are complaining about.'

Anyway, we took the troops to Honolulu and came back with some more evacuees. We paid off then and they put us into a hotel at Oakland called the Hotel California, where we waited to get repatriated. It was May [1942] before we left San Francisco. We got onto a ship called the *Uruguay*. They gave us $5 going up the gangplank to keep us quiet, because these Aussie jokers, they moaned and groaned all the

Wellington Harbour in October 1943, showing the floating dock and Aotea Quay lined with American ships and military stores. Alexander Turnbull Library, Wellington Harbour Board Collection, F-31273-1/4

time. Us New Zealanders, we just used to take things as they came, but the Aussies were on the backpedal all the time. They were loading up the *Uruguay* with American troops. There was about seven or eight troopships, and we actually came into Auckland. We were with the first American troops to come into Auckland, in June 1942.

When we got to sea we found there were only two meals a day, and one day it was sauerkraut and weenies. Of course, the Yanks like their sauerkraut. I'd never tasted it before and it was a heck of a long time before the next feed came about. Anyway, these Aussies decided they were going to go up and see the captain. We were right down in the bowels of the ship, right down above the propellers. They knocked on the captain's door and the captain didn't even know we were on board, that's how much the captain knew. We finished up in Auckland. I went along to the Cunard Shipping Company and got a train passage down to Wellington, and that was me back home.

In late 1942 John spent several months working on the Wellington floating dock.

I was working on a ship called the *Tainui*—the *Empire Trader* it was called by that time—and we were digging the bilges out; they hadn't been dug out for years. I had my name round all the shipping companies to see if anything was going. Then at the beginning of November '42 there was a message from the New Zealand Shipping Company saying there was a vacancy on the *Ruahine* as a fireman. So we left New Zealand and went to Britain. I had my 19th birthday in the Caribbean. Then we went up to New York. It was wintertime, of course, and it was freezing cold.

We came out of New York and formed up a convoy outside, then we went across the Atlantic. It was a rather dangerous period then. There were all kinds of ships getting sunk. Of course, they didn't put out any news bulletins or anything. You didn't know what was going on. But one day during the trip from New York to Glasgow—it was mostly Cockneys on the *Ruahine* at that time—this fellow came in and says, 'You'd better get up, Kiwi, there's one going down alongside.' It was a whaling factory ship, with bombers and that on the deck. It had been torpedoed.

We left Scotland again about 23 January 1943. The convoy went into storms, calm, fog, everything you could think of going across the Atlantic. Anyway, we managed to survive. They took us through the Cape Cod Canal, down Long Island Sound and into New York, which was rather strange. They didn't tell us what was going on or why they were doing things. We didn't have any communication at all, really. Just as well, I suppose, because a joker was nervous enough anyway. You knew you were likely to get blown up. Working on the boilers, you were right in the middle of the ship, which was the point they tried to aim for.

Most of [the British seamen] couldn't swim. They never got an opportunity to swim where they lived. We each had a bag with all our personal belongings in it, called a getaway bag. You slept in your good clothes all the time. You never took your clothes off when you were at sea, particularly in the Atlantic. You were all set to go, because in an emergency you didn't have time to get your clothes on.

We went to Melbourne and round to Sydney, and we actually brought back the crew of a New Zealand ship, the *Limerick*, that had got sunk off the coast of Australia. Bill Shand, one of the crew on the *Limerick*, had been on the *Te Aroha* with me. I was up seeing him of a night-time and I got told off for being up in the passengers' quarters. Even though they were seamen, they were still passengers. They had all these rules, British seamen. We had a bit of a dispute with the second engineer there once, and he just turned around to these jokers and said, 'Are you going to turn to?' They couldn't do anything, because their wives were depending on their money. When we got into Melbourne the engineers said, 'Back-ends and tubes in the morning.' Crikey dick, we've got the fires going flat out. Cleaning back-ends and tubes was a 'job-and-finish', because it was that blimin' dirty. And we still had steam on, it was as hot as anything, and the fires still had sparks in them. 'Crikey, we're not going to do that, are we?' 'Oh yeah, what can you do, Kiwi?'

What did you wear when you were on watch?
You had to wear trousers and boots, because it was that hot. You wore boots to keep your feet cool, actually. Most of the time it was pretty warm down below. In the tropics we'd try to get the ventilators turned around so we got a bit of a draught, but as soon as the ship got into the cold weather the draught used to whistle down.

You were pretty busy when you were on watch, you had to punch carbon back and things like that. Each boiler had a periscope with a light behind it so you could look up and see if it was smoking. If you saw some smoke, you had to find out which burner was clogged up. Smoke was a danger to the ship; you had to keep the smoke down all the time. Of course, most of the fuels they used were pretty low-grade oils too.

A fellow on the *Aquitania* taught us all about burning the oil. [The *Aquitania* and *Ruahine*] were both originally coal-burners; they'd been converted to oil-burning. Another job we had was to go in and scrape the boilers. You had to take all the water out and go through a small hole to get into them and scrape them. And the engineer would go in and make sure you'd done it. How we used to get in and out, goodness only knows. You'd wriggle your way through and back out again. If it wasn't right you'd have to go back in and do it again.

The *Ruahine* was under the Board of Trade regulations. A tin of condensed milk had to last you about two weeks, and you got so much sugar. You weren't allowed to have meat unless you had offal, so they'd give you a big chunk of old ox liver and a little wee strip of bacon. But we weren't too bad on the *Ruahine*, the cook there was a good cook. He'd put chips on for us, as long as the jokers off watch could peel the spuds and that—he'd do a bit extra for us. We got eggs twice a week, on Sundays and Wednesdays. Board of Trade regulations were pretty strict, really.

During the Ruahine's *visit to Auckland in 1943, John left the ship to see his family in Wellington. When he failed to report back on time he was arrested for desertion.*

They called it desertion, but what it was really is failing to fulfil a contract. It wasn't actually a crime, it was more or less a civil action between the shipping company and you, but they made sure the Englishmen always got a month's jail. I went in there and I tried to explain to the magistrate. The old magistrate was sharpening his pencils and he looked over his glasses, and said, 'A seaman doesn't take his bags off the ship unless he's going off.' He banged me down for two weeks in Mount Crawford prison, and to be 'placed aboard the first available ship'. I thought, crikey dick, I'm going to get deported from my own country! Anyway, they didn't.

When I was in San Francisco I got some American seamen's papers, so I went up to the American consul and applied for any job on an American ship, because the money was twice or three times more than the British. I was working in a butter-packing place, under the Internal Marketing Division, and I got home one night and my mother said, 'The American consul rung you up. If you want the job you've got to be there first thing in the morning.' The consul said to me, 'There's a job out at Miramar Wharf on an oil tanker. If you take it, you know we'll be watching you. We don't throw our seamen in jail. We just call it "failure to return".' 'No, you won't get that from me,' I said. So I went out to Miramar and I saw the first engineer on a tanker called the *Schenectady*. Turned out it was the first T2 tanker that was built, and it broke in half on its sea trials

The Schenectady, *the first of nearly 500 T2-SE-A1 tankers built in American shipyards during the war, had snapped in two soon after being launched in January 1943 but had later been repaired. The T2s were capable of carrying almost six million US gallons (22 million litres) of oil.*

The first engineer (he was the equivalent of a second engineer on a British ship) said to me he only had a cleaner's job available, but that he'd give me the first fireman's job that came along. It was an oil-burner. I signed on as a cleaner and we went from Wellington to San Pedro [Los Angeles], picked up a load of oil and came back to Wellington. While I was in San Pedro I had to go along and get an

Right: *An unidentified oil tanker discharging at Burnham Wharf, Miramar, Wellington.* Alexander Turnbull Library, The Press (Christchurch) Collection, G-41284-1/2

identification certificate from the Coast Guard. At the same time I had to get a certificate to say that I was a fireman. The Coast Guard fellow said, 'Have you got any qualifications?' I said, 'I've been on a couple of British ships.' 'You were a fireman on British ships? Oh, you don't need any examination.' So he just signed the paper.

We had a refit in America and they put extra escape hatches in the cabins, so we knew we must have been going on a pretty long voyage. When I went up to sign on again the joker said, 'What's your rating?' I said, 'Cleaner.' He said, 'No, you're down here as fireman. You've got the qualifications, you're entitled to the job.' If that had been a British ship they'd have never bothered. So I always admired the Yanks, I liked working for them, because if you said something they trusted you. Whereas in England they wouldn't even ask you. That class distinction thing on British ships I could never understand at all. On American ships, if the captain saw you ashore he was only too pleased to speak to you. It was just the difference between the two cultures.

Of course, the money was extra. I was getting $112 a month plus war-risk. The world was split up into 25 per cent zones, 50 per cent zones and 100 per cent zones. In the Panama Canal and in American ports you didn't get any war-risk. Most of the places were 50 per cent, so you got $112 plus another $56, and then you got overtime as well, which was for doing back-ends and tubes and things like that. They used to play an awful lot of poker too, no-limit poker. I learnt to play that fairly quickly. I did reasonably well. Once in the Indian Ocean I won £130. Of course, by the time I got to port I'd given it all back. The poker school would go all night, nearly every night. We played with reals, Australian pounds, rupees, all kinds [of currency].

When we left America we were away for 12 months. I did five trips to Abadan in the Persian Gulf. There were 27 loading docks there. The Shatt-al-Arab is the name of the river up to Abadan, where the Tigris and the Euphrates join. When you got up there the temperature in the boiler room (the fireroom they called it) was unbelievable—the thermometer went up to 149° [Fahrenheit], and the little wee bubble at the top would be full. You'd be dripping sweat all the time.

On one trip we came down to Sydney and dropped off some oil and went round to Adelaide, then up to Port Pirie, which had a big zinc smelter. When we went into Port Pirie our navigator decided he wouldn't go round the island like the chart said, he'd go in between it, and we actually ran aground. It was a sandy bottom, thank goodness. I was off watch at the time and I heard the thing going whirr, whirr, and grind to a halt. I went down below and they put her in reverse and managed to drag her off.

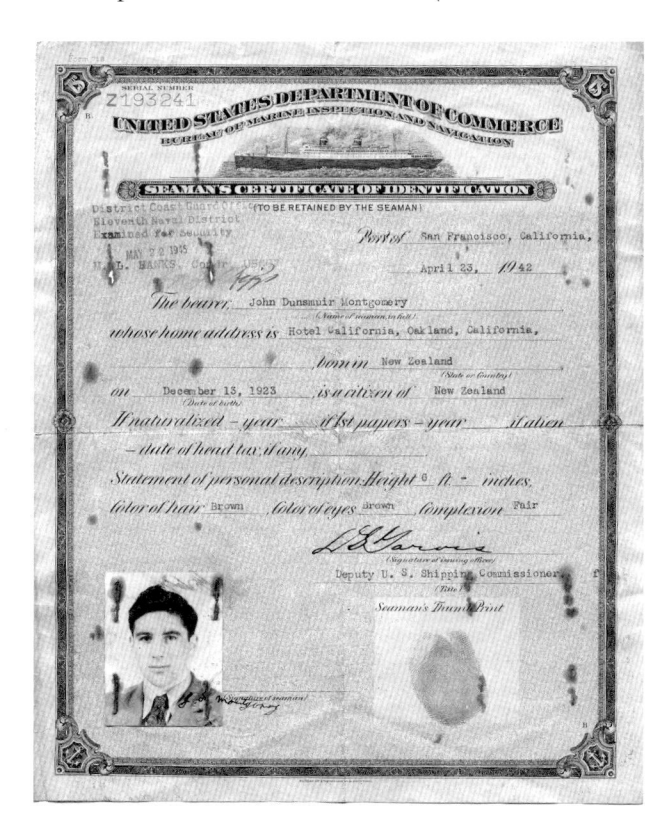

John's United States seaman's identification certificate.
Montgomery collection

Everybody was pressure-cooked. Sometimes if we didn't see the sun for two or three days we'd end up miles away from where we were supposed to be going. That made it a bit exciting. When we'd left the States a new second cook had signed on, and the chief cook said to the second cook, 'You'd better get your dough ready.' He said, 'Dough, what's that for?' 'You signed on as second cook, didn't you? You got to make the bread.' 'I don't know how to make bread.' So he had to show this joker how to make bread.

On one trip in 1944 we came into Wellington and I got a bit of shore leave. Merchant seamen had to sign customs forms and that, but if a serviceman took goods ashore he wouldn't get stopped. We were out at Miramar and I had a tennis racket for my sister and a cowboy suit for my youngest brother, a box of cigars and some silk stockings. It was worth about £5. I was going off on leave and one of the American naval sailors—we had almost as many Armed Guard as we had crew on there—said, 'Do you want us to take your bags ashore?' I said, 'No, no, I'll be all right.' So I walked ashore, and a joker with a cap on came along on his pushbike and said, 'Where are you going?' 'I'm going home for a couple of days.' 'What you got in the bag? Oh, you'd better come along with us. This is serious.' So I finished up getting fined £5 and they confiscated the lot. Apparently, the last time the *Schenectady* had come in, there were all kinds of American cigarettes floating around Wellington and they had to have come off the ship. This customs agent was watching to try and see someone coming ashore with smokes.

We went down to Lyttelton and Dunedin and were headed back to Abadan. We were going through the Bass Strait—I was on watch—when this joker said, 'You better put the bigger burners in, they've sighted a submarine.' They started shooting at this submarine. We had a 5-inch gun on the back, a 3-inch one on the front and all these Oerlikons along the side. Crikey dick, the noise of this 5-inch going off, you didn't know whether we were getting blown up or whether it was the gun going off. Anyway, they said later it was one of our own submarines that we were shooting at. But at that same time there was a German submarine off Hobart and we were just past Tasmania. They fired about 12 shots at it altogether. I asked one of the ABs, 'How close did they get?' 'Oh,' he said, 'they never got within half a mile of it.' Thank goodness for that.

When we were going to Abadan we used to go right over to Madagascar and up the African coast, to try and keep as far away from the Japanese as possible I suppose. But German submarines were operating off that coast there, off Mozambique and Madagascar. We didn't know that, of course.

In 1945 the Schenectady *made several trips to the Caroline Islands in the western Pacific, delivering oil to the huge American-led armada assembled for the invasion of the strategic Japanese islands of Iwo Jima and Okinawa—operations of even greater complexity than the Normandy landings.*

We went to Curaçao and picked up a load of oil there, came back through the Panama Canal and headed off. We finished up at a place called Ulithi. They were organising the invasion of Okinawa. There was about the largest group of ships that's ever been in the history of the world. There were British ships there too, aircraft carriers, the *Indefatigable*, *Indomitable* and others. The HMNZS *Gambia* was there. There were all these oil tankers. The kamikaze bombers came from a place called Yap, which is only a few miles away from Ulithi. Of course, they headed for the aircraft carriers, which was their main target. We pumped our oil into a navy tanker—they used to refuel the warships at sea—and then we headed back to the States. It was May 1945.

We set off from San Pedro again with a load of oil and took it back to Ulithi. After you'd pumped the oil out you had to get rid of the gas out of the tanks, using what they call the Butterworth system. Anyway, they said, 'Well, you can't do it here. You'll have to get out.' So they kicked us out of there. We had a tanker full of gas—it would have only taken a spark and the whole lot would have gone up. We went round to Port Moresby and had to follow another tanker through the Torres Strait to Darwin, then we took off for Abadan, past Sumatra, which was still Japanese-occupied.

We loaded up in Abadan and we were coming back past Sumatra again when the wireless operator tuned in to Chungking [Chinese radio]. They said, 'The Japanese have packed it in. The war's over. People are going mad in the streets.' We tuned in to America and England and couldn't get a peep out of them. Anyway the announcement soon came over—the war was over. The first thing they said was, 'Don't give up your blackout because the Japanese don't know it's finished yet.'

We went into Darwin and got instructions to go to Manila. We had an Australian escort through the Arafura Sea. That was the first time we'd ever had an escort all the time I was on the tanker. They used to let us go on our own, because the T2s did 15 knots loaded; they were quite fast. Anyway, we got to San Francisco where they were laying up the tankers on the beach and paying the crew off. It was time to go.

Right: *The battleship USS* New Jersey *(centre) surrounded by an enormous fleet of aircraft carriers, cruisers, destroyers, tankers and other vessels in the sparkling waters of Ulithi lagoon in the western Caroline Islands. Able to accommodate up to 1000 ships, Ulithi was the main base for the American conquest of Iwo Jima and Okinawa in 1945.* Australian War Memorial, 302686

'The Old Aquitania'

After signing off in November 1945, John got on an American ship bound for Brisbane, disembarked in Fiji (where he celebrated his 22nd birthday), and hitched a ride on an RNZAF flight to Auckland. In 1947 he married the daughter of a shipmate from the Aquitania, *and the couple raised four children in Wellington. John spent 25 years working for Steel Case Engineering in the Hutt Valley and a further 15 at General Motors' Trentham plant. In recent years John has appeared in several television commercials, and he was an extra in the film* The Lord of the Rings: The Two Towers.

Going to sea was a whole lifetime of experiences in those four years. It was all experience. Talking to you now about it, it's just as if it happened yesterday. But there are things that have happened in between that seem an awful long time ago, you know. The jokers who were the same age as me, some of them got to Italy, but most of them were only just 21 when the war finished. You couldn't go overseas in the army until you were 21, of course—I was only 21 when the war finished.

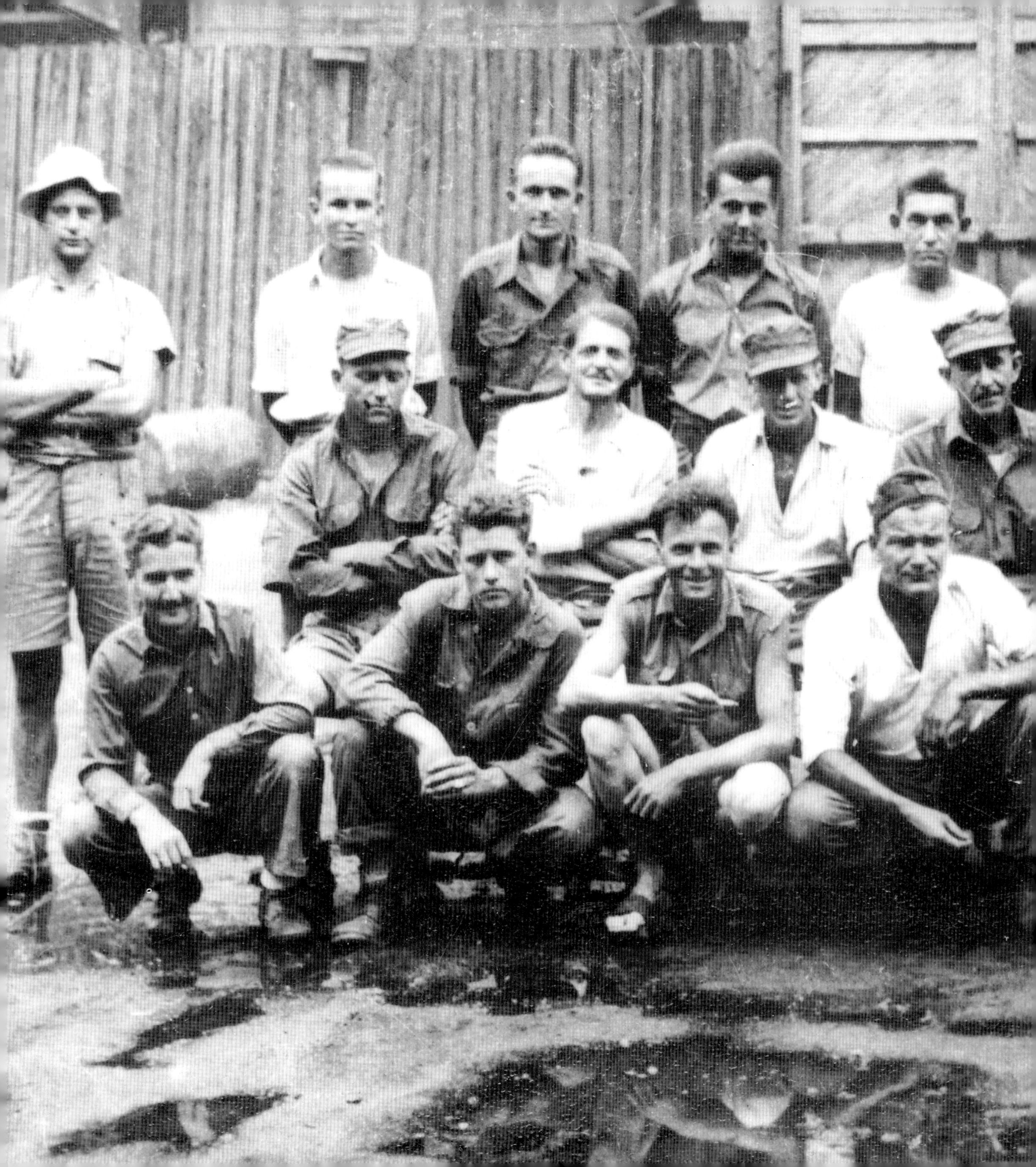

'CAUGHT BY THE JAPANESE'

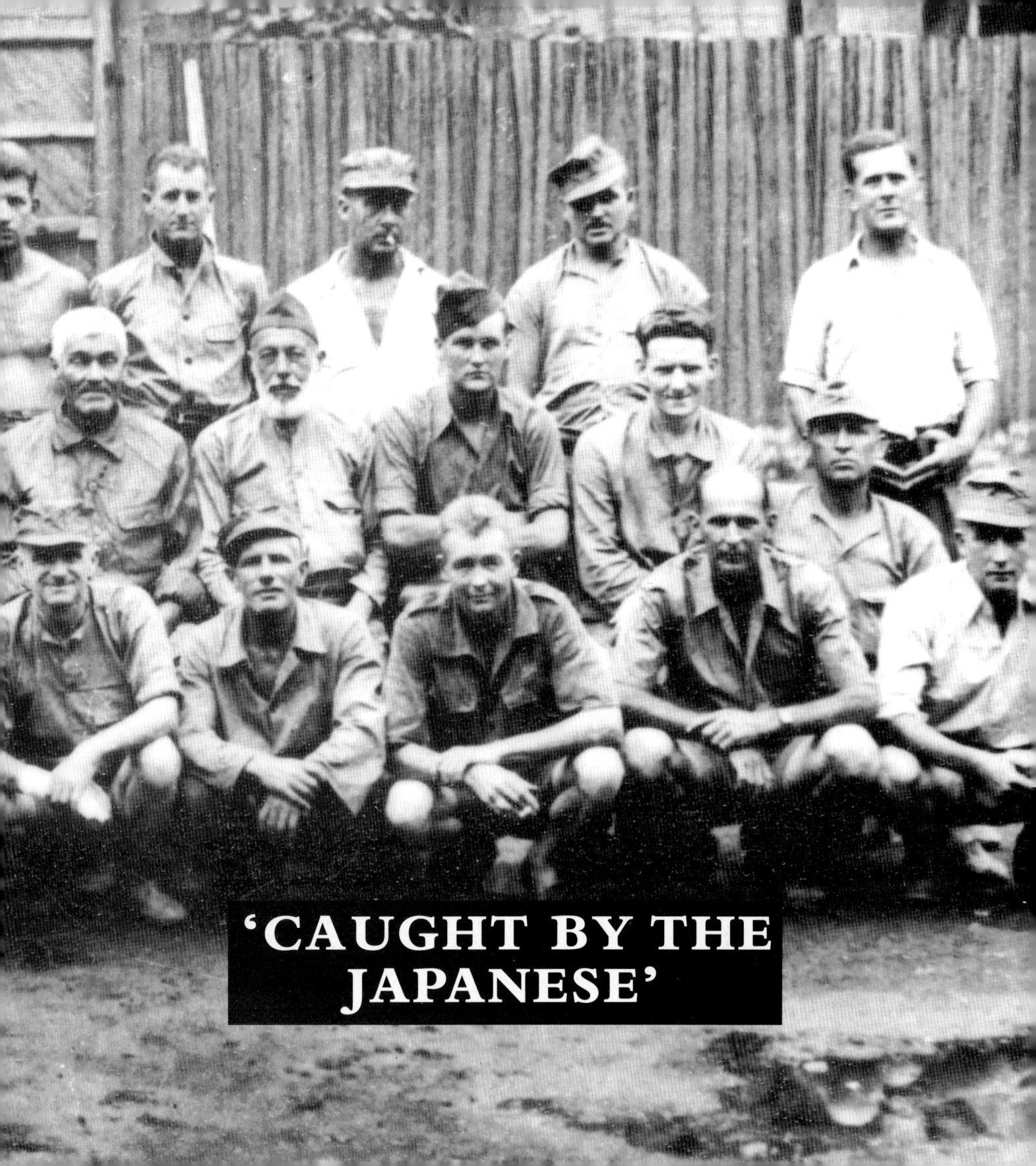

BILL HALL, Engineer Officer

William Peebles Hall was born in 1911 in Port Chalmers, where his father worked as a foreman-tradesman at the Union Steam Ship Company's repair works. Although his parents hoped he would train as an architect, Bill decided at an early age that he wanted to go to sea.

MY YOUTH IN PORT was a happy time. Money was very scarce, but that seemed to make for companionship and it was a very sports-minded little town. I served my apprenticeship with the Union Company and then went to sea with them. I trained and qualified as an engineer, passed all the examinations, and went to sea in 1934. I was about 23. They were the Depression years, so I had to scratch around a bit to get a start at sea. And I stayed at sea for the rest of my career.

Bill's first ship was the 5282-ton SS Maheno, *which had been launched in 1905 and served as a New Zealand hospital ship during the First World War.*

I was a junior engineer; there were eight engineers and I was the eighth. It was a passenger ship, an old coal-burner—the last passenger coal-burner the Union Company had. I worked with a senior engineer at the start. We had two four-hour watches.

I'll never forget my first day at sea. I was seasick and quite lost in the turmoil of the stokehold. The ship burned about 120 tons of coal a day through six boilers, with four furnaces for each boiler. Cleaning

Previous page: *Bill Hall (standing, far left) with 16 of his* Hauraki *shipmates and American and Dutch prisoners at Ohasi, northern Japan. This photograph was taken on 28 August 1945, after the Japanese surrender but prior to the prisoners' liberation. The ship's chief engineer, Bill Falconer, sits fourth from left in the middle row, Captain Albert Creese fourth from right.* Royal New Zealand Navy Museum
Above: *Bill Hall in Japan, August 1945.* Royal New Zealand Navy Museum
Right: *The engine room of the Union Company's* Awatea, *photographed on the ship's completion in England in 1936.* Museum of Wellington City & Sea

fires at the beginning of each watch was . . . well, like Dante's Inferno. The almost molten clinker was pulled out onto the cast-iron plates below each furnace, dowsed with water by the trimmers, then shovelled into the injectors and overboard. With the roar of the fans, the whole stokehold full of steam and the men stumbling and swearing, I can say I was scared as well as seasick.

[The firemen] were pretty rough, I suppose, but on the whole we got on pretty well. They worked hard—it was a slave-labourer's job on a big coal-burner. Strangely enough, I enjoyed my coal-burning days. There was always uncertainty and fun on watch. Sometimes the coal was poor, sometimes the fire bars melted and dropped—it was a terrible job to replace them—and you never seemed to know how much steam you would get and therefore how many engine revolutions you would log on your watch. Sometimes there were fights and a little blood about, but there was also singing and laughter. Men would faint [from the heat], but were just placed under a ventilator until they recovered.

I was in that ship for about six months, then I moved to smaller ships. Then I worked my way to England for a shilling a month on a Port Line ship, and worked in the shipyard at Barrow-in-Furness. The trip was really to gain a bit of experience in a shipyard, on the big stuff. I worked on the building of the [Union Company's] *Awatea*, and I came back on her as a junior engineer.

We were so proud of that ship. In 1936 she would have been one of the most modern and luxurious ships in the world. I was on her in the exciting days of competition with the Matson vessels on the Tasman, the *Monterey* and *Mariposa*. We made several attempts to take the Tasman record. Each time the weather stopped us, but we were successful in October 1937, when we averaged 23.1 knots Auckland to Sydney. And then, until the end of her short life, she carried a stainless steel greyhound on the foremast. This record stood for 24 years.

We tried to race the Matson ships, always

unofficially. During one trip, as I was going on watch at four o'clock off North Cape, the man who called me to relieve him said, 'Do you want to see a ship passing us?' I could not believe him but it was the *Mariposa*. She was racing and had caught us with our pants down. At 8 a.m. she was hull-down ahead. The chief engineer was awakened and we got permission to raise steam on another boiler. That gave us five boilers; the other one was undergoing an overhaul. There was great excitement on board—amongst us mainly, but also the crew and passengers—and ever so slowly we overhauled her. We caught up only two hours from Sydney Heads, the *Mariposa* gave a toot, and we were top dog. I remember the junior engineers took over the steaming and we had the safety valves feathering—it was great fun.

Then I was at sea in various ships until the war, on inter-island and small coastal ships, mostly cargo.

And when the war started you decided to stay at sea?
Yes. Well, everyone was supposed to take part in the war and I just kept on with my job. The armed forces wouldn't take me, because marine engineers were so scarce [and therefore could not be replaced]. I did look at the air force, but they just said if you're a marine engineer you're wasting our time, just stay where you are.

In the early days of the war I was wrecked on Dog Island, off the Bluff, on the *Waikouaiti*. At this period of the war ships mined or torpedoed around the UK were named publicly. I was in my bunk listening to my wee radio before taking up the 12 to 4 watch when there was a great crash. My first thought was, 'Now us!' I jumped out and saw just fog outside, so I was below in seconds. The engine was still turning. She must have rolled on her side and blocked the circulating water, as the engine room was full of steam. I stopped the engine and found a very white-faced fourth engineer trying to find the water in the boilers. He thought one had blown up.

The crew were put into boats while the fourth and I kept enough steam to supply lights until dawn. This was scary work as the stokehold bulkhead was showing signs of collapse. We would run in together, throw some coal in the furnace and duck out again. In the daylight, with the fog lifted, things didn't look too bad. The two of us were left on board all that day until the ship was handed over to the underwriters.

I spent time in various ships and got my diesel time in *Karitane*, and passed my first-class steam and motor certificate. I joined the *Wahine*, which was taken off the ferry run to take Public Works

Top: *Bill was on the Union Company's* Waikouaiti *when it ran aground off Dog Island, near Bluff, on 28 November 1939—one of three Union ships lost to accidents during the war years.* Alexander Turnbull Library, F-22914-1/2
Above: *Launched in 1922, the 7113-ton trans-Pacific freighter* Hauraki *was the Union Company's first motor ship.* Alexander Turnbull Library, PAColl-7985-27

Department people to build the airstrip at Nadi. We almost lost the ship with a fire while bunkering at Suva. We were very, very lucky. The electric wiring was burnt out in the boiler room, and we got back to Auckland with hurricane lamps over the boiler gauge glasses with an almost-dark boiler room. It was very hot and uncomfortable.

In 1941 Bill joined the Union Company freighter Hauraki *as third engineer.*

She was a motor ship, one of the first, early motor ships. She was certainly unique. The engines, for the power they developed, were massive: two eight-cylinder four-stroke engines with blast injection. The engine room was in a blue haze all the time. It was a move forward for marine shipping, but it wasn't a hell of a lot cleaner. The early motor ships were a lot of hard work; they're very greatly improved now. They cut the crews right down, as they didn't need anyone firing steam by hand. A motor ship would only have perhaps a dozen engine-room staff, perhaps one engineer and about three others on each watch; coal-burners had about 12 or 15 firemen and trimmers.

The *Hauraki* was running from Vancouver to New Zealand, and then she was taken over by the British Ministry of War Transport to run stores to the Middle East. I didn't have any trouble until about the last

'Caught by the Japanese'

three years of the war, when we were caught by the Japanese. We were on our way from Sydney to the Middle East. Our undoing was the most severe storm I think I have seen at sea, in the Great Australian Bight. We took a sea through the engine-room skylight which stopped both engines, and believe me it was a hectic half-hour getting them started again, with the ship beam on and rolling 30 degrees. The crew's quarters aft were flooded and the lifeboats stoved in, so we put into Fremantle for repairs.

On 5 July 1942 the Hauraki *left Fremantle for Egypt via Colombo, with supplies for the Allied forces. On the night of 12 July it was intercepted by two 10,000-ton Japanese armed merchant cruisers, the* Hokuku Maru *and* Aikoku Maru.

Do you remember much about that night?
No, because I was on the 12 to 4 watch, and it was about 11 o'clock and I was in my bed. The Japanese had a couple of big armed cruisers and they put shots across the bows. We stopped. We didn't know at that time whether they were American or British or what. We were blinded by their searchlights. The *Hauraki* had a gun aft and there was a gun squad, but it was a pitch-black night and they didn't know who had stopped us. If they'd have fired the gun the Japanese would have just sunk us.

They brought us into Singapore and unloaded the cargo. We were running the ship, with a Japanese crew aboard, and they wanted the ship up in Yokohama, Tokyo. We were a long time getting up there, about six months. We must have spent three or four months in Singapore. The Japanese thought they could use the engineers, so they took us and one or two others up to Japan. I think there were 24 taken up altogether, and I think I'm the only one still alive.

The remainder of the Hauraki'*s 56 officers and crew were imprisoned in Singapore's Changi jail.*

We set off for Japan, but very slowly, as she was an old ship. The Japanese watched us, so we couldn't do any actual damage to the ship. But after a while we found they'd got careless, so we dropped spare parts and bits over the side at night-time, and all the plans of the engines. When we got to Yokohama

Left: *After being landed in Singapore, the* Hauraki'*s deck and engineer officers, seen here in their white tropical uniforms, were photographed with some of their captors from the* Hokuku Maru. *The Japanese armed merchant cruiser was sunk with heavy loss of life a few months later.* Australian War Memorial, P02087.002

she'd been stripped bare as far as the spares were concerned. My last act was to run a ton or so of diesel oil into the lubricating oil in the crankcases. Then I started to worry that she would blow up before we got taken off.

The Japanese told us they were going to have the ship back at sea in a fortnight, but we could see her from our shipyards in Yokohama and she lay for about a year up there, fitting out. They had trouble with her when they ran her, because she was an old ship, with old diesel engines.

Renamed the Hoki Maru, *the* Hauraki *was eventually pressed into service as a Japanese military transport. In February 1944 it was sunk by American torpedo bombers at Truk in the Caroline Islands.*

This big shipyard we were in was the Mitsubishi shipyard. We had to build ships for the Japs. They had collected mainly people with a trade background from among their POWs: Americans, Army Ordnance, survivors from the *Prince of Wales*, *Repulse*. There must have been about 500 or so in the camp when we arrived. We worked with several thousand Japanese, but we didn't have much communication with them. They didn't want to bother. Some of them were kinder than others, but not much.

The Japanese didn't pay us at all—it was starvation labour. It was a pretty long, slow life. We didn't have much food—a handful of rice three times a day, that's it. Our quarters were about a mile or two from the shipyard, in a converted shed or warehouse. It was very hot in the summer and very cold in the winter. There was no heating, nothing; there was just one rug they gave us to sleep on. It was terrible. We had a bit of our own clothing and a bit from the Japanese. They gave us a boiler suit to work in.

We marched [to work each day], right through the main town. The locals didn't worry us much; we never had any bother from them. Of course we had guards from the warehouse where we lived to the shipyard, and they kept an eye on us. They were a mixed bunch, not bad I suppose. One or two of them were very hard. The Americans tried them all after the war. There were some Americans on the shipyard squad, and they came back from America and gave evidence at the trial.

How many hours did you work?
I think they were only eight-hour days, but they worked us 14 or 21 days at a time, with no breaks. That was the hard part. On the one day off we had, we had to clean up the camp. If you got any spare

time you stretched out and rested, saved a bit of strength for the next day. It was as bad as that. There was no leisure, nothing like that.

I was the most senior one working in the shipyard—well, the chief engineer, Bill Falconer, was taken too, but he was given a job separate from me—so the Japs put me in charge of a squad of about 25 POWs, a very mixed group of Americans, Dutch, Scots, English, Aussies, the lot. I learned to speak a 'pidgin' Japanese. They would write out the work we were to do and I was supposed to get the boys to do it. We got to the stage where we would do the least work we had to. Sabotage was out of the question, but I found that the engineers on the small craft—tugs, etcetera—were not very knowledgeable. So they'd bring in a ship for a job that should have taken a week or ten days and sometimes it would take two months—that was a sort of sabotage.

A lot of POWs died in there. A lot of them died of what they called malnutrition, but it was just starvation. Luckily I could live on the small amount of rice they gave us, but others just couldn't manage. I was a good age to go in, too. I was about 30, I was mature. Some of the young ones couldn't see any end to it and didn't live too well. When a chap gave up there was just nothing one could do. We did have a doctor, but he had no medical supplies at all, not even aspirin or bandages.

Did you ever get Red Cross parcels?
No. Well, the Japs did. Red Cross parcels came in, because we were given one or two after the war was over. They just used them, I suppose. The Japs were hard people to understand. About the last year of the war, some of us were allowed to send one message home [via shortwave radio]. I didn't send one, but some of the others did and they said, 'Bill Hall's with us'. So my family knew that I was alive in Japan.

From mid-1944 the Japanese home islands, including the Yokohama shipyards, were the target of increasingly heavy attacks by American B-29 Superfortress bombers.

During the first years of our captivity we saw nothing, as the Americans needed to build up their forces. Then they bombed the shipyards, and we were running around like rabbits inside. We were lucky we stayed alive. They didn't bomb us much in the daytime, the bombs came at night. You'd hear the sirens go and you knew you'd be in for another night. The Japs made us build little slit trenches and we hid in there with a folded blanket over our heads. But you went back to work just the same the next day, even if you didn't sleep all night. They didn't always come to our area. Tokyo's a big place—sometimes they came over the shipyard, sometimes they'd go someplace else.

We had some frights with the bombing, but we were always pleased to see it, because we knew the war was going our way. Time and again they bombed the shipyard, so much so that the Japanese gave up building ships, because they couldn't get them into the water. So we were herded into a train and taken north to a steel mill at a place called Kamaishi for the last six months of the war.

The conditions were not quite so bad there, but the work was just as heavy. I had several jobs: one riveting in the railway repair shop; one striking for a Korean blacksmith; and, later, driving a winch at the top of a mineshaft. As I was only about seven stone, I was almost bouncing off the rivet gun and often would miss the anvil, let alone the tool. Things were better at Kamaishi because it was a long, hot summer and on my last job, as winchman, I was out in the open. We were set to work putting a tunnel through a mountain. I never found out where it was going or what it was for. We didn't have air raids, but worse was to come.

On 14 July and again on 9 August 1945, the day the second atomic bomb was dropped on Nagasaki, Kamaishi was shelled by Allied warships.

They came in from the sea twice with a task force. There was a New Zealand ship in there, the *Gambia*. They lay off about four miles and belted us with 16-inch shells. They were so close you could see the big shells in the air, and the damage and chaos were unbelievable. They dropped a shell within a few feet of me and that's why I'm deaf. I was deaf for two or three days. It improved later but it's slowly got worse as I've got older. They shelled us for about three hours and killed a lot of people, a lot of Japanese. They burned down our camp and laid the whole mill and town to waste. In the bombardment we lost 34 of our boys.

Among the victims was the Hauraki's *fifth engineer, W.H. Brodie of Lyttelton, who died on 10 August; four of his shipmates had already succumbed to malnutrition or disease in Japanese captivity. A few days later, the surviving prisoners were moved inland to a camp at Ohasi. On 15 August, Japan surrendered.*

'Caught by the Japanese'

Part of a task force that included the battleships USS Dakota, Indiana *and* Massachusetts, *the cruiser HMNZS* Gambia *shells the steelworks at Kamaishi in northern Honshu, Japan, on 9 August 1945.* Royal New Zealand Navy Museum

How did you find out the war was over?

It was a funny thing. We knew the war was coming our way, the way they were bombing and shelling, and the Japs were hardly even returning fire. We didn't get any news or anything, but we knew the Japs were getting more and more worried and irritable. This particular night we found the Japanese camp commandant talking very seriously to his men, and then the next day we didn't go to work, so we knew then something must have happened. After a day or two they admitted they'd signed a peace settlement.

Then the Japanese gave us a couple of Red Cross parcels. I think they were trying to save face. It was about four weeks before the Americans found us, because with the best will in the world they didn't know where we were. They knew where there were possible prisoners, so they scanned Japan from the air, picking out camps. We were allowed to write 'POW' on the roof of the camp, and the Americans found us because of this. They got word to us—live as well as you can and we'll drop supplies.

With typical American thoroughness bombers were soon overhead and the bomb bays opened and the valley was scattered with food, blankets and clothing. They caught us by surprise. Our greatest fear was that we would be killed by a tin of Campbell's soup after the war was over! Next time the bombers came over we hid under a railway bridge until it was over.

It was a good spell for us to really rest up. We just had to wait to be found. But that was the hardest part for our parents; they didn't know if we were alive or dead. When they found the camp they took us back to the coast—we were about 200 miles north of Tokyo—and they sent in a hospital ship, the *Rescue*, with a small force of destroyers, a frigate or something, to take us back to Yokohama. We were taken to the *Rescue* first and they had a row of doctors ready. They tied a tag on our wrists with our particulars and each doctor examined you for a particular thing, and you passed along the chain. Then the sailors said, 'Dump all your clothing'—into the shower—and they rubbed lice powder or something in our hair. Then one gave you a pair of pants, another a shirt, and so on, and in about five minutes you came out looking like a naval rating. The last one put a gob hat on my head.

In all my time as a POW I had not been off work, but while waiting to be picked up I stood on a nail. When I was examined I was limping a little, so they wrote on my tag, 'Tetanus shot and bed on the *Rescue*.' After what we had been through a little prick on the foot was nothing, but I can still smell the fresh linen on my hospital bed, and I thought the nurses looked like film stars.

Then they took us to the Philippines for a fortnight and we were vetted by the doctors there. It took quite a while going home, six weeks, and we were fully rested by that time. We came back to Sydney on an English aircraft carrier and then to New Zealand.

Bill arrived in Sydney on 15 October aboard HMS Speaker, *and a week later reached Lyttelton on the* Andes.

My father was dead, but my mother still lived at Port. When I came through the gate, yellow with Atabrin [anti-malaria medicine], just a stubble of hair, a tooth missing in the front that a Nip had knocked out, and dressed in American jungle gear, she thought I was a Chinaman.

I had about three months at home and then I went back to sea. I spent over two years in the *Narbada*, running up to India, all over the place. I rose to chief engineer and spent some time on the coast and the Tasman, and then was sent to the UK in 1948 to stand by [supervise] the building of our new collier fleet at Leith, near Edinburgh. I came back to New Zealand in the *Kaitawa*, [which was later] lost with all hands off North Cape.

Not very long after this, I settled down to the Lyttelton ferry service: *Rangatira*, *Hinemoa*, *Maori*, *Wahine*. Eventually I was the senior chief engineer of the whole Union Company. They sent me back to England two or three times to stand by the building of new ships, and I looked after them on the delivery voyage. The last ship I stood by the building of was the *Rangatira* [II, in 1971–2]. I was a chief engineer for 25 years on different ships. I retired when I was 64, in 1975.

For the last few years Bill has lived at the War Veterans' Home in Levin.

I was very lucky. I'm old and frail now, but I haven't had any illnesses so far. It affected some POWs very much. Some of them didn't live very long after they came back. I don't worry about the Japanese now. I'm not one to worry unnecessarily. I can't do anything about it. But they were terrible people, bloody awful; they beat us up and all sorts of things. They were worse in the first year, then from then on they realised they mightn't be winning this war—at the start they thought they were going to take the world. If [the Americans] hadn't dropped the atomic bomb and they'd had to invade Japan, there wouldn't have been a prisoner of war come out alive, I'm certain. We couldn't have existed much longer, but the bomb dropping stopped the war suddenly.

The trouble was the low amount of food and the hard work. They really bloody worked us like slaves. It was a great strain living and working in those conditions. You didn't know if you were going to be alive the next day. It was just a matter of staying alive, day by day. I'd say, 'I'm alive for another day.' Conditions were so grim. It was a hell of a life.

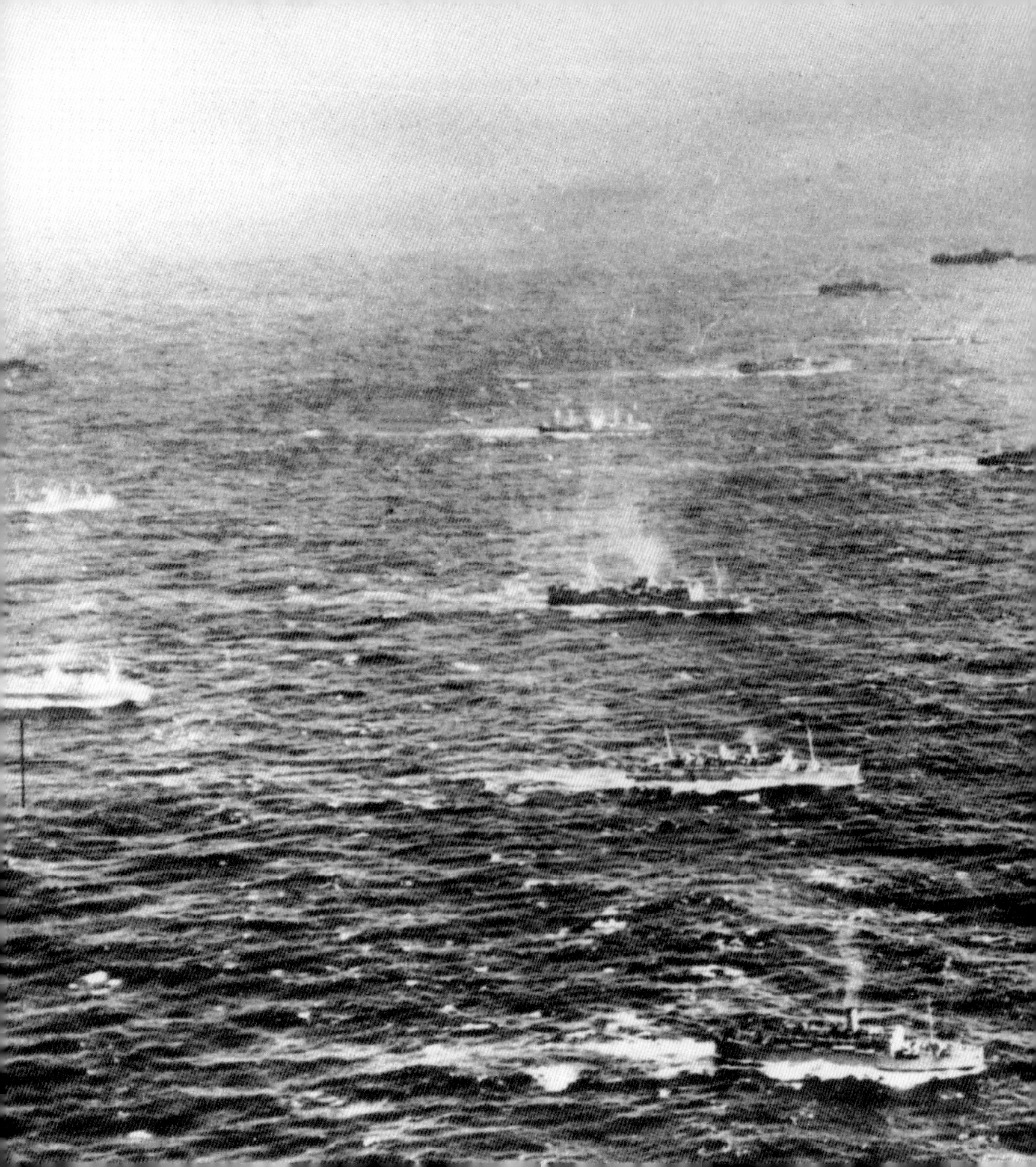

'FIVE HUNDRED SHIPS'

PAT O'SHEA, STEWARD, PANTRYMAN

Born in London in 1917, Patrick O'Shea came to New Zealand two years later with his mother Florence and father Joseph, a war invalid, on the troopship SS Remuera. *He was raised in Gisborne and Wellington, and attended St Joseph's Convent School in Upper Hutt.*

I LEFT SCHOOL WHEN I was 13. Mother took me down to Wellington and I stayed in a little wee house there with her. I didn't know my father very well. I only met him briefly. He left Mum and went back to England on another ship about 1923. He had a war wound from the First World War, by his ear. This used to affect him a good deal and he drank a lot. Meantime, Mum got a job wherever she could. We were very poor. She was on very low wages, I think she was getting 15 shillings a week. That's how tight things were. When I was 14 I got a job selling sweets in a theatre, the Majestic. It was very tough in those days. We lived from hand to mouth.

Did you have any thoughts then about going to sea?
I knew a chap, Len Malmo, who lived in a little cottage in Aro Street, and we lived close by. I got in tow with him; he was selling sweets in the theatre too. He decided to go to sea because his father was at sea—he was a chef on the *Maunganui*, which was running from Wellington to Rarotonga, Tahiti and San Francisco. I joined that ship, the *Maunganui*, as a bellboy in 1936. I was about 19 then. Wages were very poor in those days. But the passengers were wealthy people generally, and we used to make a few bob in tips.

As a bellboy you waited on passengers, bringing whatever they may want to eat and drink or anything. We worked all hours. I did the one trip on there, then they put me off the next trip. They still wanted

Previous page: *A convoy of large troopships—part of an invasion armada of 500 merchant and naval vessels—heads for the North African coast during the Operation Torch landings of 8 November 1942. The* Awatea, *fitted out as an LSI (Landing Ship, Infantry) and carrying 3000 assault troops, is the second ship in the second column.* Museum of Wellington City & Sea
Above: *Patrick O'Shea, steward.* Phillip O'Shea collection

young fellows, though; they'd engage them to go aboard and work on the ship when it was in port. We used to clean everywhere. A ship would only be in port for 24 hours, and you'd go onto another ship the next day. Or we used to get a job on the wharf or on the railways, loading the railway trucks with flour and whatever.

The next ship I got a job on was the *Makura*, another San Francisco passenger ship. I did a couple of trips on her. In September 1936 I was working on the *Makura* at the slip wharf, Evans Bay. We had just completed the last trip to San Francisco and our job was taking off stores and stripping the vessel of expensive items and fittings—because in those days of carrying passengers from Australia to the United States, we had a very high standard. I got a call to report to the shipping office to sign on a new ship, the *Awatea*—it was a job in the pantry, just working as a ship's boy in the pantry. Well, in those days to get a job was something. Mum said I was made after all. I earned £7 a month. The *Awatea* was a money-saver for our family, and with the advent of the Labour government wages were rising at sea. From then on Mum collected her regular money, an allotment, every two weeks at the Union Company office.

The *Awatea* had a big complement of staff. She used to carry 500 passengers between Wellington or Auckland and Sydney in two-and-a-half days—that was fast. The pantry was rather big; it stretched from one side of the ship to the other. That was the first-class pantry; second-class was down the other end, and the third-class had nothing very much, just barely something to eat. That ship had everything on her. We had electrical cutting machines, automatic coffee machines, automatic toasters.

My first quarters were down aft, eight boys in a cabin. You used to get called to work at six in the morning. They gave you a piece of deck to scrub, and you had to do your little bit. We used to do everything for the passengers, go in and clean the cabins out. We did work in the pantries and helped in dishwashing, all that sort of thing. We wiped the dishes and stacked them all. Everything was spotlessly clean, they were very fussy.

In 1938, when his mother decided to visit her sister in England, Pat worked his passage there and back on the Shaw Savill & Albion liner Mataroa.

My mother sailed for England on the *Rangitata*. I duly followed on the *Mataroa* two months later. My experience on *Awatea* helped me no end. Sailing up the coast of England, through the Solent, towards Southampton, the excitement was intense. Not only me, but all the British crew, who'd been away for

The Awatea *passes under the Sydney Harbour Bridge in the late 1930s. The Union Company liner set new standards of speed and comfort on the Tasman crossing—until war intervened.* Phillip O'Shea collection

six months, were being paid off. We boarded a train for London. Mum and Aunt Carrie were there to meet me. Well, it went through my mind I was born here.

Late August 1938 I received a card from Shaw Savill advising there was a job on the *Mataroa* and to report. So I said to Mum, about time I made my way back. I was sorry to say goodbye, but I would be back one day—little realising I'd be back all right, on the *Awatea* to Liverpool, 1942, with half the docks on fire. On arrival in Wellington I paid off. I must say that was a great bunch of guys, I was sorry to say goodbye. I was a little worried at this time. War was in the air, time was moving on. Mum had her booking back, on the *Rangitiki* this time, and I met her in Auckland and we came down in the train together.

> *When war broke out in 1939, Pat was serving as a waiter on the Union Company liner* Monowai. *Soon after, the ship was taken over by the New Zealand Division of the Royal Navy for conversion into an armed merchant cruiser. After some time working ashore, Pat returned to the* Awatea.

I joined the *Awatea* again in the pantry. We did a few trips, Sydney across to Auckland and Wellington, then the war started to interfere and we started to go here, there and everywhere. The Navy, the British, powers that be, decided she would be in the front line.

We sailed from Auckland with a ship full of young New Zealanders and Australians to be trained in Canada for the Royal Air Force in Britain. This was the Empire Air Training Scheme. We made a fast trip to Vancouver, about two weeks. We were escorted by an Australian warship [HMAS *Sydney*]. About this time, between Suva and Auckland we all but ran into a German armed raider. Luckily we had the speed and got out. Meantime, they sank five ships around Nauru. We were lucky this time. Because the *Niagara* got sunk, they put paravanes on the *Awatea*; I think it might have been the first New Zealand ship they put them on. We had a gun, a 4-inch or something, on the stern.

Now where to? Back to Wellington after lay-up in Sydney, then orders to Manila in the Philippines to rescue women and children from the Japanese, as they were about to invade. Then back to Brisbane, Melbourne and Sydney. That was a hard trip. We'd turn to at five in the morning, work until ten or eleven at night. We didn't mind, as women and young children needed to be fed.

With that voyage over, we went from Sydney again, then Auckland to Vancouver across the Pacific with young trainees for the Empire Training Scheme, 1000 or more, the pick of the universities and colleges. After a week storing, further orders—this time to Los Angeles, Panama, England. This was in 1941. I did not fancy the Atlantic too much, but the *Awatea* at a pinch could do 26 knots—that was warship speed in those days.

But it was not to be. Sailing day arrived, and leaving Vancouver in the open sea an American tanker crashed into us, port side, and ripped a bit of the side off. We heard it, of course; we were living for'ard then. Well, back to Vancouver for three months' repairs. [During this time] the passenger accommodation was ripped right out and replaced with hammocks and bunks to accommodate soldiers and airmen. Our galley, butchers' shop and pantry did not need much alteration.

Our staff was mostly single, with no ties. We were to carry troops and airmen to a war zone, so married men and those with families had the option of returning to New Zealand. Others stayed, like me. I was single and young and didn't know any different. I never went back to New Zealand. I was in touch with Mum all the time, wherever possible. But you couldn't sign off at random. When you were on there, you were on there. Some of our lads wanted to join the navy. They wouldn't even allow that, no way. Why would they take staff from the *Awatea* and put them in the navy? So we stayed put.

In October 1941 the Awatea *left Vancouver for Hong Kong with 2000 Canadian soldiers on board.*

My job was overseeing the feeding of the troops, so after three months' repairs—and with guns everywhere on the side for [use against] aircraft—we sailed for Hong Kong. [We spent] a week there unloading equipment for the hundreds of Canadians on board. We learnt soon after that the Japs wiped the lot out. This upset me. I had been living on board with chaps my own age, I got to know many. This was real murder. From Hong Kong we went to Singapore. We picked up women and children to take them to

The Awatea *in Vancouver in September 1941, showing damage to the port side following a collision with the American tanker* M. E. Lombardi.
Museum of Wellington City & Sea

Pat O'Shea (centre, raising glass) enjoys a drink with some of his Awatea *shipmates during a stopover in Cape Town.*
Phillip O'Shea collection

England. We hoped this was going to be a safe voyage. With women and children it was going to be a bit precarious, but we survived.

We always knew we had to be very careful [in the Atlantic]. You never went anywhere without your lifejacket. If you were going to have your meal, you had to have your lifejacket on. If you were down below, you put your lifejacket on. You went to bed with your lifejacket on. We lived with those bloody things. And when they gave orders, you obeyed them. Yes sir!

The Awatea *had a close call nearing Britain in January 1942.*

A submarine fired a torpedo at us and it missed, fortunately, and we got in to Liverpool. The ship's cargo was very precious: we were full of tea from Ceylon! They could do with it, too. At Liverpool many of the docks were still smouldering after German bombing the previous night.

After discharging cargo we sailed for Scotland, getting ready for a voyage somewhere. Well, this time we went to Bombay through the Atlantic and Indian Oceans with stops for storing and refuelling in Cape Town and Durban, someplace for our troops on board to stretch their legs. In Cape Town, coming back to the ship one evening I came across our assistant butcher lying across the railway lines dead drunk. He had met a brother from England in the forces, whom he had not sighted since they were kids in London. So I half-carried him to the *Awatea* and his bunk. Next day he could not thank me enough—a little episode of a night in Cape Town. They treated us well.

In Bombay the Awatea *took on board several thousand Polish airmen and troops who had reached India after an epic journey across the Soviet Union, Caspian Sea and Iran. Unfortunately, they were probably responsible for a smallpox outbreak on the* Awatea *that was to kill two crew members and subsequently affect hundreds of people in Scotland.*

The Polish soldiers! I was an assistant in the pantry, I was really something by then. We were very busy. We had Polish soldiers on board, we'd picked them up from Bombay. They were going to the Middle East or Britain to join the free Polish forces. They went from us onto another ship. We offloaded them in South Africa. We didn't know where we were going, you didn't know from one minute to another.

Anyhow, with the Polish we had smallpox on board the ship. Some of those affected were put off but they let the rest of us go ashore in Glasgow, and we scattered everywhere. I went down to London because my aunt was down there. The smallpox got very bad—of course, most of us got out of it, but several of the crew died. It was dangerous.

After another minor collision off West Africa in June 1942, the Awatea *was involved in a third, much more serious incident in August, when the destroyer USS* Buck *ran across its bows in heavy fog.*

Opposite: *Surrounded by some of his crew, the* Awatea*'s 'old man', Captain George Morgan (centre left), offers thanks to the master of the Dutch trooper* Marnix van St Aldegonde, *which evacuated the New Zealanders from the Mediterranean to Liverpool. Remarkably, all of the* Awatea*'s crew survived the sinking, although several were seriously wounded.* Museum of Wellington City & Sea

'Five Hundred Ships'

That was the bad one. It was night-time. We were in convoy off Halifax, Nova Scotia. That night, at 11 o'clock, 'wumph'. We were living up for'ard, and we went up and stayed the night on deck. We were on standby all night. We went to Halifax for repairs. We were very lucky. It would have been curtains for us if there'd been submarines around. They were thick off Halifax and New York then. We were in Halifax for six weeks or something. They put a new bow on. They were getting short of ships then, they lost a lot that year. It was a bad year.

Then we went to Glasgow for another refit. We didn't know where we were going to be sent. I had an idea, because I got all the milk. I said to my mate who was the boss then, if we need so much milk we must be going somewhere down the Atlantic. And that was it. We were in a big convoy, hundreds of ships. We went through the Straits of Gibraltar at night-time. Five hundred ships, I think, in the convoy. We were told to watch ourselves: keep those lifejackets on, go to bed with them on.

This was Operation Torch, the successful Anglo-American invasion of Vichy French North-west Africa (now Morocco and Algeria) on 8 November 1942. After landing 3000 British commandos and US Army Rangers near Algiers, the Awatea *carried another load of troops and equipment further east. On the evening of 11 November, the ship came under intense attack from German and Italian bombers.*

Of course the ship got it in the Mediterranean. That was bad luck. It was at a place called Bougie [now Bejaia], I won't forget that. We had landed all the troops we took over, thank God. The bombers came in, they were all over the ship. There were hundreds of them, it seemed to me. It was five o'clock in the evening, and we were getting ready for tea. I thought, I wish those bastards would get out of it while we get the tea on.

Although the Awatea's *gunners shot down several planes, the ship was raked by bombs and holed by an aerial torpedo.*

They had dive bombers and torpedo bombers, the whole lot. The bottom was blown out of the ship. She went down, she went to the bottom and that was the end of it. It was 11 November 1942—Armistice Day.

I managed to climb into a lifeboat. I remember I put the plug in the bottom of it. I was right in the middle of the lifeboat and I saw water coming in the bottom. You talked to your mates on the ship in all sorts of language, you know, 'We've got to get off this bloody thing!' We got off all right, floated away in the lifeboat. I don't remember much about that. I felt lucky to be alive. We weren't very far from shore. In fact, the 'old man' was trying to get inshore to beach her.

All the crew got off. They were bloody lucky. We should have got blown to pieces on that ship. They lost the ship's cat; he spent most of his time on the bridge, because the 'old man' used to feed him, used to give him the best of steak! The 'old man' was Captain Morgan. I lost everything: clothes, shoes, socks, watches, everything. At the time I had on khaki pants, old shoes that leaked and a singlet, that's it. But the weather was pretty warm.

We got ashore in Bougie. Bombs were still dropping round the town. The German air force gave us hell that night. We had ships called monitors, they were just gun-loaded barges, and they fired at these planes. They got God knows how many planes. We ended up on a Dutch ship the next day, the *Marnix van St Aldegonde*. We were all together then. Some of them went on board that first night, but I went to another ship that night, a British passenger vessel; it was full of Hindus. Any bed you could find, you'd go for your life.

Anyhow, we got back to England on the Dutch ship, and had a bit of a break there, a couple of weeks or something. I was paid off with a few bob, went to the sick bay, got some clothes and was off to London. Was Aunt Carrie pleased to see me! By this time Mum in New Zealand had received word I had reported and was alive and well. Then we sailed from Glasgow on a British ship that they put us on as crew. We came back to New Zealand via Panama, back to Wellington—and wasn't it good to see Wellington after all that time.

After a spell on the government's Pacific islands supply ship Maui Pomare, *Pat spent most of the next two-and-a-half years on the Union Company's* Wahine, *ferrying troops around the Pacific. He came ashore at the end of the war and spent a decade in the hotel trade, then returned to the Union Company in Wellington, working at head office and doing relieving work on various ships. After retiring in 1977, Pat settled in Levin. His son Phillip became the New Zealand Herald of Arms Extraordinary to Her Majesty the Queen.*

JOHN GREGSON, Apprentice, Mate

John Gregson was born in January 1924 in Bombay, India, where his father was working as an architect. He was raised in Yorkshire, England, and educated at Pangbourne Nautical College in Berkshire.

THAT WAS A SECONDARY SCHOOL where you went when you were about 12 or 13; it was just like a normal school but with a nautical flavour. It educated a lot of boys wanting to go into the Royal Navy or the Merchant Navy. I was still at school when war broke out in 1939, and we used to do firefighting watches and things like that in case of air raids. It was almost a year later when I went off to sea, when I was 16.

I didn't go into the Royal Navy, which a lot of them did, but I wanted to get away and to do my bit, so I elected to go into the Merchant Navy. I got an apprenticeship with the Blue Funnel Line, a Liverpool shipping company. They were taking on apprentices all the time. You signed indentures for three years. When you were serving an apprenticeship you weren't really paid at all—I think you got £9 for the first year and £12 the second year and £24 the third year—but you did get a war bonus. You signed with the employers to obey all the lawful commands of the owners and masters, refrain from alcohol and not frequent 'houses of ill-repute'—I remember that bit! They undertook to teach you seamanship and the work of a sailor in all respects. Some companies had what they called cadets, some called them apprentices, some called them midshipmen, but they were all basically the same.

I joined my first ship in Glasgow in September 1940. Of course, it was all wartime conditions, ships were all painted grey and everything right from the start. The first three months or so you weren't allowed much on the bridge. You only went on the bridge to scrub the chartroom, scrub the wheelhouse out,

Previous page: A cluster of bombs explodes alongside the Federal Line's MV Dorset *during the Pedestal convoy to Malta in August 1942.* S.D. Waters, Ordeal by Sea (1949)
Above: John Gregson, apprentice, in London in 1943. Gregson collection

and that sort of thing. As an apprentice you were in between the officers and the crew, and a lot of the time we worked with the crew. In those days, of course, the lifeboats were very important and had to be kept up to top scratch, so you worked on the boats a lot, rigging gear and everything. The third mate was supposed to teach you a bit of navigation and stuff like that, which you picked up as you went along. Blue Funnel was a very good company, they encouraged you to study. You had one afternoon a week when you had to sit down with your books and study navigation and seamanship.

The food was pretty rough, I do remember that. I think we had roast chicken on a Sunday. These chickens must have been specially bred with a hundred legs because you never ever saw a breast of chicken, you only got legs. So food was pretty basic. As apprentices we used to go and get it from the galley. I think we had our own little messroom, and usually a four-berth cabin.

The first year I don't think I did much on the bridge, but after that you did take watch on the bridge, when you were in convoys particularly. In those days you sailed in convoy across the Atlantic all the time, big huge convoys. As apprentices you were doing a lot of the signalling, so you were on the bridge. It was complete radio silence, so ships communicated by flag signals with international flags, but we had a special convoy code and codebooks. When the commodore ship would hoist a signal, perhaps signalling the convoy to alter course 20 degrees to port or something like that, we had to pick up the signal as quickly as we could with a telescope and put the answering flags up, or put the same signal up to transfer it to other ships in the convoy. If you were too slow you'd get a hurry-up from the captain. You really got expert at it, because you were doing it for days on end, and there was quite a competition between the ships to see who was the first one to answer the signal and transmit it on. Also we did a lot of Morse code signalling with Aldis lamps.

The first ship I sailed on was called the *Dolius*. The *Dolius* was quite an unusual ship because it had an experimental engine, known as a Scott-Still engine. There were only three ever built. It was a diesel engine, but it used the heat from the exhaust to run a boiler to inject steam into the bottom end or something. They were not very successful, they were always breaking down.

We went out east to Singapore, because at that stage the Japanese weren't in the war. We used to go right around the Cape of Good Hope. A voyage then was probably about seven or eight months, then you'd come home and join another ship. The second ship I joined was called the *Alcinous*. Again, I was mainly sailing around the Atlantic and the Indian Ocean.

In early 1942 John joined another Blue Funnel motor ship, the Mentor. *On 28 May this was torpedoed by* U-106 *in the Gulf of Mexico.*

We were running across the Atlantic, and submarines were very active off the east coast of America at that time, after America came into the war. We'd actually been to New Orleans and loaded a cargo; from memory I think it was for India. We sailed from New Orleans and were more or less right in the middle of the Gulf of Mexico when we were torpedoed. I remember it was about six o'clock in the evening. The torpedo hit us in the engine room, and of course the ship stopped. It was obvious that the engine room was flooded. I can remember going to look down and the engine room was filling up with water and steam. The captain ordered 'Abandon Ship' and we launched lifeboats.

We lost the engineer that was on duty, the fourth engineer, and three of the Chinese crew in the engine room. After we were torpedoed we pulled away in the boats. The ship sat there quite steady, low in the water. The radio officer had been left behind—he was busy sending out a distress message and we hadn't known. We suddenly saw him running along the deck and he jumped over and swam to a boat. Then we were going to go back. I was with the chief officer and he said, 'We'll go back on board and see if we can find the missing men.' We were just starting to go back when the submarine fired another torpedo into the ship from the other side, and a few minutes after that the ship went down.

It was dusk, just before dark, and the submarine came up. This was quite common, because they often used to take the captain and chief engineer prisoner and take them back to Germany. So he approached our boat and asked for the captain, and we told him the captain had gone down with the ship, which was completely untrue. Then he asked us if we had food and water—we said we were okay—and he took off.

We launched four boats, but one filled up with water so we had to transfer all the people from that boat into the other three. We would have had about 30 in each boat. We stayed together through the night, then we separated and set sail. We knew we weren't very far from land, about two or three hundred miles, and we knew that if we sailed east we'd hit Cuba. It was hot in the daytime and cold at night, but the main problem was the boat was so crowded. With so many people in a small boat, you couldn't lie down; it was very uncomfortable. My main recollection was the fact we were so crammed in.

I just had the clothes I was wearing. We had lifeboat rations. We immediately rationed out the water. You'd have a small beaker-full twice a day, and there were biscuits and some concentrated chocolate stuff. On the fourth day we were picked up by another ship and landed in America.

'The Santa Marija Convoy'   117

What did you do in the lifeboat all day?

Well, there wasn't much you could do. We had a sail up and we took it in turns steering. Because the chief officer trusted me I used to take my turn steering by compass. But really there wasn't much you could do. You'd tell stories, and doze off and sleep in bits and pieces. We didn't give up. We were pretty optimistic that in another two or three days we would possibly have struck land. But we were very pleased to be picked up.

We were taken to Key West in Florida and landed there. They fitted us out with clothes—just the bare necessities, trousers and a couple of shirts. Then eventually we went up to New York and then went on a ship back to the UK as passengers. It took us a long time to get home. I had two or three weeks' leave at home and then went to sea again.

Left, and below: *A boatload of survivors from the torpedoed MV* Mentor—*including 18-year-old apprentice John Gregson—about to be rescued by another Blue Funnel ship, the* Antilochus, *after four days adrift in the Gulf of Mexico. John was to survive another sinking three months later.* Gregson collection

John's next destination was the beleaguered Mediterranean island of Malta, which had been heavily bombed for two years and faced desperate shortages of food, fuel and ammunition.

I joined a ship called the *Deucalion* and we went to Malta in that well-known 'Pedestal' convoy. Everything was very secret. Nobody was supposed to know anything. You weren't allowed to take cameras away or anything like that. But when I joined the ship in Glasgow the rumour was that we were going to Malta. Everybody seemed to know; even the wharfies loading cargo would sort of know. Sure enough, we did go to Malta. This was the last big convoy to Malta: there were 14 merchant ships and nine were sunk; only five got through, and three of those were damaged. So that was quite exciting.

The old convoys were very slow, with 30 or 40 ships, governed by the speed of the slowest one, but this was a very special convoy and all the ships were capable of doing 16 knots. They were more modern, faster ships. The *Deucalion* was a motor ship and quite modern. Every ship carried a mixture of

The Deucalion *wallows in the calm Mediterranean after being damaged by enemy bombers on 12 August. As the rest of the convoy presses on towards Malta, the destroyer HMS* Bramham *ushers lifeboats back to the ship.* Gregson collection

the same cargo. In the early days of the war, one ship would have all the food, one all the bombs, and one this and that. This time every ship had so much food, so much ammunition, and we had petrol in cases and cans, because Malta then was in a pretty desperate situation.

> *Among the fast cargo-liners selected for Operation Pedestal were many familiar names from the New Zealand refrigerated trade: the* Waimarama *and* Wairangi *(Shaw Savill & Albion),* Port Chalmers *(Port Line),* Brisbane Star *and* Melbourne Star *(Blue Star), and the* Dorset *(New Zealand Shipping Company/Federal Line).*

We sailed from Glasgow right out into the middle of the Atlantic and we had a huge escort, something I'd never seen before. To start with we had two battleships, the *Nelson* and the *Rodney*, but they later dropped off. We had three cruisers, the *Manchester*, *Nigeria* and *Cairo*, and when we came back in towards the Straits of Gibraltar we were joined by three aircraft carriers, *Victorious*, *Indomitable* and *Eagle*. And 15 or 16 destroyers at all times. We knew then we were going to Malta.

We were pretty well armed. We had a 4-inch gun on the stern, plus a Bofors anti-aircraft gun and two Oerlikon guns. We had Oerlikons on the bridge as well, and we carried a squad of army gunners. I was the sight-setter on the 4-inch gun on the poop—that was my action station. We did a lot of gun drill on the way down there, gunnery practice. In the early part of the voyage I was on the bridge, signalling. Then we went through the Straits of Gibraltar in the middle of the night, in quite a bit of fog, and we ran into the Spanish fishing fleet—there were all these little white lights dotted about—so we knew very well that we were going to be reported. We knew that the message would get back to Germany that a convoy was going through the Straits. Once we got into the Mediterranean we were on doubled-up alert.

We were attacked many times in the first two or three days. All day there would be high-level air attacks and dive-bombing attacks. The threat of being torpedoed from submarines was there all the time, and the destroyers were always dashing around dropping depth charges as the convoy zigzagged and carried out emergency turns. The noise of the dive bombers and the bombs and all the ships firing with all their anti-aircraft guns and everything they had was deafening.

On the second day I was at my action station on the poop when I heard three loud explosions and saw that the aircraft carrier *Eagle* had been torpedoed and was heeling over to port more and more. I'll never forget seeing the aircraft sliding over the deck and into the sea and her crew jumping off as she heeled right over and sank within six or seven minutes of being hit.

The ship I was on, the *Deucalion*, was the first ship to drop out of the convoy. We were actually straddled by a cluster of bombs. One of the lifeboats was totally destroyed and another bomb went straight through the deck and right out through the ship's side under water before it exploded. Two of our holds were flooded and we were slowed right down, so we had to leave the convoy and proceed with one destroyer along the North African coast. The *Bramham* was the destroyer that came with us. We were going to see if we could get to Malta on our own.

After we were attacked, which was during the day—and I didn't know this until afterwards—some of the crew got into lifeboats and pulled away. At that stage we were stopped in the water. Then they came back. I think the *Bramham* chased after them and brought them back, but I don't even remember that part. So we carried on.

Then that evening we were attacked again by a couple of aerial-torpedo bombers, and they hit us and set the ship on fire. I was on the poop and the torpedo came right in just underneath that, so I was knocked out. I must have been out for a wee while, I don't know how long. When I came around there were only three of us left and the ship was blazing. The whole of the after part was blazing—we had petrol on deck which all caught fire. I was a bit groggy, I suppose. I looked along the deck and there was no way I could get along to the midships, it was just a mass of flames.

I realised that the gunlayer (I think he was an army man) was still there and he was trapped under a raft by his leg. There was another guy with me and the two of us realised we had to get off the ship quickly. It was then dark, and we managed to get the raft off him and get him over the side. He didn't want to go so we had to heave him over the side. I jumped in after this fellow and swam with him, towed him away from the ship as far as I could. The weather was good, it was summertime, and I was quite a good swimmer then. I saw the *Bramham* in the light from all the flames and swam with him to the *Bramham*, and they pulled us up.

Opposite: *A German reconnaissance photograph captures a huge column of black smoke rising from a bombed tanker in Valletta's Grand Harbour. Arrival in port was no guarantee of safety for the ships and seafarers of the Malta convoys— between 1940 and 1942 Valletta was one of the most heavily bombed cities in Europe.* The Air Battle of Malta (1944)

'The Santa Marija Convoy'

How far away was that?

I don't know—half a mile, something like that. Afterwards they said I'd saved his life. I didn't think I had, I was just saving my own life and saved him as well. He couldn't swim—he had a broken leg amongst other things. I had a cut above my eye and I remember a guy putting a couple of stitches in that, and I think my legs were badly bruised. I can remember having difficulty walking for a day or so.

On 12–13 August, relentless attacks by German and Italian bombers and motor torpedo boats claimed another eight merchantmen, including the Dorset, Wairangi *and* Waimarama.

On the *Bramham* we had survivors from the *Dorset* and an American ship, so we had quite a few survivors. You slept wherever you could, sometimes on a coil of rope; you just lay down where you could on the deck or anywhere. We then went and towed the *Ohio*, the tanker, into Malta, which was quite exciting. We went alongside the *Ohio*, and I can remember going aboard. We all went aboard looking for food actually, raiding the stores for food.

The *Ohio* was a tanker loaded with aviation fuel and it was very important to get her in. She'd been attacked several times and the engine room was out of action; she had a German plane that had been shot down on the fo'c'sle head, and most of the crew were on the *Bramham*; they couldn't do anything. We had the *Bramham* tied up on one side, another destroyer called the *Penn* tied up on the other side, and another one towing ahead, and every time the Germans came over we had to cut the ropes and split off, then come back.

But we managed to tow her into Malta and we got a good reception when we got there, I remember that. As you came into the harbour the piers and the harbour entrance were crowded with people. The population obviously knew we were coming, and it was crowded with people all cheering and waving as we came in. It was a special day, a saint's day—they called it Santa Marija, the 15th of August. It was known as the Santa Marija convoy after that.

Malta itself I've not got much memory of, except it was a desperate situation—it had been bombed to bits and there was very little food there. Most of the buildings were ruined and there were piles of rubble everywhere. We were landed at a submarine base and given some clothes. I got a pair of shorts and a shirt or something. I recall we got half a loaf of bread and a bowl of soup a day; there wasn't much else around. We were there for four days, and they were trying to get the survivors off as quickly as possible because there was no food. In fact, if the convoy hadn't got through—I didn't know this at the time, of course—they actually had planned that in another month they would have had to surrender the whole island.

Then I went back to Gibraltar on the *Penn*. I stayed in Gibraltar for a couple of days, I remember, then went back to England on another ship that was going that way.

> *Despite Pedestal's terrible losses, the arrival in Malta of the* Ohio *and four freighters helped ensure the island's survival. John Gregson's effort in saving the* Deucalion's *wounded gunner, described by the ship's master as 'a really gallant and plucky action by a boy of only 18', would see him awarded one of the British Empire's highest civilian decorations, the Albert Medal.*

Did you have any idea that you had been put forward for a decoration?
No, I didn't. I didn't know until six months later, when I was notified. Somebody must have recommended me, I suppose.

And what was your reaction?
Surprise, really. I didn't consider I'd done anything particularly gallant. I mean, there were many, many people who deserved it more than I did. Possibly the fact I was only 18 might have had something to do with it too. But I was just in the right place at the right time, or something.

I was awarded the Albert Medal, which was a civilian medal for saving life at sea, and also the Lloyd's

John, wearing his Blue Funnel apprentice's uniform, with his parents outside Buckingham Palace on the occasion of his investiture with the Albert Medal in 1943. Gregson collection

War Medal, which the Lloyd's insurance company awarded. I went to Buckingham Palace and was invested by King George VI. I went with my mother and father. I think by then it was 1943. It was a great occasion too. That was very exciting.

> *The Albert Medal became obsolete in 1971. Surviving recipients have since been treated as holders of the George Cross, although John has never exchanged his medal for the latter decoration.*

I wasn't home for long, then I went back to sea and joined a ship called the *Rhesus*, another Blue Funnel ship, a very old ship. We were running down to West Africa and across to America. This was in 1943, and there were still a lot of submarines about. I can remember on one convoy from Freetown in West Africa to the UK, we got badly attacked night after night. Every night a ship would be torpedoed—you'd see it on the other side of the convoy and hear the explosion—and in the end the convoy had to scatter and we ended up on the other side of the Atlantic in Halifax. We were told to go over there and then come back to England from there. Some funny things used to happen.

These convoys, of 30 or 40 ships, they were amazing things. We were all in formation. By that time I was a senior apprentice and used to help with station-keeping on the bridge. The ships were quite close together: I think you were five cables apart, beam on, between the columns, and the ships astern and ahead of you were supposed to be only three cables apart—so quite close. So you used to have to adjust your speed by revolutions, up three revs or down three revs. You got used to it, but it was quite a feat. There were a few collisions, and ships would get out of station, especially at night-time or in fog. When you got into fog you put a little fog-buoy over the side, which was like a scoop which sent up a column of water (rather like the jet tail you see behind power boats), and you towed that several hundred yards behind you so the ship astern could see it. They used to steam alongside it really.

After I'd done three years as an apprentice I went ashore, during 1943. I went to school in Newcastle-upon-Tyne for about three months and then sat and passed my second mate's certificate. I left Blue Funnel then and joined another Liverpool company called Brocklebanks as third mate. Brocklebanks was running out east to India most of the time and had Indian crews. By that time the Japanese were in the war so we were still in danger when we were in the Indian Ocean.

At sea during the war you had to have complete blackout at night. On some of the older ships you had the engine room in the middle of the ship and then an alleyway each side on the deck and accommodation outside the alleyway. And with the blackout we had to have screens across each end of the alleyway, which stopped the air running through. There was no such thing as air conditioning or anything like that so it used to get very, very hot, and you had to keep your portholes shut. Around West Africa and the tropics it used to get terribly hot. You were glad to get out of the cabin and on deck.

I was navigating by then—as third mate I'd keep my own watch as navigator. I was in charge of cargo as well, supervising the loading and discharging of cargo. I stayed with Brocklebanks for three years, and I got my first mate's certificate in 1945. After the war a lot of guys left and went ashore, but I thought, well, I'll carry on at sea. I just kept on going and made it my career.

John got his master's certificate in 1949 and spent three years as an officer on the Orient liners Ormonde *and* Orcades, *voyaging between London and Sydney. During this time he met his future wife, Mary, a New Zealander returning from a year in England.*

We corresponded for quite a while, and then when I came out here I met her again. I'd always wanted to come to New Zealand and I just decided one day I'd come out. So I came to New Zealand in 1952, and once I got here I stayed. I worked my way out to Singapore delivering a vessel and then travelled via Australia to New Zealand. I just arrived here—there was no thought of immigration procedures or anything like that in those days. I worked ashore for a while, out on a sheep station, and then I realised I should go back to what I knew best and went back to sea with the Union Company. A lot of the officers on the Union Company ships were from the UK, a lot of them had come out after the war. That was quite noticeable.

After marrying in 1954, John and Mary bought a house in Wellington and had two sons.

I was at sea sailing around the New Zealand coast for seven or eight years, right through the '50s. I was on the Shell Company tanker, the *Tanea*. In those days there was no refinery here. The overseas tankers brought petrol out to Wellington and Lyttelton and Auckland, and we just had this one little coastal tanker that used to deliver it all around New Zealand. I started on the ship as third mate and finished up as master.

Then in 1961 I got a job in Tauranga as harbour pilot, piloting ships in and out of the port at Mount

The Shell Oil tanker Tanea, *which John captained in the late 1950s, alongside Burnham Wharf, Miramar, Wellington.*
Alexander Turnbull Library, W.H. Raine Collection, 20798-1/4

Maunganui. It was a very small place in those days, just a holiday resort. In 1961 the wharf was only capable of accommodating three ships. From the time I arrived they never stopped expanding the wharf, trade increased, and shipping got busier and busier. The log trade was building up all the time. In those days you could have five, six, seven ships anchored outside waiting for an empty berth. It would be nothing to have ships waiting outside for up to a week. Today it is a major port, of course.

In 1977 John went back to sea, spending ten years as an officer on the Union Company's coastal tankers Kuaka, Kotuku *and* Amokura.

The refinery had been built by then, so we loaded at Marsden Point and delivered petrol all around New Zealand. I enjoyed it. I mean, conditions had changed so much. You had far more leave, but it was still hard work, especially on the tankers. You'd go away for six weeks and you wouldn't have a day off. The tankers worked 24 hours a day, seven days a week. Then I retired—at that time it was compulsory retirement at 63.

John and his wife still live in Mount Maunganui. He looks back on his seagoing career with satisfaction.

I've never regretted that I went to sea and made that my career. I suppose because of the war I was never a teenager in the modern way, because I went to sea when I was 16 and the next thing I was well in my 20s. There were bad times, but I never regretted it. I don't really think about the bad times, the bad food and all that.

When I look back on it, I think I was very fortunate I survived the war, with all the people who were killed. I think back to the Blitz and the huge number of civilians who were killed in London alone. It was terrible really. [But being] brought up during the war you didn't think about it much. You just learned to live with it. All through the war at sea you knew you were a target. You knew you could be torpedoed any time, day or night, because you couldn't see the submarines. I remember we often used to turn in with our clothes on, so we could leap up in the middle of the night. You didn't dwell on it, but you were aware of that all the time. In fact, [as a proportion of the number who served], the Merchant Navy lost more men than any of the other services.

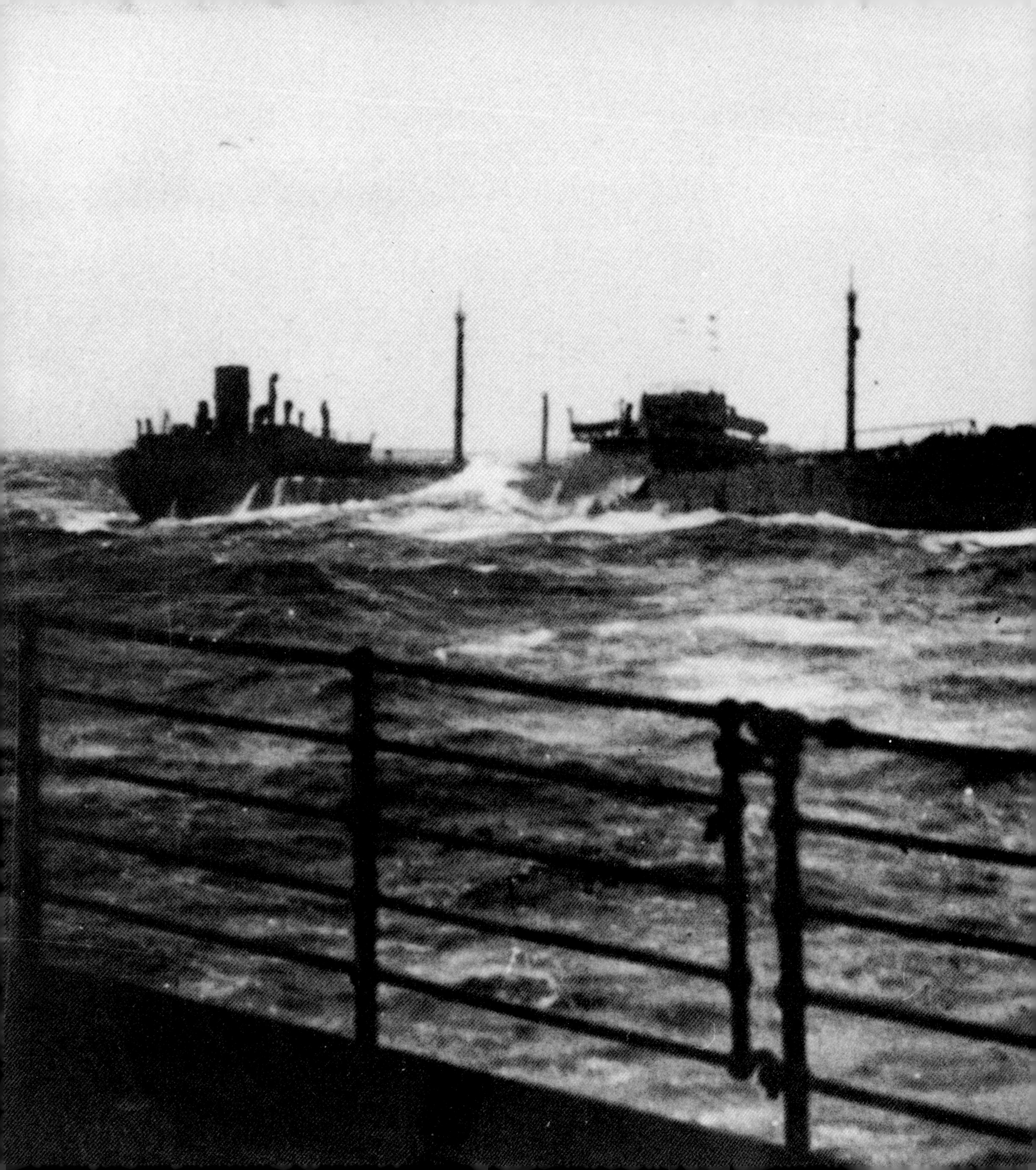

'FOUR DAYS OF HELL'

LES WATSON, Steward

Leslie Arthur James Watson, the second-eldest son in a family of four boys and a girl, was born in Dunedin in September 1922. His father, Ernie, played rugby for Otago, and the Watson boys—Albie, Les, Eric and Len—were all 'sports mad'. When the war broke out Albie joined the navy and served on the cruiser Achilles. *Les tried to enlist in the army, navy and air force, but was turned down because of an arm injury he had suffered playing rugby.*

THERE WERE THREE BOYS from Dunedin—Jack Cameron, Bill Webb and myself—who said, 'Let's go to Wellington and we'll get a ship.' So we worked our way to Wellington and we got a ship, the old *Raranga*, from where a lot of crew had deserted. They called her a 'blood ship', because nobody stayed on her more than one trip. She was an old coal-burner that was brought back into action for the war. But she was sound, and I managed to get a job to go to England. And believe it or not that was the worst journey I had all during the war, that first trip; it petrified me.

I signed on as a steward. We left Wellington about two days before Christmas [1942]. We had Christmas Day at sea, and a vat on the stove in the galley overturned and burnt the cook. We put him off at the Chatham Islands and he died. When we went to the Chatham Islands they thought we were a German raider. I'll always remember this: we went into a bay and a big whaleboat came out and they had a white flag there. I can't say exactly what went on, but I heard them talking in the officers' mess. They thought we were a German raider and they were going to surrender the island.

It took us nearly 35 days to get from Wellington to Panama. The seas were rough. The Pacific is not noted for being as rough as the Atlantic, but it was. When we left Panama we waited about seven

Previous page: *A convoy of cargo ships and tankers ploughs through the North Atlantic towards Britain.* Royal New Zealand Navy Museum

Above: *Les Watson in his deck steward's uniform on the* Ceramic (II) *in 1948.* Watson collection

Opposite: *The Shaw Savill & Albion coal-burner SS* Raranga *(10,040 tons) in Wellington Harbour. Despite its age (it was built in 1916) and modest top speed, the* Raranga *proved to be a lucky ship, safely crossing the Atlantic many times during the Second World War.* Alexander Turnbull Library, G-15983-1/2

days to join a convoy slow enough for our ship. Our top speed was nine knots. So they said to us, you go ahead of the convoy and head for Florida and we'll pick you up during the night. Well, the convoy passed us during the night and they were attacked. We got straight through to Florida and then New York all right. From New York we went up to Halifax, where the convoy was made up. All the captains went ashore for a meeting about what we were going to do in the convoy and what positions we were to take, and then we took off.

In late February 1943 the Raranga *sailed for Britain in a slow convoy of about 60 ships, convoy SC121.*

I'll always remember that, because I'd never been in action before. I know I stood on the deck and I thought, I'm going into action—all brave, you know. This was before I even knew what war was about.

It was one of the worst convoys; a lot of stragglers got sunk. It was a mixture of the world's shipping at that time. In wartime there were many ships brought back into service that had been taken out of service. Because we were getting so many sunk they were bringing out anything. The ship that I was on, we had a boat drill and all our oars broke—they were warped, everything was old. Yet the same ship was one of the few that maintained its speed across the Atlantic in all weathers.

Anyway, they were rough seas—mountainous seas. The ship would go right down in the troughs and the waves were higher than the ship. And it was freezing, bitter. There were ropes down the gangways to hold onto so you didn't get swept overboard. The hatch cover shifted and it was pretty dangerous with the water coming over. So the 'old man' got all the crew and firemen to lift the cover bodily back on top of the hatch. We'd have been sunk if we hadn't put it on. The whole cargo shifted. You couldn't explain to anybody what it really was like.

As the ships of SC121 battled through a force ten storm, two German wolf packs—a total of 26 U-boats—were gathering to attack.

Some of the sailors were talking to me and I said, 'Would we get an attack in this type of weather?' They said, 'Not very likely, the submarines wouldn't.' But they did—we had four nights and four days of hell. The German wolf packs would get ahead of the convoy and then turn their engines off and drift underneath us, then pop up and sink a ship and then submerge again. We only had about four corvettes looking after us. In those days they were struggling for escorts.

I asked these sailors, 'How long will a ship float [if it is torpedoed]?' They said, 'Well, if you've got a cargo

An Atlantic convoy in fine weather, seen from an escorting corvette. In the early years of the war the Allies were desperately short of suitable escort vessels. Coastal Command (1944)

of rice, when water gets in the rice will swell and it'll burst the ship.' 'But we've got a cargo of butter,' I said. 'How would we get on?' They said, well, butter could sort of seal the hole. In the finish they were telling me to shut up because I was saying all these despairing things to them. But I was so green I didn't know what to do.

I was out on the deck one night and the chief officer came out and said, 'What are you doing out here, son?' I said, 'I'm making sure there's nothing in the way to my lifeboat.' He said, 'Don't stay out here, because if we get hit you'd get blown into the water. Stay under cover.' So I never went out again, for four days and five nights.

When we got to Belfast this joker said, 'You had a pretty rough time, steward?' I said, 'I'll be honest with you, I was so frightened I don't know where we are.' Then we went into Bute Street docks at Cardiff and I paid off. I thought, I'm not going back to sea. But blow me down, I get to London and German bombers are coming over. I thought to myself, out of the frying pan into the fire. Then I got scared and I thought, I'm going home. But I found out, going up, you couldn't go to sea and come back. You had to do a round trip, you couldn't sail one way to New Zealand. So what I would have to do was jump ship. Well, I thought, I'm not doing that, I'll just have to carry on. But after those first two or three voyages they got control of the U-boats in the Atlantic and it was quite good at sea then. We got on top of them.

Can you tell me more about your job as a steward?
I looked after the captain on the way, Captain Ireland. I never even had a chance to get seasick; the 'old man' really had me that tied up I had no time for anything else bar doing my job and doing it correctly. In the morning we got up at seven o'clock, and everybody on the ship had a job to do, like wash down some steps or a corridor, you all had a part to do. Then I'd make the 'old man's' bed, and help with the meals: I did the officers' mess and the 'old man'. I had a special job, which was to carry the water for his bath from down in the officers' quarters up to the 'old man' on the bridge. I had to put the hot water in and cool it off. One morning I didn't cool it off, and he had a bit of gout, and he came in and put his feet in the hot water. I tell you, I never went back to his cabin all that day. I hid for the day. I thought he'd kill me.

He did say to me, 'Son, have you been seasick yet?' I said, 'Sir, you're not giving me a chance to be seasick, you're making me that frightened.' I'll tell you a little thing he did. I used to have to leave a tray up on the bridge for his cup of tea at night-time, and once I forgot to leave a teaspoon. The seaman on watch came down to my cabin, at two in the morning or something, and said, 'Steward, the captain says he hasn't got a teaspoon on his tray.' I said, 'Well, go to the galley, pick up a teaspoon and take it up to him.' He sent the sailor back: 'He says, "You tell that steward to get up and bring it up to me himself".' That was the type of man he was. But really he did me a favour, he made me grow up.

You'd do ten hours a day straight, seven days a week—70 hours. [In your spare time] you'd write home, or do your dhobiing—your washing—and all that stuff. You had to look after yourself. We were pretty tired at the end of the day, we'd be straight in the bunks, have a read, write home and things like that. There was not much playtime. Even in port, everything was a rush. We bolted our meals down, because we couldn't waste time, we wanted to be ashore. You might only be there for a couple of days.

What was your food like?
Being a steward we got better food than the crew did. The crew used to bring their dishes up to the galley and fill them and take them back down. That's where the trouble was. During the war they had run out of good cooks and they had pressure-cooker jobs jacked up, and some of them were pretty hopeless. My meals were quite good; I ate what the officers ate. But there was some terrible food went to the crew. I'd be in the captain's cabin when crew were bringing up their food to him, and they were saying, 'Captain, how could you eat this stuff?' The captain would say to me, 'Son, don't stay in the cabin when these men come to see me.' On the *Raranga*, when the firemen and trimmers used to come out after their watch they looked like skeleton wrecks. They were just bones. The conditions were shocking, but they survived.

Where was the crew's accommodation?
The seamen and firemen lived for'ard. We were aft with the galley staff. In the Atlantic the waves came over and flooded our cabin. I was on the top bunk—I remember this to this day—I was sitting there and there was no way I was going to get out and paddle in the water. Even if the ship was sinking I was staying in the top bunk!

In convoy there was [another] job we had to do: put our lights out, all your lights had to be out. I'll always remember one night, I had an English mate and I said, 'You do my blackout tonight and I'll do yours tomorrow.' And he didn't do it, and the commodore of the convoy threatened to fire on us to extinguish the lights, because it was pretty bloody bad—all the U-boats needed was a light. I remember going out on the deck, him and me were going to have a fight. I was genuine about doing my job properly, I didn't want to dodge things.

> *In late 1943 Les was sent to the United States on the* Queen Elizabeth *to join a newly completed Liberty ship, the* Samavon, *at Portland, Maine. He then sailed to India, where he had a narrow escape from the devastating Bombay docks explosion in April 1944 which wrecked two dozen ships and killed at least 800 people.*

When we got to Bombay part of the ship's engine was crook, so instead of leaving us tied up at the wharf they told us to go out in the stream, drop the anchor and wait there till we got the parts. It was just as well, because in the meantime an ammunition ship blew up in Bombay Harbour. We were in the stream, we were lucky. The joke was you could have got a gharry to Calcutta for nothing, every Indian would have pulled it [to escape from Bombay].

I had my appendix taken out off that ship, in Baltimore. They wouldn't let me sail because if I got sick at sea, well, we had no doctors. So they put me off at Baltimore and I had a spinal injection—I'll always remember that. I was sent to a Norwegian sailors' home and from there up to the sailors' home in New York. Then I was put on the *Empire Beresford* to go back to England. It was a tanker, carrying high-octane. I'd never been on a tanker, and I didn't know till I was on it, because I was just sent: 'Go on the *Empire Beresford* back to England, then you can get back on the Pool.' I sweated every day going across the Atlantic that we wouldn't get attacked. She was a floating bomb.

We had a Pool in England. I got a Churchill 'V'-sign put on my identity card, and that meant I had to take any ship that they asked me to take without any quibbles. Actually, I joined one to go to Murmansk, but I took crook and I'm glad to this day that I never went to Murmansk. I nearly joined the *Newfoundland*, a hospital ship, and she was sunk in the Mediterranean. I think she was one of the first hospital ships to be sunk. Something diverted her and I didn't join her. So really I had a bit of luck.

> *Instead, in mid-1944 Les joined the* Île de France, *a 43,450-ton French luxury liner commandeered by the British for use as a troopship.*

Two of the world's finest pre-war ocean liners, the Île de France *(right) and* Aquitania, *on troop-carrying duty in the Indian Ocean in February 1943. Together with the even larger* Queen Mary *and* Queen Elizabeth, *these ships—known collectively as 'The Monsters'—safely transported several million Allied service personnel during the war years.* Australian War Memorial, 029566

The *Île de France* was one of the biggest ships in the world. My job was to look after the chief engineer, Harding. It was a great job. I just about made up my own menu: I'd go down to the galley and say, 'The chief engineer would like a couple of fillet steaks tonight', or something. He was a good man.

I went adrift [AWOL] in New York—actually I was courting an American girl. They said, no shore leave. I thought, Oh I'm going, so I went ashore just for a couple of days. But when I came back, the ship had gone from New York over to New Jersey. So naturally I just said, 'Where's the *Île de France*?' Next thing a jeep came up, carrying MPs and all that, and they put me in it. To speak the name of a ship during wartime was like telling the Germans that the *Île de France* was in port, you know, and they'd wait outside for it. I was taken in to the chief engineer and he brought out his uniform and said, 'Give it a good brushing down.' So I brushed all his uniform down. He says, 'You'd better go adrift more often. That's the best you've had my uniform since we sailed.' He was a good joker.

We used to do things for the Americans—we used to take [up to 10,000] troops across to England every time from America. If they wanted to have a shower, they couldn't, so I let out the chief engineer's shower at 50 cents a shower. Then the chief said to me, 'How are you doing on the uniforms, son?'

'How do you mean, sir?' He said, 'Pressing any American uniforms?' So I found out this was another racket, you did their uniforms and charged them a dollar. Anyway, all I used to do with those American uniforms—I couldn't improve them, because the Americans always kept their clothes very good—was button them up, hang them up in a wardrobe, bring them down at night-time, and take a dollar.

There were a lot of queers on there. When I joined the *Île de France*, this joker came on board and I said, 'What are you?' He said, 'I'm the butter queen.' He delivered butter to all the troops. What a great job he had! There were some bloody hard cases, and some good cases. Our chief steward, he was queer, and he used to get all the New Zealanders in a group, take us ashore and shout for us. But he'd pick out somebody in the group who'd be more compatible to a queer, you know.

How were homosexuals treated by the other crew?
Oh, all right; like a sheila, you know, you'd have them on. But they existed. I had a couple of experiences with them. On one ship I was on I belted one. He was having a go at me. I think he fell over and broke his ankle, up on the deck. When I told the 'old man' why all this happened, he defended me, he was on my side.

What did you usually do when you went ashore on leave?
Well, first thing, we went straight to a pub, to have a beer with all the boys. I've been round the world that many times and yet I didn't really sightsee these places. It was the seaman's way of living; get ashore, have a few drinks, go to a dance. But in New York I used to get around and see different things, Radio City, all those places. New York was wonderful. We'd drink in Jack Dempsey's bar and all these other famous bars. You could go to a theatre: I saw Red Skelton, Joe Brown and all the top bands, Tommy Dorsey, Gene Krupa. It was brilliant. Then we went to the Atlantic Club, which was a club for seamen, and there was the Stagedoor Canteen and all these big clubs. We got on well with the Americans. I spoke home to New Zealand through Nola Luxford's show. She [broadcast on the radio] to New Zealand, so we could speak to home.

In England we used to go to Romford, just outside London, at night-time and meet in this pub; no girls were allowed, but every sort of servicemen, troops and sailors. We got together and drank till ten o'clock, then went over to a dance. We got on good as gold. I loved the pubs in London during the war, with all the singing. It was a wonderful atmosphere.

The New Zealand-born actress Nola Luxford surrounded by New Zealand and Australian servicemen in a Manhattan radio studio; the men in civilian clothes may be merchant seamen. During the war Luxford's Anzac Club in New York provided hospitality to thousands of visiting service personnel, many of whom—like Les Watson—broadcast messages home to their families. Alexander Turnbull Library, F-17618-1/4

I sailed with this London boy and we stayed in their home every time we came back. His mother was wonderful. We were allowed to take a food parcel from New Zealand, so I took it to her in London. [Elsewhere] I stayed in the sailors' missions. I had no problems, even up in Liverpool. They had the Red Ensign Club, we stayed there. The only thing was you had to have your wits about you. Say you went in for a meal, [you had to pay a] deposit on your knife and fork. And people would pinch your knife and fork to get the deposit. Everything was a fiddle.

Did the crew visit the red-light districts in port?
Yes, oh yes. I'll always remember my mate, the Londoner, in Santos, Brazil, and we couldn't find him. So we went into a brothel and I said, 'Have you seen Ray?' 'Yes,' she said, 'we've put him to bed.'

'What have you put him to bed for?' She said, 'Oh, he's a lovely boy.' So we had to drag him out of the brothel—he was getting it for free. He had high cheekbones and blue eyes.

Near the end of the war, when we went to the Argentine, Buenos Aires, or to Rio de Janeiro, Santos, Rio Grande do Sul, they had warnings to stay out of places that were [pro-]German.

In mid-1945 Les was serving on the Balfe, *voyaging to South America.*

We were off Rio Grande do Sul on the SS *Balfe* and we picked up 30 survivors off a Brazilian cruiser, the *Bahia*. Somehow it had been sunk, with their own depth charges, I think. They were all lying on rafts, and they'd been on these rafts for four or five days, so they all had salt sores. The 'old man' said over the speaker that nobody should go over the side because there were sharks about. They were shooting at them. We threw a rope to one raft and a Brazilian fellow dived in the water, and I guarantee he swam 15 yards there and back and was never touched. Yet when he got back on board, the water was thrashing with sharks. We were supposed to get a decoration for that [rescue].

I spent VE Day in London and VJ Day down the Argentine. We went adrift down the Argentine on VJ Day. This was on the *Balfe*. When we came on board Captain Sweeney was going to log us. The boy who was with me was from London, and he turned around to the captain and said, 'I don't care what you do to me, sir. My family's been getting bombed since 1939 and this is the end of hostilities. I don't care what you do, my people are safe.' And Captain Sweeney let us off, he realised that the boy was genuine. I always admired those people in London. One doodlebug or rocket would just about wipe out a block. You didn't know where they were going to come down. I admired the English people for what they had to put up with.

I didn't meet a lot of New Zealanders [during the war]. I never sailed on a New Zealand ship. Actually, it was pretty hard for a Kiwi, because the Poms gave us hell on the ship and if you didn't stand up for yourself you had a pretty hard life. But there was a code of ethics on a ship. You never thieved on a ship, because you're all in close quarters and the whole ship would condemn you. I felt there was a character to them, merchant seamen, and yet they were classed as the scum of the world. But they had a great code of ethics—their own code, but it was an honesty code. I had no problems. Mind you, on ships you couldn't have a Liverpool crew and a Scottish crew together—Liverpudlians and Glaswegians, that would be dangerous.

I played a bit of soccer on the English ships. Down the Argentine all the ships had a team; a lot of good football was played down there. On the *Waiwera* we got to Australia and went up to Port Alma and Gladstone, and there was nothing to do at these places. They had a ship's soccer team, but there were a lot of Stornoway fellows, from Scotland, in the crew, who weren't playing. I went down to them and said, 'Listen, if we make up a team would you jokers play [against] the ship's team?' They said, 'We've got no gear.' So I wrote up to Rockhampton and got some—like the All Blacks, the colours were all black—and boots and that, and we played the ship's team. These Stornoway fellows would only play for me, they wouldn't play for the ship. I said, 'Now look, you can all play football.' 'Of course we can.' 'Well, why not play for the ship?' 'Nah, officers.' But they said, 'All right, we'll turn out for you, Kiwi.' Eventually the ship's team grabbed our strip and then I got into that side as well. So I got really interested, you know. I was always interested in sport, always competitive.

We brought the 'Kiwi' [2NZEF rugby] team home after the war, on the *Moreton Bay*, Charlie Saxton and all those jokers. I was a second steward by then, so I got better jobs. I got on the *Ceramic*—it was a modern ship, had just come out of the yards; the old *Ceramic* had been sunk. We took it out on its maiden voyage [to New Zealand in 1948]. I got a deck steward's job; it was a wonderful job, and good money.

Les (second from left) and other stewards on Shaw Savill's Ceramic *(II), during the liner's maiden voyage to New Zealand in 1948.*
Watson collection

I met my wife in Gladstone, Australia, and she went through two romances. I was in love with a girl in New York and was writing to her, and she dumped me. Then I was in love with a girl in London and she dumped me, and all this time I was writing to my [future] wife and treating her like a sister. My brother said to me one day, 'That sheila you're writing to in Australia, why don't you put the hard word on her? Come over and get engaged, one way or the other.' That's what I did and she accepted, and I've had 52 years married—brilliant. So I'm glad all the others fell through.

So you decided to leave the sea then?
Well, no way was I going to go to sea and leave my wife at home, because I'd seen that much going on in the Merchant Navy. It's no place to be, at sea and letting your wife run wild, or vice versa. I think I'd have stayed at sea if I hadn't been courting. By this time my family had just about forgotten me. I hadn't seen them much for years.

I did it the right way. I went down to the Pool office and said I'd like to get home. They said the only way you can do it is if there is someone who can replace you. You go one way and they go the other. And that's what happened—someone had been in hospital out here. I was very fortunate really, because otherwise you had to keep doing the round trip and I would have had to jump ship.

> *Les signed off his last ship, the* Waipawa, *in Napier in February 1950. After some time in Christchurch and Otaki, he returned to Dunedin, where he worked at the City and Wain's hotels and later ran a successful restaurant business with his wife Val. He played soccer for Technical Old Boys and was later active in coaching and administration, helping Dunedin City win the Chatham Cup in 1981. Meanwhile, his brother Eric became a leading rugby coach, eventually coaching the All Blacks in 1979–80. In 1995 Les Watson was one of the New Zealand veterans selected by ballot to attend the celebrations in Britain marking the 50th anniversary of VE Day.*

It was one of the greatest trips. We had army, navy and air force people picked out from all over New Zealand. In Hyde Park they had a big gathering. I met people I'd never have a show of meeting in the world. I met Vera Lynn. I even proposed marriage to her (she'd already been married three times). I had a few beers in me by then! And Cliff Richard, he sang in Hyde Park. We had the Queen, all the royal family. We met everybody. That trip was brilliant. You can't put it in words.

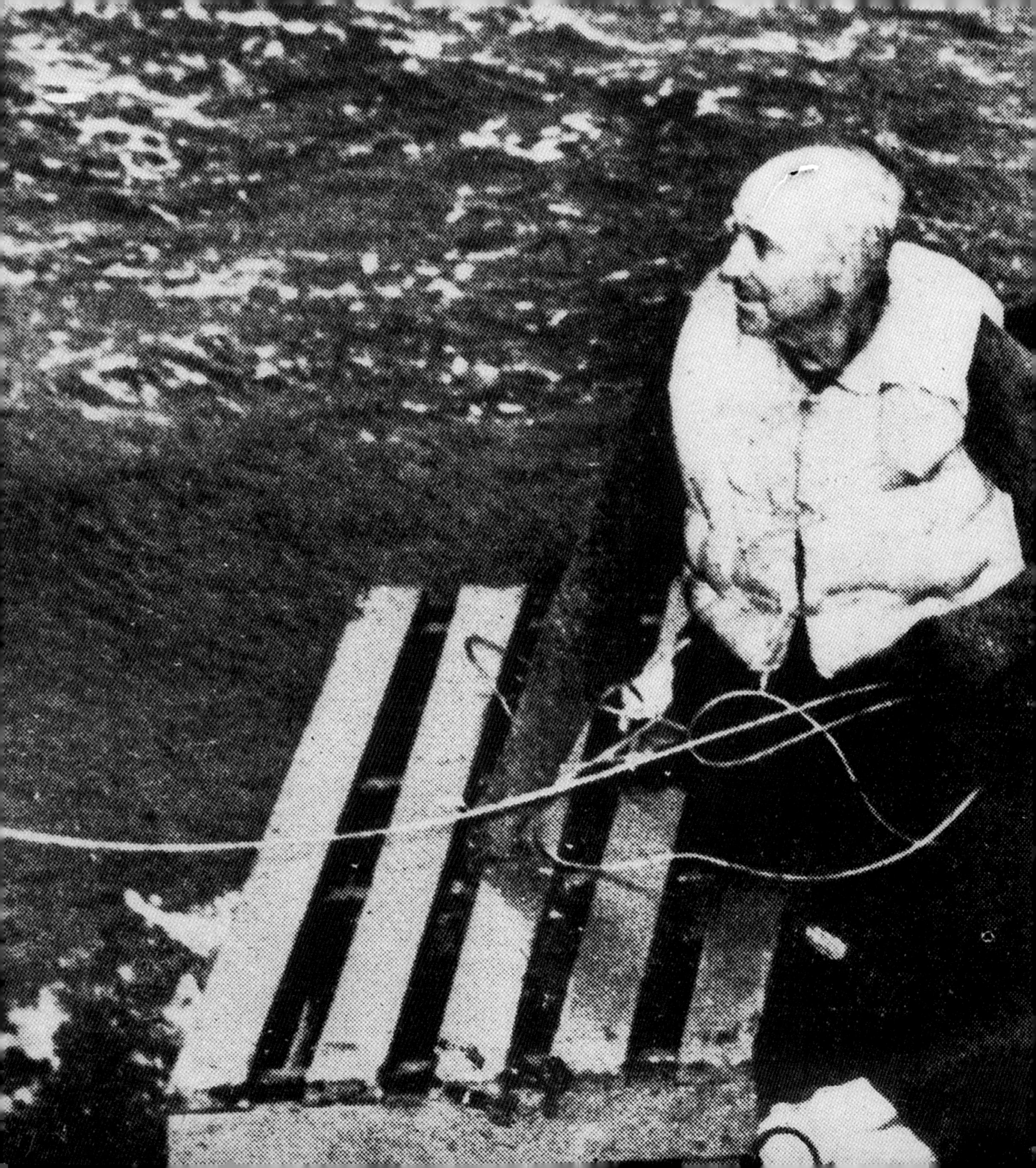

'IT SEEMED LIKE AN ETERNITY'

DARCY HOFFMAN, Boy, Seaman, Bosun

Darcy Hoffman's paternal grandparents came to New Zealand from Germany in 1872 and settled in Southland, where his grandfather worked on the construction of the Dunedin–Invercargill railway line. Darcy, born in Gore in November 1924, was the son of farming parents. After attending primary school in Mandeville and Gore and the technical high school in Invercargill, he started a joinery apprenticeship in 1938.

Do you remember hearing about the outbreak of war?
Very much—oh yes, it was a big thing. All the young fellows wanted to go. But I wasn't old enough to go, according to my parents. So I served three-and-a-half years of my trade, then I went away to sea in 1942. It was either the navy or the Merchant Navy—my choice, nobody else's. I went to one of the shipping companies, Blue Star. There had been an accident on a ship, causing a few casualties, and they were short of deck hands and men down below. I was fortunate I got an appointment with the chief officer and he 'liked the colour of my shirt', so I got the job. It was in Bluff—on the *Canadian Star*. They loaded frozen meat in Bluff and Port Chalmers and then went to England.

I was a deck boy, just running around behind the ABs, doing what they were doing, whatever they wanted done. Once I was on there six months I was promoted to ordinary seaman. It doesn't take you long, really. I forget the pay now; there was a war-risk bonus though, which was quite good. I think it might have been £12 a month and £10 war-risk or something. But you got your keep and a bed and all the rest of it. The accommodation was aft. It was quite good. It was one of the modern ships at the time. The food was reasonable, but not as good as you get at home.

Previous page: *Survivors from a torpedoed merchant ship about to be rescued by a US Coast Guard cutter in the North Atlantic in 1943.* Australian War Memorial, P02018.187
Above: *Darcy Hoffman, seaman.* Hoffman collection
Opposite: *The Blue Star Line's 8293-ton refrigerated freighter MV* Canadian Star *off the New Zealand coast in 1942.* Alexander Turnbull Library, G-25195-1/2

'It Seemed Like an Eternity'

We had a 4.7, a 12-pounder and two old Hotchkiss machine-guns. When the ship got to England I was going to be trained to get a gunlayer's ticket to operate these guns. But I'd had word from home that my brother Paul, who'd gone away earlier, in 1936, was in London. I asked the chief officer if I could go down and he said, 'No trouble, you can do the gunlayer's ticket some other time.' But I never got round to doing it, and a damn good job I didn't too, because [later] we had an accident with that gun, the 4.7, that killed a few men.

Then I was asked if I wanted to come back on the ship. Well, I didn't know anybody over there, so I signed on the Pool and came back. We loaded in Swansea first, then in Liverpool, and then came out. It was a fairly fast ship and they didn't bother about a convoy first off—it could do 18 knots.

In late 1942 the Canadian Star *returned to New Zealand with a cargo of arms, ammunition and crated aircraft, and then shipped supplies and personnel to the Middle East. For the return voyage from Australia to Britain the ship took on 27 passengers, mostly service families who had earlier been evacuated from Singapore. In February 1943, near Panama, the breechblock of the 4.7-inch gun*

A naval corvette swings around to pick up survivors on a liferaft in calm conditions. Heavy seas of the kind encountered during convoy HX229 in March 1943 made survival aboard rafts and rescue operations of this kind far more hazardous. Coastal Command (1944)

> exploded, killing three crewmen and injuring several others. On 8 March the Canadian Star sailed from New York as part of the fast convoy HX229.

The time we got torpedoed was when we were in that convoy. But it might have been worse if we'd have been on our own. [The convoys were] for security, and if anything happened you had a better chance of getting picked up by one of the escorts. We left New York to go to, I presume, Liverpool. We were in a nine-knot convoy. At that particular time the submarines were getting very cheeky, they were coming right into the convoys.

It was late in the day. I'd been wet, so I came in and got changed, and then the bloody alarm went again. I shot up on deck and I left my papers and everything, hoping that I'd get back into my cabin again, which I didn't. The third officer [New Zealander Reg Keyworth] spotted a periscope and I tried to get the Oerlikon onto it, but the gun was too bloody high and I couldn't [depress it enough]. If I'd have shot I might have hit one of the other ships in the column. Then I saw the furrows of two torpedoes coming and I thought, oh my God, we're not going to dodge this. [The helmsman] tried to put it hard a-port to see if we could get round them, but no. We were going too slow; if we'd been going a bit faster perhaps it might have been different.

Anyway, we lost a few fellows. And two boats—the explosions blew them up, they were out over the side and they were blown to bits. Myself and a man called Joe Cormack, another AB, lowered the only boat that got away, the No. 1 boat. The one behind it was No. 3 and as it was being lowered people were coming out of the lower deck and getting into the boat, and I don't think the fellow [lowering it] could hang onto the rope, and he let it go and tipped them all out. I think that's what happened.

So myself and Joe got down to the foredeck and by this time it was lifting pretty high, as it was sinking by the stern. We cut a raft and let it go and then jumped down to it. It finished up with quite a few of us on it, 13 I think—not a good number. The sea was rough as hell. After we got out of the lee of the ship, it just kept turning the raft over. That's where quite a few were lost. It was very cold in the sea.

What were you wearing?
We had old kapok lifejackets, probably the worst things you could have, after a few hours, because you'd go down with it. I had boots on and that's the first thing you had to kick off, so I had nothing on my feet, just ordinary light clothes, and a lifejacket over the top.

Did the escort ships come back looking for survivors?
Not straight away. They were busy trying to bloody locate these submarines and dropping depth charges and God knows what else. I didn't think we were ever going to get picked up because she was getting pretty dark. It was late in the afternoon. I thought, oh well, I might be finished now, because it was that cold, I could hardly hang on any longer. But with that, a corvette with the name of *Anemone* pulled alongside and just dragged us aboard. I think there were only eight of us left.

How long were you on the raft?
A couple of hours, perhaps. It seemed like an eternity. Well, if you understand, a raft's a very small thing. In the reports from the captain [of the *Anemone*], one of his lookouts thought he saw something in one of the troughs of the waves—they were big waves—and they went over to inspect it. We were very, very lucky. We could have been missed, you know.

There would have been 200 survivors on the corvette. We just lay down where there was a bit of room, just on the sealed deck. They didn't have any blankets or dry clothes, because the ones who got the best attention were the ladies and those who were injured. They got the officers' cabins—the officers gave up their beds, which was excellent. Anyway, it was warm enough in there, with that many of us huddled together. They went into action against a submarine, got it on their Asdic gear and went over and dropped depth charges. But we never saw any of it. They wouldn't let us out on deck at all. If we'd have been hit I don't think any of us would have got out.

We got a good meal once a day. But you understand that's a hell of a lot of mouths to feed. In the end they had to leave the convoy, when it was sort of out of danger, because they had no more food or water left. They took us to a place called Gourock [in Scotland] and they gave us clothes to wear and a bit of a clean-up, because a lot of us were still covered in bloody oil.

> *Twenty-three of the* Canadian Star's *crew (including three New Zealanders) and seven passengers went down with the ship. In just four days, HX229 and another eastbound convoy, SC122, had lost 22 merchant ships amounting to over 146,000 tons.*

I think you were given a couple of weeks' survivor's leave, and a ticket to wherever you wanted to go. I wanted to go to New Zealand! They said, 'We'll give you one after the war.' But it was sort of funny.

'It Seemed Like an Eternity' 149

You see, [with a name like] Hoffman, coming ashore, of course quite a few heads popped up. 'Hoffman?' 'Yeah, yeah.' 'Where's some identification?' I didn't have any. I got a piece of paper to say, 'This man claims to be a British subject', and that was it until my papers came through.

Then they gave me another ship. I was quite keen to get back to sea again. It was the *Fort Louisbourg*, a Canadian-built ship. I was on it for eight months, out around West Africa. I contracted malaria out there and was in hospital in Lagos for 12 days. I didn't think I'd ever get out of there. Hell, it was hard.

I had a monkey for three or four months. I got it in West Africa, and all the fellows liked it. There was an Australian who knew all about monkeys, and he was helping to train it. But anyway, the authorities in India wouldn't let it in. That was the law in India; you can't bring in an animal from another place. The skipper sent for me and said, 'If you don't catch it and drown it they're going to come aboard and shoot it.' I said, 'Oh well, okay.' That's the rules. There were bloody cats and dogs on a lot of the ships and nobody did anything, but I suppose a monkey could be different.

Then I joined the *Empire Tamar* in Glasgow. We got it all ready, it was going on engine trials and the bloody things broke down, so they paid us all off. I was only on her about a month and then I joined the *Ocean Faith*. [The 'Ocean' ships] were American-built coal-burners. I spent 15 months on that ship. I was an AB by this time, and when we were in Bari and Brindisi we lost some fellows and I was promoted to bosun. I was bosun for the rest of that trip, about a year. The pay was better and the accommodation was better.

You were pretty young to be a bosun, weren't you?
Yeah, I think one or two of [the crew] must have thought that, too. Oh no, they were all right. I used to do quite a bit of boxing when I was away (as a boy I went to a boxing school in Invercargill). I had gloves and a punchbag and everything, and I think that might have helped me.

When Darcy boxed in wartime Britain he changed his German-sounding name to Jim Gordon, hence the 'JG' on his shorts. Hoffman collection

I did offer some of them the chance to spar with me, but they turned me down. Some of the engine crew, they'd come up and spar.

I boxed quite a lot over there, when I was on leave in England and Scotland. I fought in some of the boxing booths at fairgrounds. They travelled around in great big marquees, and you challenged the boxer. Even some of the good champions did their training in there. I had to change my [German-sounding] name over there, or I'd have got thrown out. Oh hell, yes. I changed it to Jim Gordon.

On the Ocean Faith *Darcy took part in the Allied amphibious landings at Anzio, Italy, in early 1944, and then in the South of France in August.*

We carried troops on both those trips. At Anzio we had Americans. We were due to leave, and then all of a sudden an American came down (he had all sorts of gold braid) and he said, 'You're taking barges to Anzio.' Anyway, they towed these things alongside us and I said, 'What weight are they?' 'Oh, I don't

A shore leave permit for the southern Italian port of Brindisi, which Darcy visited aboard the Ocean Faith in April 1944. Hoffman collection

Opposite: *Merchant ships and military vehicles assemble in an Italian port in preparation for Operation Anvil, the successful invasion of southern France by American and Free French forces in August 1944.* Australian War Memorial, 305172

'It Seemed Like an Eternity'

know, 100 and something ton.' I said, 'Hell, that lift we've got is only 80 ton.' And he said, 'Well, we'll see if it'll do it.' They didn't seem too bloody worried, you know. We got them on anyway. Then in the South of France we had Americans and Free French. They had wee rubber boats; we got in as close as we could.

Did you come under attack from German aircraft or artillery?
Pretty often, yeah. It wasn't easy, especially when you're just sitting there and they're banging away at you. I was only on the Oerlikon, I never got onto the bigger guns; the only training I had was on the small guns. And if you were bosun you wouldn't want to be bloody tied up with a gun, you'd be the first repair party if anything happened. That was a very happy ship, a lucky ship I would say. Because how the hell we weren't sunk I'll never know.

>*After the French landings, the* Ocean Faith *continued to transport supplies around the Mediterranean and Middle East. In 1945 Darcy joined the* Empire MacKendrick, *one of the MAC ships (Merchant Aircraft Carriers)—bulk grain carriers fitted with flight decks to provide air cover to convoys.*

These ships carried grain from Canada. They built them just for a few aircraft. We did a trip to Canada, and I was in Montreal on VJ Day. They barred all shore leave to everybody who was in there, as on VE Day there had been a couple of ships in Montreal and the crew just about wrecked the town. We brought grain back, and then they welded cleats on the flight deck and we took a load of Thunderbolts back to Baltimore and put them ashore there. They were six-month articles, and by the time we went up to Montreal and loaded grain again my six months was up, so I left there.

Then I joined a ship called the *Mapleton*, and I went to Scapa Flow on an ammunition ship for six months. The war had finished, but they still had to have people to maintain supplies. After that I was sent in a scratch crew to Hamburg to bring back a ship called the *Salzburg* to England. It had been built for the United Fruit Company but had never been to sea. Hamburg was pretty knocked about. There wasn't a hell of a lot of it left.

I couldn't come back [to New Zealand yet], because when you joined you got a number. In 1939 you'd have been in number one group, at Christmas time you'd be in number two group and the next year you'd be number three. Well, I was '23', and I had to wait on that number before I could be discharged. I applied for repatriation back to New Zealand, and the only reason I could get out of going back to sea was if I took a job in essential industries. So I went to Hall Brothers in Aberdeen and I worked for them for eight months in the joinery. That was added to my training time when I came back to New Zealand, which was really good.

Darcy returned to New Zealand in September 1946 and resumed his apprenticeship in Invercargill. A couple of years later he moved to Dunedin, where he married and then ran his own building business for 38 years. He continued boxing until 1949, when he fought for the New Zealand light-heavyweight championship. In later years he pursued his love of flying, holding a pilot's licence for 21 years and building two light aeroplanes, including a replica 1930s Piper Cub.

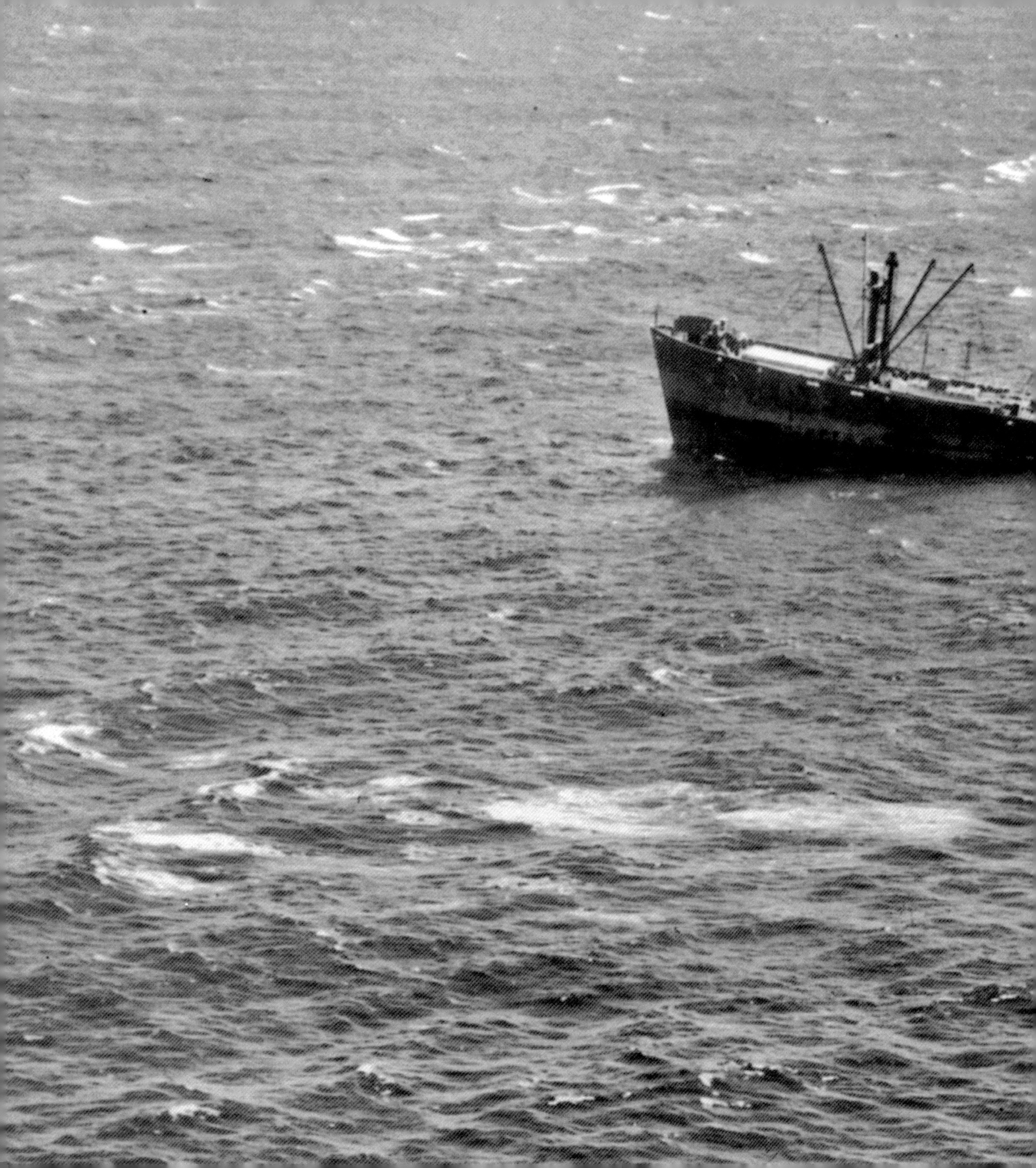

'I DON'T LIKE THE LOOK OF TONIGHT'

ALLAN WYLLIE, Steward

Allan Wyllie was born in 1921 at Mangapapa, Gisborne. His family had lived in the area for generations—he is a descendent of the Scottish-born trader James Wyllie and his wife, Keita (Kate) Halbert of Rongowhakaata, who were married in Poverty Bay in 1854.

MY FATHER HAD A HOTEL outside Gisborne, Waerengaokuri Hotel, and 40 acres of land and 12 cows. I went to the school there. There were only 15 [pupils] in the school. The master of the school came from Auckland and he lived in the hotel with us. My brother and I—I was nine, my brother was seven—milked 12 cows night and morning. My father died when he was 38. He had bubonic plague. He was a policeman in the First World War and he carried the germ until the early '30s. It broke out and he was dead within three days. He went black, I saw him.

So I left school then—I was 14—and I had to go to work. I worked in New Plymouth for Farmers' Co-op, driving the van. I got my licence on a Model T Ford. I left there in '37, came down to Wellington and did a couple of jobs here. The last one was for Jack Shelly, of Shelly Motors. Then I went away to sea as a bellboy on the *Awatea* in 1938.

Why did you want to go to sea?
Because when I was a kid I worked on a bread run with a man called Gordon Durie. He drove the van and I worked every Saturday with him. He said he used to go to sea and he gave me an introduction to the secretary of the Cooks and Stewards' Union in Wellington. So I got in the union (because you had to be in the union first) and they let me know when there was a job, and that was it. That's how I got away.

Previous page: *The American Liberty ship* Starr King *sinks after being torpedoed by the Japanese submarine* I-21 *in the Tasman Sea on 10 February 1943.* Australian War Memorial, 128144
Above: *Allan Wyllie in his bellboy's uniform aboard the* Awatea, *1938.* Wyllie collection

> *The* Awatea *has often been described as the finest passenger liner ever to fly the New Zealand flag.*

She was very good, yes. We went backwards and forwards to Australia, Wellington–Sydney and Auckland–Sydney, alternate trips. We carried a lot of passengers then. Two-and-a-half days it used to take us. Once she broke the [Tasman] record, doing 26 knots; her average speed was 23. She was a good fast ship. [But the stewards' quarters] weren't very good, because we lived right for'ard. There was about nine or ten of us in the 'glory hole', as they called it.

What did your job involve?
As a bellboy you answered all the bells, and you went into cabins and did what [the passengers] wanted and so forth. From bellboy I went to second-grade steward, then I went to first-grade and I ended up captain's tiger on the *Awatea*—the captain's steward. I was very young then. I said to the second steward who wanted to put me up there, 'No, that's an old man's job.' He said, 'No, the captain wants someone he can train.' It was Bill Martin—he'd come off the *Niagara*, after she'd hit a mine off North Auckland. He was a good fellow too, to look after. I used to do all his washing and ironing and all that.

In 1940 we went up to Manila and evacuated British army wives and families. They came from Hong Kong to Manila, we picked them up there and dropped them down in Brisbane, Sydney and Melbourne. Every night I used to run [Captain Martin's] cocktail parties for the colonels' and generals' wives, about ten of them.

> *After signing off the* Awatea, *in December 1940 Allan joined the MV* Limerick.

Well, I was doing a line with a girl who worked in Wellington dry-cleaners, and she went back to the States. One of the fellows there arranged for me to get a ship to go up and see her in San Francisco. So that's when I got aboard the *Limerick*, running up to the States. I met her up there and so forth, and that was it. But I kept on the *Limerick*, and we went up to Fiji and carted sugar from Lautoka to Canada. We called in at Rarotonga and Tahiti on the way up. Then we went up to Ocean Falls and Powell River [in British Columbia] and picked up newsprint and brought it back to New Zealand.

I was on the *Limerick* until '43, when it got torpedoed. The Union Company ran her, they had all the ships then. That was the only company I worked for in those days. As a steward, you had so many

The trans-Pacific freighter Limerick *(8684 tons), which Allan joined as a steward at the end of 1940.* Alexander Turnbull Library, C-23271-1/2

rooms to look after and so many officers or engineers to look after, and you ran them on their meals, on the table and so forth. You wore a white jacket and black pants.

Between September 1941 and April 1943 the Limerick *made several trips to the Middle East.*

We took supplies to the New Zealand troops. We went to Aussie first and had a bit of a survey in Sydney, about three weeks, and then we went on our way to Fremantle to load up there. Then we went up to the entrance to the Red Sea, Aden, and had to wait for clearance. We went up the Red Sea into Tewfik, through the Canal to Port Said and then up to Haifa. We took a lot of bags of sugar from Australia up to Haifa.

She had a 4.7 gun on the stern and [anti-aircraft] gun nests all over while running out to the Middle

Allan on board the Limerick. *Although nominally owned (from 1938) by Irish County Steamers and registered in London, the ship remained under Union Company management and was crewed mostly by New Zealanders.* Wyllie collection

Opposite: On 14 May 1943, several weeks after sinking the Limerick, *I-177 claimed a more infamous victim off the Queensland coast: the Australian hospital ship* Centaur. *Though clearly marked and illuminated in accordance with the Geneva Convention, the* Centaur *was torpedoed without warning and sank in minutes. With 268 lives lost, this ranks as the Tasman Sea's greatest maritime disaster.* Australian War Memorial, 043235

My little mate, Andy Gilligan, he was hanging over the side and he said, 'Come on sport, you'd better jump.' The screw was still going around, one propeller turning (we had twin engines), so I thought, all right. I got on a rope and I went down, and I held on too hard—I never thought [about friction burns].

Later on we yelled out, 'There's a couple of us over here.' And a joker replied, 'We're not in a lifeboat, we're in "Wouldn't it".' That was the barge they hung over the ship's side for painting. (One of the ABs was good at signwriting and he wrote on it, 'Wouldn't it'—as in wouldn't it do this to you, wouldn't it do that.) As a rule it used to take about six of them to lift it, but this time it just took two of them. They lifted it and just threw it over the side.

He said, 'You'd better swim to us.' So we swam and got in it, and then he said, 'You'd better start bailing too, there's water in here.' I started with my hands and I thought, God, where'd they get this insulation tape from? [The skin] was all hanging off my hands, and they started to sting.

How long was it before you were rescued?
Quite a few hours. We didn't get picked up till eleven o'clock the next morning. It was quarter past one when she got it. It was nice and calm when we got torpedoed, but half an hour after that it came up windy and very rough. You'd get the sea in your face, and next time you'd turn around and get it the other way.

We got picked up by a corvette, one of the corvettes that was in the convoy—the only time I had anything to do with the navy, I get torpedoed! But they looked after us well, and when we got to Brisbane they looked after us well there too. When I got aboard the corvette they said, 'Here, Doc, there's a bad case of rope burn here.' I thought, oh they've got a doctor on here, thank God for that. But it wasn't a doctor, just a first-aid man. He put some stuff on them and bandaged them up, and I couldn't do anything. I had to take a joker to the toilet with me and he had to hang it out and he'd point it at my feet and shoes or what-have-you. And I had to take a joker to the shower, and he used to pull it and say 'Flinders Street Station' and all this. They used to do all kinds of things. I went to a pub and I could only hold a glass like this, in between [the back of my hands].

Did you get survivor's leave?
Well, we got a train down to Sydney and they wanted a steward on the *Karatu*, a Union Company ship, so I volunteered to go there and they let me off in Lyttelton. You got a month ashore once you got torpedoed. I went back to Wellington on the ferry and had a month ashore.

I stayed with the Union Company all the time. Later I was on the *Waipori* and we went up to Norfolk Island. We took soldiers up to build the aerodrome there. I was in the *Waipori* for a while. She was running to Sydney, Newcastle and Port Kembla, up to Brisbane, Townsville, Cairns, and we called into Darwin towards the end of the war. Then I went on the *Wairata*, running up to the States.

I never came ashore until after the war; they wouldn't allow you to. My wife then said, 'If you don't come ashore this trip I won't be here when you come back.' So I had to go ashore. She'd arranged a job for me in the old Alhambra Hotel [in Cuba Street, Wellington].

> *After about four years working as a barman, Allan went back to sea with the Union Company. From the early 1960s until his retirement in 1984 he worked on the Cook Strait rail ferries, eventually becoming chief steward on the* Aramoana. *Following the death of his first wife, he married a stewardess he met on the ferries. Allan's son went to sea at the age of 15 and now works on the inter-island ferry* Aratere.

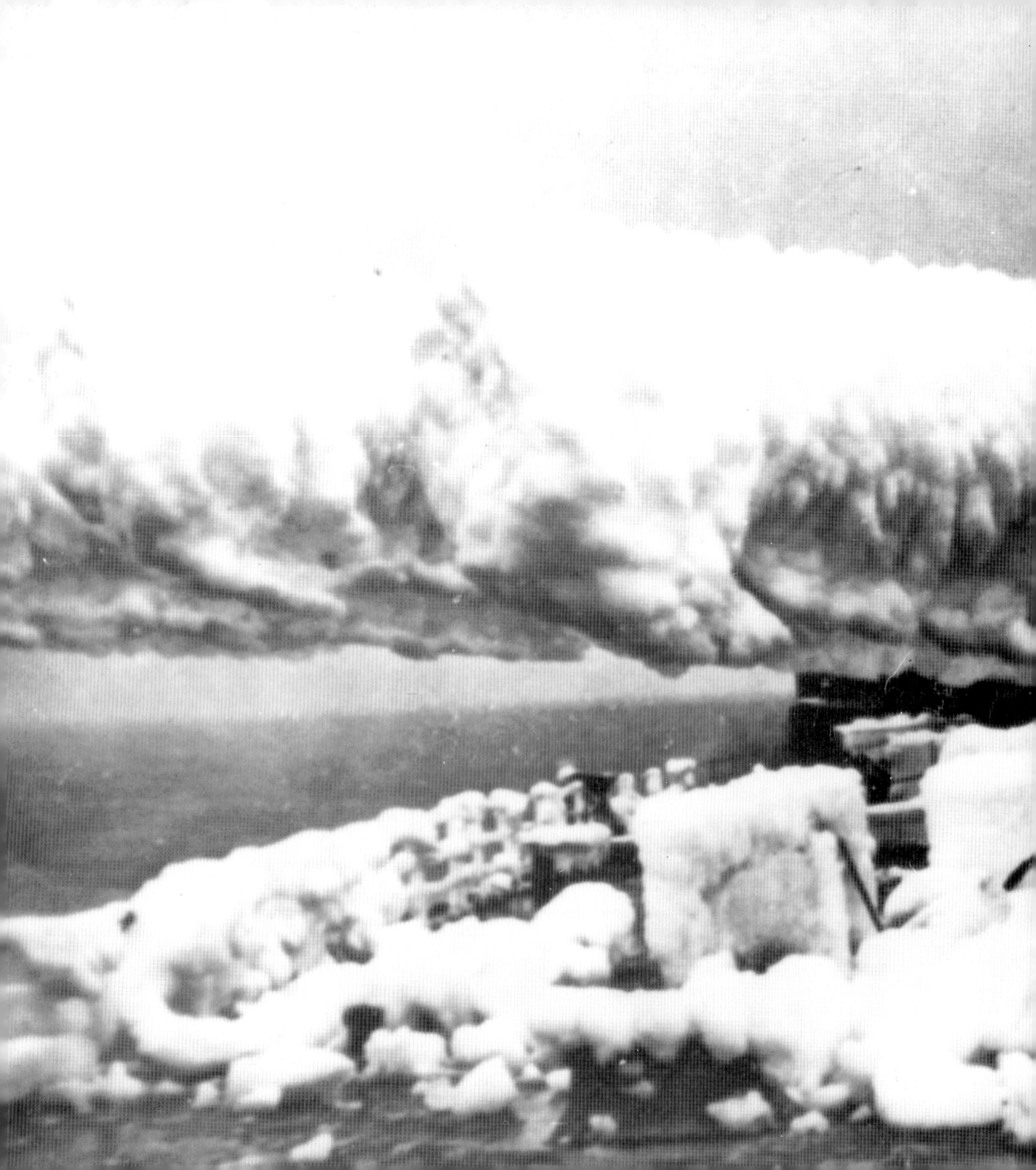

'LOCH EWE TO MURMANSK'

DAN BASHALL, Trimmer, Fireman

Dan Bashall was born at Collingwood, Golden Bay, in November 1924. His father managed the nearby Puponga coal mine, but died when Dan was four. After primary schooling in Wakefield and a couple of years at Nelson College, Dan travelled around the North Island working as a farmhand. He registered for military service as required when he turned 18, but decided he wanted to go to sea rather than wait to be called up.

I PREFERRED THAT TO THE ARMY. I wanted to go away, and I did. I think it was the best thing I ever did. So I came down to Wellington and worked there for a while. I decided I'd go down to Lyttelton and apply for a job [on a ship]. I had a [release] from Mr Stan Hunter, who was the Director of National Service, in the Hope Gibbons building. How I got that I don't know, but he said I could go overseas. So I went down to Lyttelton and worked there as a wharfie. A bloke came along and said, 'Are you the fellow that was wanting a job?' 'Yes.' He said, 'Well, there's a job on that one there. I'll pick up your pay. You go up there and fix everything up.' So next thing I was on the *Themistocles*. That was February 1943.

I went trimming coal, and as you can guess it was quite hard work, and the conditions were quite different to what I was used to. They were all Liverpool firemen on there, but I think I was lucky because they couldn't be bothered with me. I was only a little fellow, younger than they were. So they just treated me that way. But I was befriended by a good Welshman, Russell Jackson. He was a fellow trimmer. I was on the same watch as him, 8 to 12. He took me under his wing, and when we got up to Liverpool and paid off the ship, in Gladstone Dock, he said, 'You'd better come home with me.' That was the greatest thing that ever happened to me, going home with him, because from then on I used to be quite welcome in his town, Caerphilly, in South Wales. Whenever I went on leave I went there and

Previous page: *The build-up of ice on decks and superstructures was a constant problem on ships sailing to the Russian Arctic ports. This picture was taken aboard the battleship HMS* Anson, *which provided distant cover to several Arctic convoys.* Royal New Zealand Navy Museum
Above: *Dan Bashall, fireman–trimmer.* Bashall collection

it was like a home from home, instead of hanging around the seamen's missions.

We were trimming the coal with wheelbarrows from the bunkers and putting it by the furnaces for the firemen to shovel it in. It was a mighty hard job. You had to leave a relief—a big heap, about four or five barrowfuls—for the next watch to come on, so they had coal there. I had a dickens of a job getting that coal out, because I'd been feeding it all watch. But this Welsh fellow was pretty good, he used to help me do that. Each watch burnt a fire down so the next watch came on, pulled that fire when there were just hot embers in it and they built it up again. So each watch had a different fire, to keep them clean. Our job was to get rid of the ashes, for one thing. They had a 'Blow George', pumped with compressed water. You put it in, but if you put it in too quick it choked and water went everywhere. Anyway, that's how they got rid of all the ashes, straight over the side.

We got fed reasonably well, and we had a peggy who used to clean up everything after us, bring our

Built in 1911, the 11,231-ton SS Themistocles *served as a troopship during the First World War and joined the Shaw Savill & Albion fleet in 1932. The old coal-burner spent most of the Second World War on the UK–New Zealand run, surviving the conflict unscathed only to be scrapped in 1947.* Alexander Turnbull Library, W.H. Raine Collection, F-20811-1/4

meals, take the stuff away. But our quarters were up in the fo'c'sle. Oh, they were tough all right. It was very cramped. I forget how many there was, could be eight to ten people in there—not much bigger than a bedroom. They only had portholes [for ventilation]. They opened them one time in the tropics, when it was very hot. I was on the top bunk and when I came off watch at midday all my blankets were wet through, because there was a bit of a swell and she was dipping her nose in, and water was coming through the porthole. Like I say, they were very pokey places. She was very old, the *Themistocles*; she was no good.

I went on another ship, the *Empire Bittern*, after that, and she was old too. They got her out of mothballs and used her when the war was on. Our quarters were down aft and the propeller put you off to sleep. I did two trips on that one. Russell Jackson was with me. On the first trip we went to St John, New Brunswick. We came back to London and got some leave and went to his place at Caerphilly, then we went back over to America. We went to Staten Island to pick stuff up, all kinds of stuff, even had aeroplanes on the deck. When we got to Boston they loaded wheat and my mate, this Welshman, tripped on the coaming, fell down the hold and killed himself. We buried him in Boston. They only let two of us go off the ship. Two funeral directors helped us with the coffin.

The merchant ships and escorts of convoy PQ18 under attack from German bombers while en route to Archangel in September 1942. Australian War Memorial, P02018.120

Jackson's son was three months old when his father died. So when I paid off the ship I went back to them, and of course they welcomed me with open arms. I always went back there when I had some leave. The sorry point about the whole subject was, about ten years ago [the son] rang me up and said, 'Can you tell me where my father was buried?' I said, 'I certainly can, Woodlawn Cemetery in Boston.' He said, 'I'm going to go over there, me and my wife, and we'll see his grave.' He rang up about three weeks later and he said, 'When we went there the sexton checked his records and said, "I think I'd better come and show you".' So he took them in the cemetery and all there was there was a little wee mushroom with number 180 on it—like a pauper's grave. So he got the stonemason to put a stone there for him, so he's okay now. It just shows, doesn't it?

Dan's next ship, the Ocean Gypsy, *sailed from Scotland on 20 December 1943 as part of convoy JW55B, bound for Murmansk in the Russian Arctic. On Boxing Day, a covering force of Royal Navy warships engaged and sank the German battlecruiser* Scharnhorst *in an action that became known as the Battle of North Cape.*

We went from Loch Ewe to Murmansk. It was Christmas time; I think we had Christmas dinner on the ship. We didn't even know anything about the battle, because it's dark so early [in the Arctic] at that time of the year. It doesn't even get daylight, there's just twilight from about ten in the morning till two in the afternoon. They must have been going hammer and tongs. They reckoned afterwards that if it hadn't been for the navy they'd have sunk all of us, just one at a time, no trouble at all.

What was the weather like up there?
It wasn't very good weather any time. We often used to go right along the propeller shaft and up the rungs that way [to our quarters], because if you got on the open deck you'd get blown away. It was that rough up there. The shaft tunnel had just enough room for us to move in.

The snow, oh! We gave [the seamen] a hand to shovel a lot of snow off the decks, because it gets very heavy. They'd have the steam winches going all the time, ticking over, so they didn't freeze up. We weren't on the deck very much, but when you were you'd wear everything you could find—which wasn't much. I felt sorry for the DEMS gunners, they just had duffle coats, out there in the middle of the night, you know. Down below it didn't even get hot, it was just nice and warm.

Did you get ashore in Murmansk?

Yeah, we got ashore. We weren't there very long. They were very quick getting rid of the stuff. They had a canteen on the wharf, and that was it. There was a bit of vodka about. You could get a cup of coffee or tea. But they wouldn't let us go down the road. Some of the boys tried to go out and were stopped. They wouldn't let them leave the wharf. It was a miserable place, a horrible place!

You know what young fellows are like with girls. Well, they had women working on the wharves. There weren't many men about, only army. I remember a train was shunting on the wharf, and there were women on there too. I think all the men were away at the front. Anyway, this woman was working there and some sugar had spilt. I had a Woodbine tin for cigarettes (it was empty). I got the thing and filled a tin of sugar up and gave it to her, and she quickly put it into her pocket. Anyway, the next day they were cleaning up, finishing off, and I said to one of the guards on the gangplank, 'Where's so-and-so?' (I forget her name now, but she'd told me.) He looked at me and he went like this [drew his finger

Above: *The escort carrier HMS* Nairana *battles through heavy Arctic seas while shielding convoy RA64 in the winter of 1944–45. Allied convoys to northern Russia faced not just the danger of enemy attacks but frequent fierce storms and freezing temperatures.* S.D. Waters, The Royal New Zealand Navy (1956)

Opposite: *Photographs of firemen (stokers) and trimmers at work are rare—this image was taken in the stokehold of a converted coaster operating as a minesweeper for the Royal New Zealand Navy.* Alexander Turnbull Library, John Pascoe Collection, F-271-1/4

'Loch Ewe to Murmansk'

across his throat]. I felt really ashamed. It sunk in afterwards—they'd caught her with it. She shouldn't have the sugar, they'd say. She'd more than likely gone to prison or whatever.

After coming back from Russia, in early 1944 Dan joined the Fort Richelieu, *one of the 7100-ton standard merchantmen that were built in Canadian shipyards.*

I was a fireman then. They called us fireman-trimmers, so we had to do both jobs. It was quite a good job. She had been built on the Three Rivers, [near] Montreal. They were nice ships, I reckon, because they were half-and-half: the American Liberty boats were all-welded; these were half-welded and half-riveted. Good accommodation, down aft.

We went to South Shields, on the Tyne, and loaded up with everything for the troops in Italy. There were spuds there, a lot of mail, cigarettes and stuff, even rum for the navy. But we didn't know where it was all going. When we left there we went round to Oban on the west coast of Scotland, and the convoy went from there. I remember the Bay of Biscay, it was really rough.

We went through into the Mediterranean and ended up in Naples. The American Liberty boats always seemed to get preference, so we lay out on the hook for two or three days and they shifted us over to a place called Castellammare, in the Bay of Naples. It must have been close to Easter [1944]. That was when Vesuvius erupted. There was volcano ash everywhere, especially in this place. We were there for some time. They got rid of all the mail and the spuds; they had American Negroes unloading it.

We thought, gee, we're nice and safe here out of the road, because we heard a raid on Naples; you could hear them across the bay. I remember one bloke saying, 'I don't know about that. Look at this Red Cross ship.' It was tied up just by us, and a bomb had gone right through the forward part. The Germans had bombed the thing. I thought, it's a tough thing, this war.

We did a trip up to Pompeii from there, while we were waiting; they gave us leave. The funny part about it was the ship's providores must have collected some cauliflowers from there, and when we went to eat the cauliflower nobody could—it was still full of grit. The cook said, 'I washed it and I rinsed it . . .' It was everywhere, this volcanic ash, in your cabins and everywhere.

We went down to Alexandria two or three times, picked up troops and brought them back. I remember the Indians with their long hair; they used to wash their hair and drape it over the rails. We couldn't get over it. We brought a lot of people backwards and forwards, and carted a lot of stuff from

Port Tewfik, provisions for the troops. I think they were 12- or 14-man boxes with all their provisions in there, even toilet paper.

Then we went to Algiers and they rigged the ship out for troops, in the 'tween decks. Nobody had any idea what it was all about, of course. We went round to Brindisi and picked up Free French soldiers and American soldiers. The friction between the Free French and the Italians was bitter, they hated their guts really. We got mixed up in that. I'll always remember this Red Cap said to me and another bloke, 'Hey, what are you doing around here?' We were just having a look around. 'I think you better get out of here,' he said. 'I'll give you a ride down the docks. It's not safe around here.' And as we hopped on his jeep, he said, 'Get out of the vehicle! Quick, quick, run, run!' Somebody had put a hand grenade under it and blew the flippin' thing up. That bloke saved our bacon.

When the Americans came on the ship, a couple of them came down and one said to me, 'Hey buddy, where are we going?' I said, 'I don't know'—which I didn't. He looked at his mate and said, 'Anyway, it'll be much better than where we've been!' They'd come from [fighting in] Italy, you see.

As it turned out, the Fort Richelieu *was bound for the South of France to take part in the American–Free French landings of August 1944.*

There were ships by the thousands. We had to do all the work getting the stuff off the ship when we got to southern France—we had no army engineers. We landed between Sainte-Maxime and Saint-Tropez, and unloaded the troops in landing barges. We did the winching and took the barges ashore. Because we weren't needed down below we were on standby, so I had the job of helping winch a landing barge up and down. I was on the windlass in the front.

The Germans were hightailing it out of there. But on an island just across the way they must have had artillery. They were lobbing artillery shells, you could hear them whistling over the top of us. They weren't aiming at us, they were aiming at a beautiful bridge [near] the beach. You could see them smashing it up. But it wasn't long before the air force fixed them up, then there was just dead silence. [Some German] bombers came over, but there was too much resistance. You could see them dropping their stuff, but they were a fair way away from us. I remember the whole hillside was on fire. The trees must have got set alight by incendiaries, I suppose. Otherwise, it was quite a good invasion!

After this we went to Cagliari in Sardinia and loaded up with some old antique stuff, old tractors and that. They reckoned they were taking them back to Naples for the war effort, to melt it all down for the metal. Then when we left there we went up as far as Livorno, or Leghorn. They were very wary of frogmen. They had the ships' propellers just turning slowly, taking the weight on the lines, so frogmen would have a job to put limpet mines on them. They were all round the place there. One of the guards at the gate caught one: he had all his gear on and he was trying to get over the wall. They just ran out and tackled him. He said, 'I should have shot him.' 'Oh my God,' I said, 'Why?' 'He'd have blown your ship up.'

While we were going to Casablanca I got very sick. All I wanted to do was sleep. I felt terrible. No one could work out what was wrong with me, so when we got into Casablanca a French doctor came aboard. In broken English he said, 'He has chickenpox,' and they started laughing. But gee, you can get very crook with chickenpox, especially when you're a bit older. I'd have been 20 then. So they put me ashore in an American hospital there, in Casablanca. I thought this was good for two days—in 'solitary', best of food, best bed I ever had, good showers—then I got sick of it.

After being sent back to Britain, Dan spent some time on Welsh colliers, delivering coal from South Wales round to the Battersea power station in London. Soon after the war in Europe ended, he joined a ship bound for occupied Germany.

We went up through the Kiel Canal. You could see all these destroyers and little ships, hiding under the willow trees on the Kiel Canal, all smashed. The air force had got them. We ended up at the Baltic. You could see huge U-boat pens and the ten-ton bombs had smashed right through them.

I got a nice sword there, a German sword. What happened was, all the boys were up in the town drinking. I'd been on watch on the ship and the other bloke came back and took over from me, and I went up the road. It was just getting dark. I don't know what happened, but somebody had been at a girl and next thing she was in the drink. And of course, me being sober I hopped over the side. She was drowning. I grabbed her by the hair and right alongside us were the rungs of a ladder, so with a lot of help and grunting and groaning, we got her up out of the water. I went back to the ship really brassed off and changed all my gear.

Anyway, the next day a bloke came down and said, 'Who was the fellow who saved that girl?' They said, 'Oh, that funny-looking joker over there.' I said, 'What do you want?' He said, 'A special bloke wants to see you. He told me to come down and get you.' I said, 'What for?' He said, 'It'll be all right. He's very pleased at what you've done. She's the only relation he's got left.' I said to my mate, 'I'm not going up to that place. I don't know what they might do to me.' He said, 'I'll come with you.' So we went with this bloke.

Opposite: *The shattered remains of vessels and wharf buildings in Kiel in May 1945, around the time Dan visited the German Baltic port.* Australian War Memorial, UK2940

It was just getting dark, and I'll always remember this—it was just like the pictures. There were no lights anywhere, there was no electricity or anything, and this bloke took us through a door and there was a bloke with a big flash desk, and he had two lanterns. 'Come in,' the bloke said in a funny voice. I don't know to this day who he was, but he must have been pretty high up [in the local Nazi administration]. He said, 'This is all I have got to give you, but I would like you to have it. Do not be offended.' Because when we saw it, it had a swastika on it. It was a Nazi sword. It didn't worry me. I said, 'Thank you very much.' You know, they'd lost everything, hadn't they? Things were that tight. I'd seen blokes cut a Mars Bar in half and give [one piece] to a [German] bloke, and the bloke would give him a pair of field glasses. There was nothing; they had nothing to eat.

So how did the girl end up in the water, did she fall?
I don't know, or was she pushed? There was terrible hatred [towards the Germans], more hatred with some of them than others. I had a girl who was in London, and I went to her house one time when I was on leave, and I said to the mother, 'Where's Sadie?' She looked at me very sorrowful, and said, 'I think I know where she is, but I can't help you much.' She'd gone down to see her auntie and at the same time I'd come out of the Seamen's Mission—and I still remember, it was a lovely sunny morning—and one of these rockets went over, the big ones. It'd be the V-2, I suppose. I'd just come out, and it went 'wumph!' up the road. The whole vibration went through my knees. Well, that's where she was. You could put about four double-deckers in the hole. So I had my bitterness too, you know, but I never showed it like the other blokes. Sad, isn't it?

Anyway, when we left we did a trip up to Narvik, and up to a place called Harstad. It was dark [all day] up there at that time of year, but we picked up this stuff and it only took a couple of hours to load—it was that iron ore. She wasn't even half-full. And we got into rotten weather. Oh, my God. So we went with the wind, we had to. We went miles off course, because they didn't dare go into it.

Anyway, I did different trips after the war till my time was up. I had to do three-and-a-half years over there, that's what I was told. Then I went back to Wales. Funnily enough, when they fixed me up and gave me my discharge at Bute Road, Cardiff Docks, a bloke gave me a piece of white paper. He said, 'If you'd like to fill that in we'd be very pleased to let you stay in this country.' I said, 'No thanks mate, I'm getting home.'

After arriving home on the Rangitata *in October 1946, Dan undertook rehabilitation training as a carpenter. Then in 1952 he volunteered to join Kayforce, the New Zealand Army contingent in the Korean War, where he served as a driver. Back in Wellington, he got married in 1956 and continued to work as a carpenter until his retirement in 1984.*

I always look at it this way: I reckon I was one of the luckiest blokes going. Some of those trips in the Atlantic were that rough. But I was lucky, I never had to get in the water. Some of us were lucky, weren't we? We all went through the other bit, there were always alarms and things. I still remember my mate's face—me and him were down in the stokehold and there was one God-almighty noise. It was a depth charge, but we didn't realise it. And he looked at me—I can still see his face. 'Good God,' he said, 'I thought she was coming through.' The coal dust was floating down off the rivets. You know, there's only steel between you and the water. There was nothing you could do about it, was there? It's a long way up the fiddley, as they say, a long way up top.

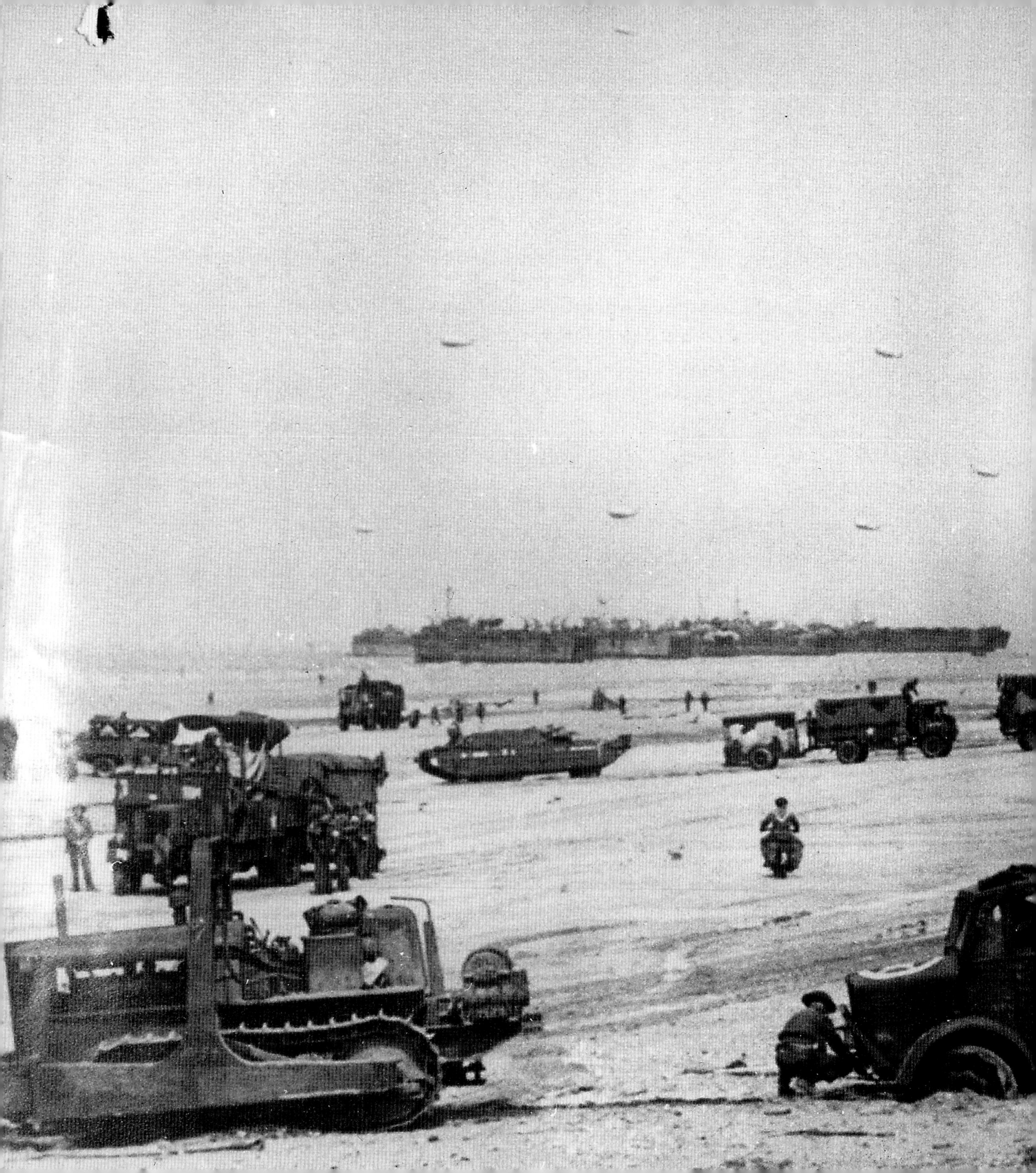

'IT WAS THE MOST ASTOUNDING THING'

DEWI BROWNE, Seaman

Born in Wanganui in June 1920, Dewi Browne is of Maori, Welsh and English descent. His great-grandparents were Paeroke Rawiri of Te Ati Awa, who was born on Kapiti Island in 1823, and the whaler William Jenkins, who arrived at the island in 1836; they married at Waikanae in 1849. Dewi's father, Theodore, went to sea as a 14-year-old in 1887 and travelled the world on sailing ships. After attending Gonville School in Wanganui, Dewi worked on a farm until 1937, when he got a job on the trans-Pacific liner Niagara. *In September 1939 he was sailing on an Australian coaster, the* Dundulla.

IN NEWCASTLE, OUR HOME PORT, we saw two German cargo ships moored side by side. Perhaps a fortnight later, on the eve of war, one of them slunk away to safety and wasn't apprehended. Pre-warned?

We were on our way from Townsville with sugar, going right around to Fremantle, and we were about opposite Newcastle when the war started. We would have heard it on the radio. I can't remember whether we expected it or not. But the point is, a chap's a seaman and you just keep going, war or no war, that's your job. You didn't look on it like it's danger, not in those days. But we didn't have it like they did over in the UK.

While Dewi stayed at sea, two of his brothers were to have very different wartime experiences. John fought with the New Zealand Division in Greece, Crete and North Africa, was taken prisoner, and later escaped from a POW camp in Italy. Mervyn, a conscientious objector on religious grounds, spent the war in detention camps in the central North Island, and Mount Eden Prison.

Previous page: *The day after: part of the vast Allied invasion fleet of landing craft and transport ships, protected by barrage balloons, off one of the Normandy beaches on D+1, 7 June 1944.* Royal New Zealand Navy Museum
Above: *Dewi Browne, able seaman, photographed in August 1944.* Browne collection

'It Was the Most Astounding Thing'

How did you feel about Merv's decision at the time?
Well, I was agin it then, and I was agin him too, but I realise now that war doesn't accomplish anything. You know, a chap could shoot a German or an Italian or whatever in wartime, and he could be a painter like me, or the same religion or same thoughts, a married man with two children, or whatever. You don't think of those things. But luckily I never had to take any lives. My brother John did, [German] paratroopers in Crete.

Dewi came back to Wellington at the start of 1940.

Dewi's first ship was the trans-Pacific liner RMS Niagara *(13,415 tons), built for the Union Company in 1913 but later transferred to the Canadian-Australasian Royal Mail Line. In June 1940 the* Niagara *became the first wartime casualty in New Zealand waters after striking a mine laid by the German raider* Orion *off the Northland coast.* Alexander Turnbull Library, G.H. Edwards Collection, G-18386-1/4

It was around about 6 January. The First Echelon was going away, with my brother. Then I joined the *Rangatira* and we made two trips to Fiji with troops. The reason I got the job on the *Rangatira*—it was a good job, just an ordinary seaman—was that there was a trial on at the court, one of the seamen was being tried, and there was an exodus from the shipping office in Wellington. I said, 'Oh no, I've come here to get a job.' So I didn't join the exodus, I went to the shipping office and I got probably the best job I ever had. Then after that I became an AB and was on various ships around the coast. It was quite a happy life on the coast, as long as you're single, I suppose.

I was on some of our ships that used to run over to Australia; that's a good run, you do some of the Australian ports, including Tasmania. On one New Zealand ship, one of the crew was a most obnoxious, useless chap, a young chap. We were in Adelaide and I don't know whether it was a long way from pay day and we didn't have much money, but we must have been aboard this night, and you could hear this fellow coming along the wharf, shouting and abusing everyone. When this young chap came aboard, the bosun—he had liquor in him but he wasn't drunk—seized hold of this chap and knocked him down under the bunk. When the fellow was only halfway up he hit him again, a couple of his teeth went flying, and the bosun screamed at him, 'You,' he said—and I've never heard the term since—'You . . . We were two men short the minute you joined.'

How long were you on New Zealand ships?
All of 1940, '41 and '42. In October '42 I joined a British tramp ship, the *Cornish City*, in Wellington. It was, you might as well say, a modern ship, only six years old. It had all the modern equipment for winches and so on, but I can't remember a tap. At a certain time of the afternoon, say four o'clock, we had to go along to something that was like a village pump, and pump up a bucket full of water for whatever we wanted it for. Anyway, I went away to sea as an AB. Perhaps I'd been a bit spoiled on the coast, because we used to have tablecloths, towels, sheets. On board this British ship there was nothing like that. I never had a towel. I don't think I even had soap. I used a cotton shirt for a towel all the way to Panama.

In Cristóbal, the Panamanian port, a Welsh fellow and I were given the job of painting, or patching up with paint (red lead, I suppose), near the stern of the ship. I got the Welsh fellow to pull the stage as far back as he could and I painted, in eight-foot letters, 'hungry' on the ship. I was a rebel, you see. We went like that in convoy, and when the skipper was going ashore to a convoy conference in New York he noticed it. Oh boy, he came back furious. I was logged £6 over that. Because that word 'hungry' could have [been a coded message meaning] New York, you see, where we were going to. I couldn't see I was doing anything wrong. I was a Kiwi.

I had the wheel coming into New York, up on the monkey island, which is a bridge above the bridge; it was wide open, and the pilot was up there, and the captain too. We were coming into New York in a fog, and how the pilot knew where he was I don't know, but every now and again I'd get a helm order, to put the wheel over: 'starboard ten', 'steady', all this sort of stuff. By gum, it was cold. We lay at anchor there for ten days, I think, waiting for a convoy [across the North Atlantic].

We sailed to Glasgow and after a week or so, I went along to the shipping office to apply for a job, like I would anywhere. Wellington or Newcastle or Sydney, you go to the shipping office—only I didn't know about the Pool. I went along there and joined up with other chaps in the queue, and the

The 9152-ton Port Line freighter Port Melbourne *in Wellington Harbour.* Alexander Turnbull Library, John Dickie Collection, G-15926-1/2

Anyway, I think there were about 12 ships going up the coast there, and a few ships peeled off and went in to Beira, and we anchored. The rest were going further up the coast. And we heard later that three of them had been torpedoed that night. That's just your luck, you see.

The Mozambique Channel was a popular hunting ground for long-range U-boats in 1943. Later that year the Germans introduced a new anti-shipping weapon.

We were in the Atlantic. Some of our chaps had been listening to the news on the radio the night before, and they heard the Germans had been using a new type of bomb, a glider bomb. The next day, around about noon I think, they used them on our convoy. It was controlled by radio from the mother plane. I think it was a Focke-Wulf [Kondor]. The plane stayed on a steady course, out of range. She went over the convoy and released one of these bombs. They zigzagged, and then when they got near the ship they were intended for, they went steady. They got two ships from our convoy, and a straggler too. But I think Germany found out they weren't as efficient as they thought.

In May 1944 Dewi joined a small hospital ship, the Lady Connaught, *which was sent to support the Allied landings at Normandy. The ship had a British crew and American medical staff.*

The preparations for Normandy were so extensive. Six months, maybe a year before Normandy, a seaman could arrive at his port for a job and the official would say, 'Do you want to be a V-man?' I think it meant 'Volunteer'—you could go anywhere, any place, any time. 'Yes, okay.' From then on, the front of your identity card had a big red 'V' on it. Well, towards the tail end of May 1944, my Scotch buddy and I got offered a job in Glasgow. The official said, 'V-men?' 'Yep.' 'Righto, I'll send you down to see the mate of a ship at Partick', [near] Glasgow. We went along there and the ship was being converted to a hospital ship. You'd never seen such chaos in all your life, wires everywhere.

The chief mate, a tall English chap, looked down at us little fellows and said, 'You know anything about small boats?' My mate, he'd been used to going out to sea after lobster creels up near Aberdeen, and he said, 'Aye'. Then I remembered, what about me, all my years on boats on the Whanganui River. So we were trained as boatmen, to run into the beaches and pick up the wounded off the beach. They were specially built boats. They were fitted out to carry seven wounded on stretchers, on slide-in fittings, and we could also take four walking wounded, so that's 11. But after the first once or twice we hardly ever did that. [Instead, the wounded] were brought alongside in big barges.

For Operation Neptune—the maritime component of Overlord, the D-Day landings—the Allies assembled the largest armada in history: 1200 naval vessels, over 800 merchant ships and more than 4000 landing craft, supported by more than 10,000 aircraft.

Opposite: *A flotilla of landing craft heads for the beaches of Normandy on D-Day, 6 June 1944. Many assault troops were to make the return trip in hospital ships like the* Lady Connaught. Royal New Zealand Navy Museum

It was the most astounding thing. On the way over I had two thoughts uppermost: goodness me, there's not that many ships in the whole world; and the other thing was, all these planes going over by the hundreds, all going the same way. I thought, they're all ours, and I thought, I know who's winning the war now.

The weather had cleared up by this time and we just ambled along the beach, three hospital ships in a line, small ships. I was at the wheel and the third ship decided he'd take our place, so we just marked time and he took our place and we dropped back. Three ships, like ducks going across a lawn. Half an hour later, I was still at the wheel, and those two hit mines and we didn't. So, it was luck again you see. They got them both back to England and patched them up. Later on, we heard that another British hospital ship, a bigger one, had been mined, with large loss of life. Apparently German planes were dropping mines over the shipping lanes during the ensuing nights.

Anyway, we got to Normandy about 12 noon the next day, D+1 [7 June]. Ours was a Yankee beach, 'Utah'. Of course 'Omaha' beach was the terrible one.

How close inshore were you?
Very close, very close. We were anchored. The beach was similar to our beach here [in Wanganui] in this sense: it shoaled. You could walk for quite a while and strike a shoal. Most of the time [the wounded] were brought out on huge barges, big flat-topped things, and we'd run down the gangway. Very often I'd just have a pair of shorts on, nothing else, no shoes, nothing. I could have carried as many as a hundred or more up the gangway. We'd carry these fellows down to the ward and they'd get rolled into their bunk or whatever, and we couldn't get out of that place quick enough, out of the hospital ward.

Now and again one of our wounded died and his remains were placed on the boat deck, where there is very little space anyway. One night at sea, prior to me going on watch at midnight, I hung my washing out to dry, to be uplifted at 4 a.m., and immediately beneath my clothesline was one of these bodies.

On the night of D+1 I was on the afterdeck in the evening, and there was a group of walking wounded, about four or five of them. I suppose they were all happy they were going back, fighting finished. Most of the wounded we carried back were airborne chaps, paratroopers or glider men. They had probably landed in the wee small hours of the morning and been fighting all day. This chap took his tin hat off, and there were two holes in the back of it. You had to see it to believe it. Two holes, in and out, bullet holes. All it did was tickle [the back of his head]. Then night-time came, and he coiled up in a foxhole and pulled his greatcoat over the top of him, and a cow fell on him and broke his collarbone! That was his story. But I imagine that nearly all the wounded men would have no knowledge of how they came back. They probably wouldn't know they came on a hospital ship.

For the next two months the Lady Connaught *ferried wounded from Normandy back to England.*

The invasion had been on a while, and we're laying off the Isle of Wight, waiting to go back for more wounded, and the steward came into our messroom: 'We're having a concert tomorrow night, I want items.' Well, fancy trying to organise a concert with just over 24 hours' notice. I realised that two of my mates were good singers, and I've been proud ever since that this Kiwi stirred his mates (there were 12 in our mess) into activity. We found three mouth organs around the ship, and we opened the British half of the programme with a medley of eight tunes.

We heard later the Yankee medical staff—they greatly outnumbered us—had been rehearsing for two weeks. Their half of the programme was base. They sort of look on women as second-class citizens. Our skipper was about to go into the concert, and apparently he found some Yankee nurses out on the boat deck. He said, 'You're not going to the concert? 'No, we're not allowed.' 'Not allowed? Of course you can', and he let them in. 'It's my ship,' he said. That's how base it was. They're as low as a snake's bum, they are. Anyway, apart from me singing, our half of the programme was 'A1'. One of those English chaps was Carmen Miranda, with bananas and things on his head. Next day, when we were going back to France, I was at the wheel again, and this dear old skipper thumped me on the back: 'New Zealander,' he said, 'by gum you chaps were good last night.'

In early 1945 Dewi was serving on a British tanker.

In convoy, all the ships would get a message that at 8 p.m. every night you'd alter course, either port or starboard, to throw the subs off. Anyway, this particular night—it was dark, eight o'clock—I already had the order 'starboard', maybe ten degrees or whatever, and if you can imagine 50 ships, and at a given time they're all [changing course]. The ship had already answered the helm, and she was swinging over lovely to her new course, and boy oh boy, the ship on our starboard beam, an American Liberty ship, they didn't know their right foot from their left. Instead of going to starboard, she came to port.

Boy, she came close. And our skipper, I've never seen a man so in control of himself. He raced to the whistle lanyard and he was actually Morsing with his body, Morsing on the whistle lanyard, to turn this Yankee fellow to starboard.

About a month away from the end of the war, we were coming up towards Liverpool. I think we were only about 30 miles from Liverpool. It was tea time, and the next thing: 'Action Stations'. The ship ahead of us, a Yankee Liberty ship, she'd been torpedoed—we found out later—by a midget submarine. We just kept going. Someone would have picked them up. Anyway, I did what I was trained to do,

Ships glide through surface fog in the Arctic Sea. Dewi sailed on the tanker British Promise *in the last convoy to Russia in May 1945.* Royal New Zealand Navy Museum

we all did. I happened to be the first one to get to our gun, an Oerlikon. You throw the cover off and you pull a pin out, you elevate the gun, then you train it, and you strap yourself in. That's what we were trained to do. The other chaps arrived as quick as that. We never saw the submarine. About 20 minutes later one of the DEMS gunners arrived and he had the magazine with him—there wasn't any magazine on the gun! That should never have happened. The war was getting towards its finish and they were getting a bit lax, I suppose. They'd stripped the guns. We never noticed that jolly gun never had a magazine on it. This also happened to four other guns.

> *Dewi's next destination was the Soviet Union, aboard the tanker* British Promise, *loaded with aviation spirit. However, by the time convoy JW67 sailed from Scotland on 12 May 1945, Germany had capitulated.*

That was luck again, you see. I was on leave with my mate, near Aberdeen, on VE night. We came back to Glasgow, got back on the ship again, went up to Russia, and the war had finished. We saw some German subs being escorted back to captivity. It was summertime, 24 hours' daylight, or near enough. We went to a place called Molotovsk [now Severodvinsk], near Archangel. It was pretty nondescript, all wooden buildings. On the way in there were little ice floes floating and the water was a kind of amber colour.

After our first night ashore, we were still yarning in the messroom and drinking coffee at 3 a.m., no doubt influenced by the 24 hours' daylight and the fact that the war was over. Someone who was more wide awake than the rest of us said, 'Come on you fellows, it's three o'clock.' No response. He roared at us, 'You've got to get up in three hours' time!' Then we realised that it was 3 a.m. You see, it was a normal part of our day to be in the messroom drinking coffee at 3 p.m.

We were there about ten days, from memory. We'd go to dances they had for us, or some nights it could be a film evening. I remember one night they showed a whole lot of graphic stuff about 'One day on the Russian front'. The first night or two there the drink was vino. But about two nights later the Russians were drinking vodka. Our chaps swore that that 'vodka' was our cargo. Probably someone must have been able to leak some of this stuff out into buckets. All around the ship there were big red notices, 'No drink'—it would cause blindness, you see.

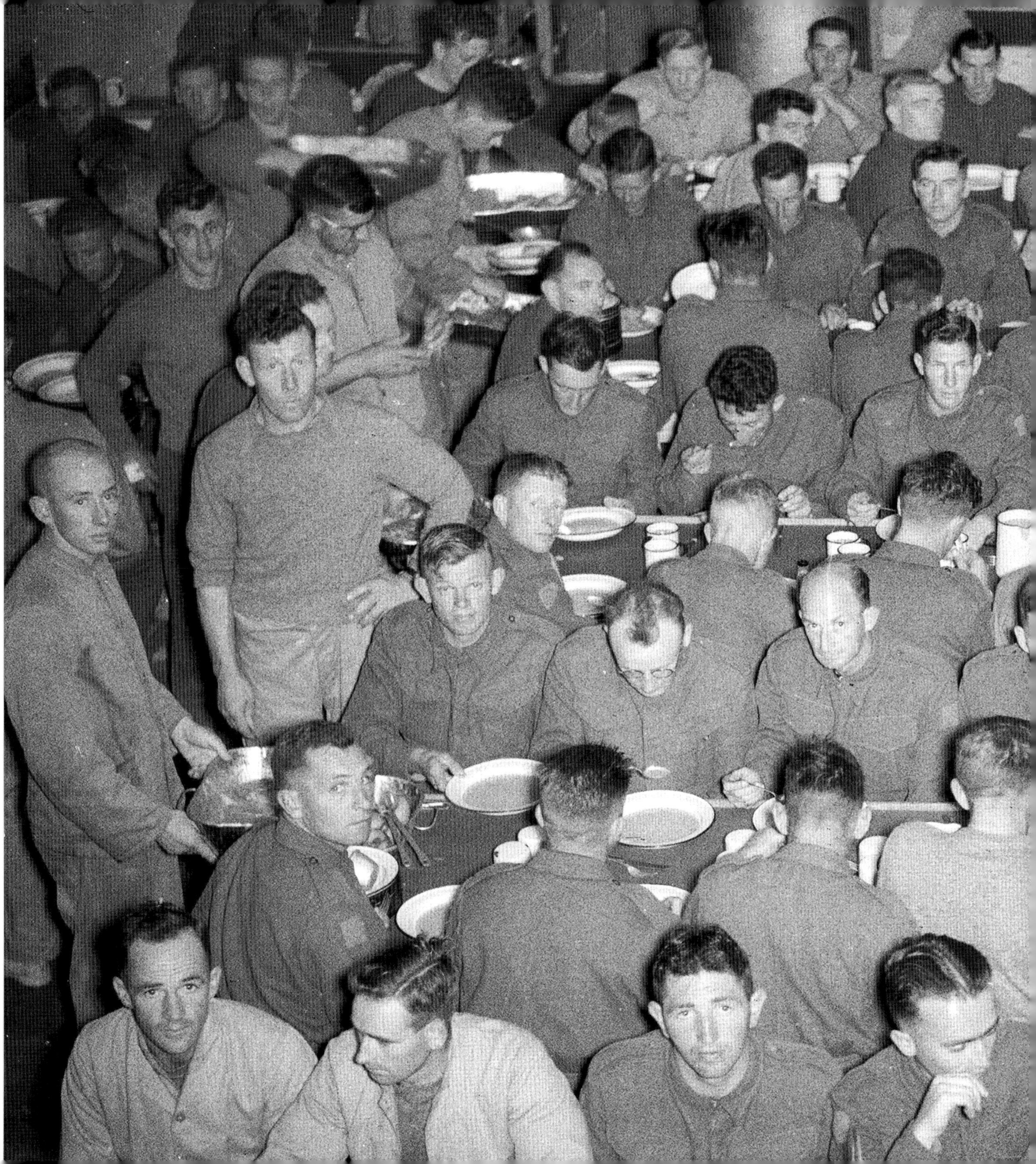

'WE HAD TO FEED THE TROOPS'

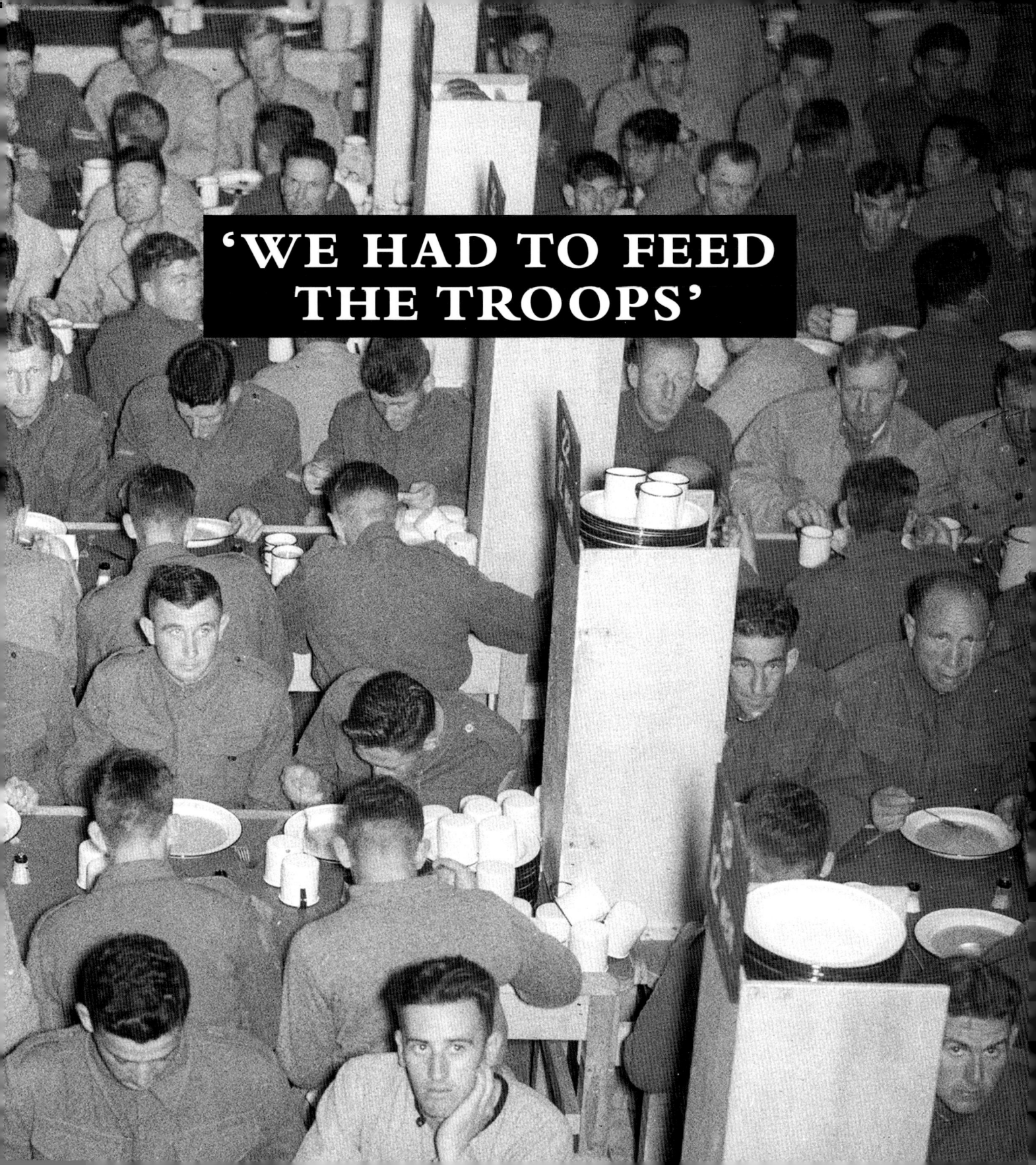

CLIFF TURNER, Steward, Baker

Clifford Harry Sidney Turner was born in Hastings in November 1921, and raised in Gisborne. Even there, the shock of the 1931 Hawke's Bay earthquake was felt strongly, and while jumping down stairs Cliff suffered a double hernia which required an operation.

My FATHER TOOK US TO ENGLAND because he was offered a job over there. But when we got there there was no job, so he had to go on the dole. Times were really tough. It was the Depression. I went to school there for a while, until I was 14.

I was 15 when I went to sea, in 1937. I was taken on as a baker's boy on the SS *Inanda*, of the Harrison Line. It was running out to the West Indies. That's where we met Jean Batten; she was a passenger. I got her autograph. We were just travelling around the West Indies, visiting all the islands. I was in the catering department all the time. We made bread and all sorts of things.

I was in Trinidad the day war broke out, on the *Inanda*. We were a bit disappointed and we had to wait there outside in the bay, and we were right alongside a fertiliser place and everything was coming over. We had to wait for the paint to come, grey paint. We had to paint the whole ship before we could leave there to go back to England.

> *Cliff then joined the New Zealand Shipping Company's SS* Rimutaka *(16,576 tons) as an assistant steward. The* Rimutaka *was bound for Montevideo in December 1939 when the damaged* Admiral Graf Spee *sought refuge in the neutral port.*

Previous page: *New Zealand soldiers cram into a troopship messroom en route to the Middle East. Feeding thousands of troops on long ocean crossings was challenging work for ships' cooks, bakers and stewards.* Alexander Turnbull Library, War History Collection, F-663-1/4-DA
Above: *Cliff Turner in front of an unidentified troopship.* Turner collection
Opposite: *In late 1941 Cliff served on the Canadian-Australasian Line's MV* Aorangi *(17,491 tons), carrying troops and evacuees between Britain and the Far East. This image was taken in the Solent in June 1944, when the* Aorangi *was serving as a depot ship for tugs and other small craft involved in the D-Day invasion.* S.D. Waters, Union Line (1952)

'We Had to Feed the Troops'

We were going to pick up some meat there. We were outside the River Plate as the *Graf Spee* went in, and the next day she came out and blew herself up. Then we were allowed in to pick up the meat and went back to England.

Then we went out to New Zealand and picked up young Kiwis for training with the Fleet Air Arm. We were on the last ship coming out of London when [the evacuation of troops from] Dunkirk was on, in May 1940. All the little ships were coming across, and we were going in and out.

When we were in Cardiff the Germans used to come over and bomb us, but we were lucky. I was in Cardiff for the first air raid [in July 1940]; my first discharge book was lost in the bombing. Not only that, I was in Liverpool when they bombed that and I was in London during the Battle of Britain. I was on leave in London on 15 September 1940. It was terrible.

The occasion of one the heaviest German bombing raids on London, 15 September 1940, is commemorated as Battle of Britain Day. Later that year, Cliff suffered a recurrence of his hernia trouble in Halifax, Nova Scotia.

I'd been in hospital in Halifax for a fortnight because I'd had a breakdown after my operation. I came back on the *Middlesex*, of the Federal Shipping Company. We left Halifax with 42 ships in a convoy. We were told to disperse because of heavy seas. I don't know what happened to the rest of them, but as far as I know, only five of us turned up in Liverpool. We lost half the bridge and all our lifeboats; they were all smashed by heavy seas. We didn't have a dry bit of clothing on board.

> *Cliff spent most of 1941 on the* Rimutaka. *Then in November he joined the MV* Aorangi, *a former trans-Pacific liner requisitioned by the British Ministry of War Transport. He was by then a first-grade steward.*

We sailed via Africa with troops for Singapore on the *Aorangi*. The causeway [to Malaya] was blown up when we got there. We dropped a load of troops, and then picked up women and children and took them to Perth, Adelaide, Melbourne and Sydney, and then came back to the UK.

> *Between April 1942 and March 1943 Cliff served as assistant baker on the* Rangitata, *then a transatlantic troopship, and the old* Ruahine, *which was on the UK–New Zealand run. The* Rangitata *could accommodate 2600 troops, and during one voyage the ship's bakers turned out 77,835 loaves of bread.*

We were working under difficult conditions. We had to feed the troops—that was the trouble, a couple of thousand troops on one ship. But we managed. You got used to it. When you're at sea you just normally take whatever comes along. You just do your shift, your day shift or night shift. And when we got near land I was on the guns. We had to do four [hours] on, four off. I had a gunnery certificate. I volunteered for training, on the 4.7, 12-pounder and Oerlikons. We had to do practice shooting, but we never had to fire them in anger.

The last two years of the war I was on a hospital ship, the *Llandovery Castle*. It was a British ship. I was one of the few New Zealanders on board. I came down on the *Winchester Castle* to Cape Town and then we went overland, three nights and two days in a train, and joined a ship in Durban. Then we went up the Red Sea to Suez, overland to Cairo, then to Alexandria, and joined the hospital ship there. We went backwards and forwards to Tobruk and Benghazi. When we were at Tobruk the Germans bombed us. We were lucky—the bombs didn't fall in the right place. We had Red Cross markings, but it didn't make any difference.

The bakery was a separate part of the galley. We had two bakers. I was second assistant baker—there were three of us, and we got a few troops to help. We wore a white uniform. Then there were the cooks in the galley, about half a dozen. I was on the day shift and when we had extra [patients on board] we worked through the night, to make sure that we got the bread ready.

[On one occasion] when we were at sea the ovens blew up on me. The bakery oven on the ship had steel tubes in it, and they used to have coke to fire them up with. We'd run out of coke, so we had to use solid fuel and of course it burnt out the tubes, and I opened the oven and it blew up. I was okay, I was lucky. We had to use the other ovens in the galley then.

> *In July 1943 the* Llandovery Castle *took part in Operation Husky, the large-scale sea and airborne invasion of Sicily. This was followed in September by landings at Salerno on the Italian mainland.*

We went to North Africa, and then to the invasion of Sicily and Italy. They brought the wounded out on barges after the landings. They were mostly British from that part of the war. We could only cater for about 400 at a time. We were taking all the wounded back to Algiers, running backwards and forwards. Where the patients went after that, we didn't know. We went over to Algiers and picked up a lot of food and we made bread en route, so when we got to Sicily again the troops had hot bread. Then we went up to Salerno and Naples in September 1943.

They had dentists on board the hospital ship as well as surgeons and doctors. One time I broke my false teeth—it was an accident, I dropped them—and they made some new ones for me.

> *One of the patients evacuated from Italy on the* Llandovery Castle *was the commander of the New Zealand Division, Major General Howard Kippenberger, who was wounded by a mine near Cassino in March 1944.*

We took Kippenberger back to England after he'd lost his feet. I was the only Kiwi aboard the ship, so when I had spare time during the day I used to go up and say hello. We took him back to Southampton, then he went on to Roehampton, where they gave him artificial feet. When I was on leave I used to go up to Roehampton to see him. He was not too bad, but it was very difficult for him to walk; he had to be in a wheelchair most of the time.

Then we were told to pick up 400 patients and take them back to Canada. They were all troops who had TB, and people were dying. We had burials at sea every day. We just wrapped them around and put some lead in, and pushed them over the side. The padre just gave a send-off for the different denominations.

We came back to Glasgow and they sent us down to Southampton for D-Day. We were there on the first day, at 'Omaha' beach; they were all Americans there. We were anchored—it was a 10,000-ton ship, so we had to anchor out quite a bit of a way. They used to bring the wounded out on barges and they were winched up on pallets. Once Cherbourg was clear we went in there, and then we took troops from all over France. We stayed there till near the end of the war, going back and forth to Southampton.

What did you do for entertainment on the ships?
We used to do items and all sorts of things. We used to have people who played violins and piano and that, who gave concerts when possible. When we were running backwards and forwards with patients we couldn't do that. When we went across the equator—crossing the line—we had special programmes. I was dumped in the water when I first crossed the line. That would have been on the *Rimutaka*.

Left: *Major General Howard Kippenberger, commander of the New Zealand Division in Italy, recuperating in England after his evacuation on the* Llandovery Castle. *Turner collection*
Opposite: *American soldiers wounded during the D-Day assault on 'Omaha' beach, Normandy, are winched aboard the hospital ship* Llandovery Castle. *Turner collection*

'We Had to Feed the Troops'

They had a plank over a swimming pool, and they just dumped you in there.

In port I went ashore by myself. I was a loner. The others all went on the drink, and I didn't drink. When we went to Buenos Aires and down to La Plata and those places, I went by myself. I used to take photographs. I went ice skating and roller skating; I used to take my skates everywhere I went. I went skating in New York, in South Africa, down in Buenos Aires. And we used to go to dances. In London I went to the Australian club, the Boomerang Club. I helped out and did a bit of baking for them. The New Zealand services' club didn't want me, they had enough people. I used to spend my spare time making things for the Red Cross, like a miniature doll's bed. I gave it to the Red Cross and they raffled it to raise funds; they got £15, I think. That was in 1944.

Cliff signed off the Llandovery Castle *in Southampton in March 1945.*

I was on some Liberty boats and went around the British coast doing a little bit of work, relieving people. That's when I met my wife—I went to a dance in Hull. She was an English girl. We were married in Hull.

On VE Day I was down in Piccadilly Circus. It was marvellous. We were marching down there with a flag and I had a WAAF on both arms. (We met one of the WAAFs again after my trip to VE Day in 1995; she was living in Eastbourne, New Zealand.) I didn't know at the time, but a photograph appeared in the *New York Times*. It went right around the world.

At the end of the war Kippenberger helped me get an overseas bursary to stay in London. I was one of the 'rehab' people. I'd decided I wanted to do something more productive while I was still at sea during the war, so in 1944 I enrolled in a correspondence course with the National Bakery School in London. And they asked me, when I got my discharge would I go there? Finally in 1945 I got my

Cliff (front row, fourth from left, holding flag) marches through Piccadilly Circus, London, on VE Day, 8 May 1945. In the following days this image was to appear in the New York Times *and other newspapers around the world. Turner collection*

VE Day revellers climb lamp-posts in London's Trafalgar Square. Turner collection

discharge in London and went to the National Bakery School. I was there for a year. Instead of going into a two-year course I went into the second year because I had practical experience. I won all the cups. I got my City and Guilds finals in bread-making, cake-making, flour-testing, and then I went to Levers' research bakery in London for a year. Then I came back here in 1947. I had to pay £35 for my wife, because I'd missed out on the [war brides'] repatriation for her.

Rehab couldn't find me a job at first. Then I found a job: I was manager of the Adams Bruce bakery for three-and-a-half years, in Majoribanks Street, Wellington. Then Charlie Griffin from Griffin's asked me if I would go out to their biscuit factory. So I spent a while there. Then I started my own business in Waiwhetu, Fairfield. I was there for 34 years.

Cliff Turner became well known for making novelty breads and wedding cakes, including the cake for the wedding of the Governor-General's daughter, Joanna Porritt. He was also active in the Masonic Lodge, Jaycees, Chamber of Commerce and the local RSA. He retired in 1987 and now lives in Avalon. In 1995 Cliff was one of the New Zealand veterans who returned to Britain to attend the celebrations marking the 50th anniversary of VE Day.

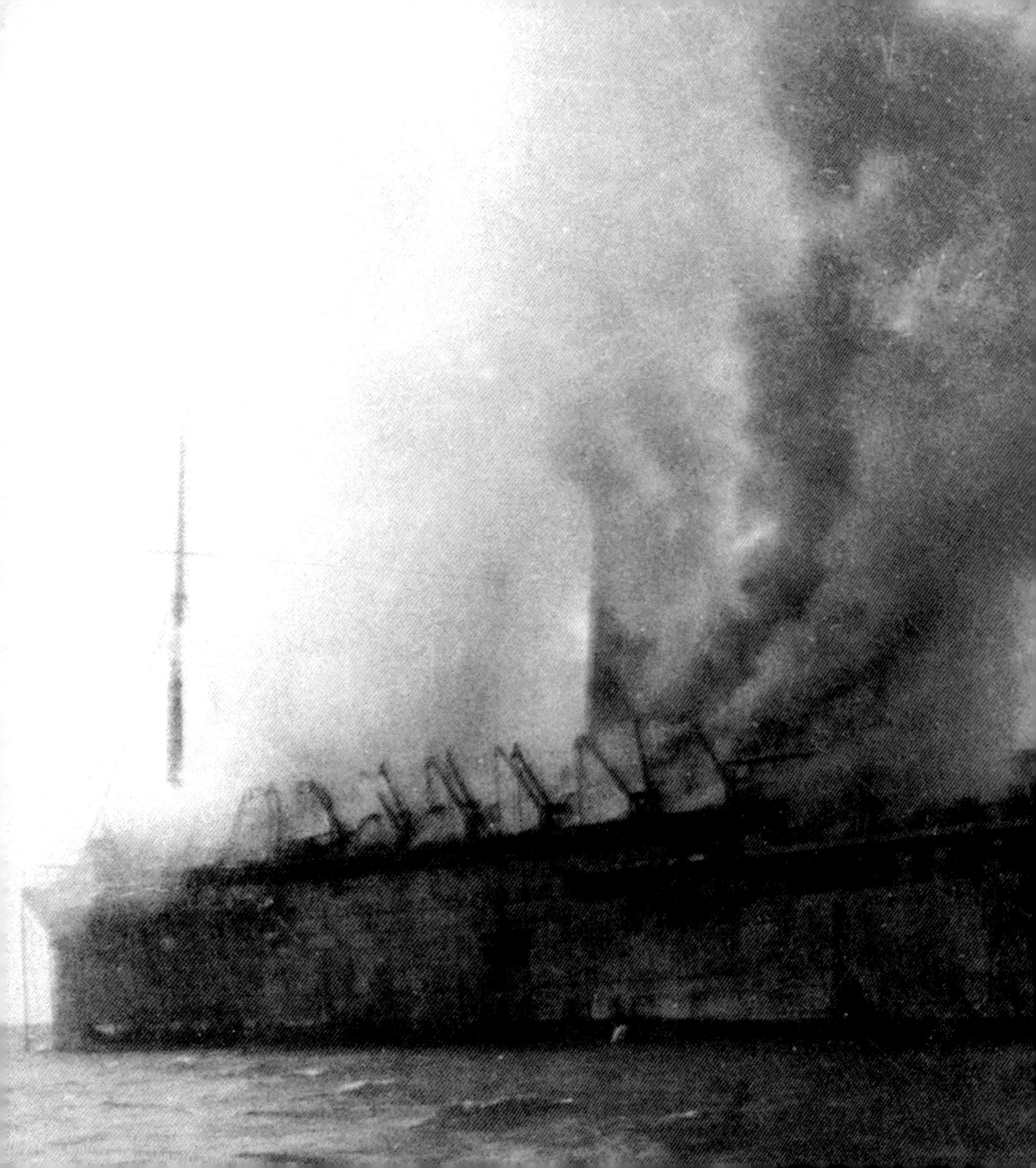

'I PUT MY AGE UP'

LOU BARRON, Boy, Seaman

Charles Louis (Lou) Barron was born in May 1926 in the English seaport of Hull. He was raised in Birkenhead, near Liverpool, during the bleak Depression years.

MY FATHER WAS A SEAMAN, and we shifted over to Merseyside before the war, because shipping was more available there. Things were pretty hard. Most people around our way were seamen. Merseyside was a great seaport, and I always had the intention of going to sea when I was young. We used to watch all the ships coming up the Mersey; in those days the Mersey was full of ships.

When the war broke out in 1939 I was still at school. I left school when I was 13 and a half. My first job was as a butcher's delivery boy, but I decided I'd try and get away to sea. I put my age up, but I was unsuccessful for a starter, until I got a job on a ship called the *Lech*, a Polish ship. I joined that ship in November 1940 as a galley boy.

Although he claimed to be 16, Lou was only 14 and a half.

We sailed from Liverpool to London around the north of Scotland. We got bombed off the River Humber in a convoy, but we didn't get any damage. We sailed into Deptford, London, and I paid off that ship with ten shillings. Then I went back to Birkenhead, and things were pretty desperate then, in

Previous page: *The troopship* Empress of Asia *burns after being attacked by Japanese bombers off Sumatra on 5 February 1942. Lou Barron had left Singapore just three days earlier on the* Duchess of Bedford. Australian War Memorial, P01604.002

Above: *Lou Barron, seaman.* Barron collection

Opposite: *The 20,123-ton* Duchess of Bedford, *which Lou joined at the end of 1940. Early the following year the Canadian Pacific liner carried 3000 New Zealanders of the Second Echelon from Britain to Egypt.* Alexander Turnbull Library, C-27877-1/2

1940. I met a friend of mine and he said we should try and get a job on one of the big troopships. So we went over to Gladstone Dock in Liverpool, and I joined a ship called the *Duchess of Bedford*. I signed on in late December 1940, and I was on that ship right up until April 1942.

We carried New Zealand troops from England to the Middle East—that was our first job. On the corner wings of the bridge we used to have machine-gun pits with Lewis guns, and they had New Zealand soldiers doing the gun watches. I was a bridge boy, running messages from the bridge, putting up the flags, making coffee and sandwiches for the officers on watch. I used to stand on the wing of the bridge with a pair of binoculars on lookout, and I got talking to the soldiers—it was the first time I'd met New Zealanders. I was talking away, and I said, 'Would you like a cup of tea?' 'Oh, yeah!' So when I'd make the officers a cup of cocoa or tea or whatever, I'd make two extra cups and give them to the two gunners. I met one of these New Zealanders again after [the war], when I joined the Ex-Prisoners of War Association. We were having a do one night and he said to me, 'I know you. What ship were you on?' (He knew I was a merchant seaman.) So I told him. He says, 'I left England on the *Duchess of Bedford*. Ah, you're the one who gave us cups of tea.' He recognised me.

A convoy in the Atlantic, around 1940. In contrast to the North Atlantic crossing, south of Freetown most merchant ships sailed independently, like the Gloucester Castle *in mid-1942.* Alexander Turnbull Library, J. Sutherland Collection, PAColl-0566-01

After we delivered the New Zealanders we carried Italian prisoners of war from the Middle East to Durban in South Africa, and then went back to England. We loaded up with more troops and sailed back to the Middle East, to Port Tewfik. Then we went back again, to Glasgow this time because Liverpool was getting blitzed, picked up more troops and sailed to Bombay. We dropped troops off there and picked up Indian troops and took them to Singapore, before the Japs arrived. We were one of the last ships to leave Singapore. There was the *Empire Star*, *Empress of Japan* (which was called the *Empress of Scotland* later on), and two American ships, the *Wakefield* and *West Point*. We left there on the 2nd of February 1942, and it fell on the 15th. Little did I think I'd be back in Singapore later that year.

We took women and children from Singapore to Durban, dropped them off there, and sailed on to England with German prisoners of war. We dropped them off in Liverpool and then I left that ship. At the time a schoolmate of mine, Chummy Weir, happened to be home. He was a young fellow like me, a seaman, and he'd been sunk on his first ship, a Blue Star ship; he was in a lifeboat for about a week. We always wanted to go to sea together, so this was our opportunity, both being home at the same time. We went to the shipping Pool in Liverpool, and they said, 'Oh yes, there's a ship here called the *Gloucester Castle*.' So we signed on, and then we took her over from Liverpool to Birkenhead and loaded ammunition and drums of aviation spirit.

> *Built in 1911, the 8006-ton* Gloucester Castle *had served as a hospital ship at Gallipoli during the First World War.*

She was a very old ship. She was the only ship I've ever been on that had wooden derricks, wooden masts and wooden decks. You could hear the waves hitting the side of the ship, you'd think they were going to come through. We lived for'ard, in the fo'c'sle, and it was pretty grim, firemen on one side and us seamen on the other side. I was an ordinary seaman by this stage.

We left Liverpool on 21 June 1942, joined a very slow convoy of ships off Belfast, went out into the Atlantic and sailed down south. There were one or two sub scares, but nothing much to worry about. We broke the convoy up off Sierra Leone and proceeded independently to Cape Town. We were about six days above Cape Town apparently when a German raider, the *Michel*, intercepted us. She'd followed us all day long, without us knowing it. She thought we were an armed cruiser, according to what the Germans told us later.

> *The* Michel *was one of nine German 'auxiliary cruisers' or raiders that together sank or captured over 140 merchant ships between 1940 and 1943. Armed with six 155-millimetre (5.9-inch) guns concealed behind false partitions, smaller arms, torpedo tubes and mines, the* Michel *also carried two seaplanes and a small motor torpedo boat.*

They came up at night-time on our starboard bow and attacked us, and really blew hell out of us. We had a crew of about 150 and there were only 51 of us saved. She really belted the hell out of us, and set all the aviation spirit in the forward well deck on fire. We were in the fo'c'sle head on the port side and the raider was on the starboard bow. They sent an MTB around onto the port side, and it started strafing us with machine-gun fire. We were still making way, but the bridge was on fire and all shot to hell. Well, our intention—me and my mate, a few of us with lifejackets on—was to dive over the side, but we didn't. We ran through the well deck and got up onto the boat deck and started lowering the boats. We had a few women passengers and they went down with the ship; I think there were two ladies saved, and two boys. The lifeboat I got into overturned alongside and I got thrown in the water. That was the last I saw of my mate, Chummy Weir. He went down with the ship.

The Germans told us they put two torpedoes and 30 shells into us, not counting small-arms fire. We just burst into flames. We had a 4.7 gun on the stern, but it was a 1904 Japanese gun and it fell to pieces every time you fired it. It could only fire in a certain arc, because there were two lifeboats alongside of it, and the German raider was over off our starboard bow. It wouldn't have done any good anyhow.

I was in the water for about three-quarters of an hour or something. I got picked up by the only lifeboat that got away. We didn't even know what had sunk us at the time. We didn't have any idea, because it was night, pitch black. But it was quite warm and the sea was just a bit of a swell, it wasn't rough or anything. The next thing we saw was a ship coming towards us and a searchlight going around, and we thought, hello, they're going let us have it, machine-gun us. Some dived over the side. I didn't, I stayed in the boat. I'd got wounded in the hand; I don't know what by, shrapnel or something. Anyhow, the next thing the light shone right on us, and a voice sang out, 'Come alongside, come alongside.' It was a German singing out, and that's when we knew it was a German raider.

We got aboard the raider and they had a ring of sailors with machine-pistols around. They asked if there were any wounded so I went up. My hand was all puffed up. All I had on was a pair of dungarees and a singlet, bare feet and everything. They blindfolded me and I thought, hell, what's going to happen here? I was shaking, I was in shock. And they took me through the ship—the idea of blindfolding me was so I wouldn't see parts of the ship—into the hospital, and the Germans were really good to us. The doctor came and had a look at my hand, and one of them gave me a cigarette and then a cup of soup. Then they gave me a needle and I didn't know anything after that, I was out like a light.

The next thing I knew was when I woke up in bed, and the first thing I saw was a big photograph of Hitler. I heard somebody saying 'Sieg Heil, Sieg Heil', but I didn't know what it was all about. Then I realised I was in a German ship. I was in hospital for a while and being a boy—I was only 16 at

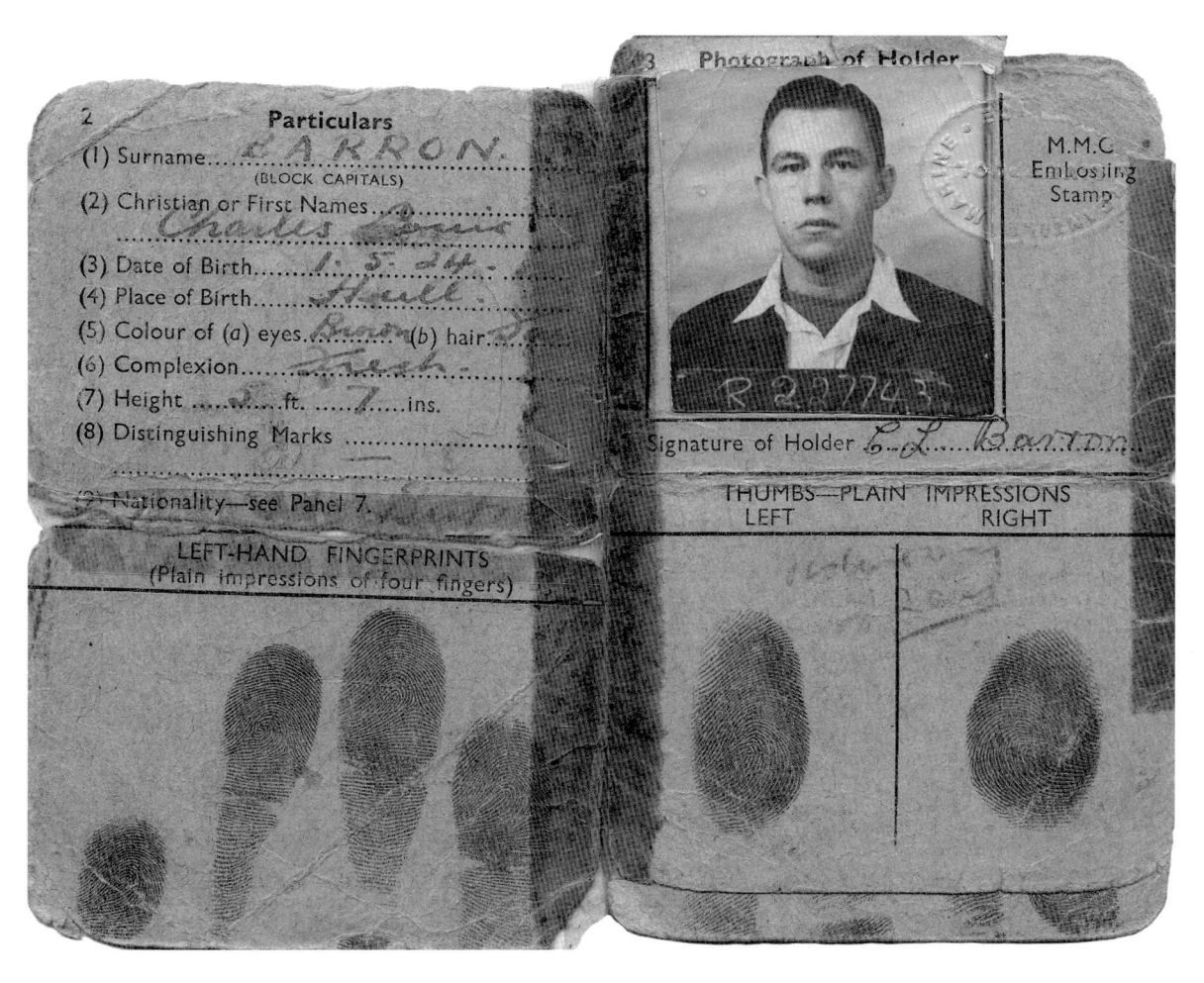

Lou's British Seaman's Identity Card, showing his birth date as 1924 instead of 1926. Barron collection

the time—they really looked after me. It was nice and clean, we had bunks with nice clean sheets and everything. A lot of these Germans were ex-merchant seamen. There was the odd one who was a Nazi, but you didn't take much notice of them. The thing we didn't like was when we were battened down, when they were sinking other ships. We were right down the bottom of the ship in these quarters, locked up. They sank another four ships while we were on the raider.

They used to allow us on deck for maybe two hours in the afternoon, in lots. When they started to get a lot of prisoners you'd only get an hour on deck. We saw some of the ship but not a lot of it, because we were only on the foredeck, more or less. We could see where the guns used to come up, and they had boxes on the deck that looked like aircraft crates, but there were guns in them. When they went into action you could hear the guns going up and then, 'Boom, boom, boom'.

After about three weeks they transferred some of us to a supply ship called the *Charlotte Schliemann*. It was a tanker, and that was a bit of a change in conditions. They put us down below in the hold and it wasn't very nice. I think there were about 200 or 300 of us altogether, in the 'tween decks. We were allowed up on deck at certain times of the day. They took us right down to the Roaring Forties, way down in the South Atlantic, and it got really cold. The food wasn't very nice. They used to send buckets of stew down and we used to have ship's biscuits, which were full of weevils, and what they called 'submarine bread' in tins—it was like brown bread, it was terrible. We were on that ship for about two months, I think. There were rats running all around. You'd be laying down in the hold on a palliasse, and the rats would be running across your feet. We used to try and have sing-songs and that, to try and keep our spirits up.

> *Rather than attempt to return to Europe, the* Charlotte Schliemann *rounded the Cape of Good Hope and headed for Japan, where most of its prisoners were interned. Lou, however, was among a group landed at Singapore.*

We thought we were going to Germany, but they told us that they were going to Japan. We were really down in the dumps because we'd heard stories about the Japs. The Germans said to us they were sorry they had to pass us over to the Japanese, because they didn't have much time for them either.

We got sunk on 15 July 1942, and it was late September when we landed in Singapore. We went past Java, up the Bangka Straits and up to Singapore. The Japs wanted 50 seamen, so we got loaded off there. They put us in trucks and ran us right across the island, and you could see all the damage that had been done. Of course I said to the guys, 'I've just left this place not long ago.' They landed us in Seletar, the naval base on the other side of Singapore, on Johore Straits, and put us on a Chinese river steamer called the *Tung Wo*. They gave us a bit of lecture that if we tried to escape, we'd get our heads chopped off.

So we settled down and divided ourselves into four watches. We had six Japanese marines in charge of us, and they didn't treat us too bad for a start. The only trouble was food. We thought we'd be on rice, but we were on semolina and split peas. This was all we had for a fortnight. We had one of our cooks off the ship and he mixed up this stuff, and in the meantime we caught fish. The Japs let us go fishing in the Strait and that was not too bad.

Then we asked if we could have some more meat. Each morning they used to put us on deck, and we had to face their ensign as it was raised and bow to it. Then they made us do physical exercises like they did, and then they lined us up for roll call. So the next morning, the interpreter (one of the Japanese could speak a bit of English) read out some names. I was one of them, and we had to step forward. The words he actually spoke I don't remember, but apparently it was an insult for us to ask for more food, so we were going to be punished. So they lined us up, ten of us I think, and one of the Japanese came back with a rope with a splice on the end of it, and gave us three right across the backside. That was our punishment for asking for more food.

Then we started to twig what the Japs were like. One minute they'd be quite good and then the next minute they'd switch. But it wasn't too bad there, and we got in contact with a lot of other British seamen. There were survivors off the *Prince of Wales* and the *Repulse* in the naval base, and we ran launches for the Japs. The Japanese navy used to come in, the big aircraft carriers and that. We did a lot of work on the *Tung Wo* to get it sea-fit again, mostly painting and chipping and all that sort of thing. The food did improve a wee bit, but it was mostly rice, plus what bit of fish we used to get.

What sort of clothing did you have?
They issued us with shorts. But we used to have what they called a 'fundoshi', a G-string, and we used that most of time because it was that hot. We didn't have any footwear. The Japs did give us some army gear that they'd captured. But we used to go around in just this 'fundoshi'.

Then after a while, about a year, they shifted us to a place called Loyang, which was a former British naval base. They had a big mine depot and a big long jetty, but they'd blown it in half before the Japs got there. The Japs had us repair all this. And they had a big warehouse there where they had us splicing wires and all that sort of thing. It wasn't too bad. We had barracks, but the food was pretty grotty.

Every now and again some of the Jap navy guys would go to Singapore on leave and they'd come back drunk and start picking on us, start giving us a bit of a wallop. They used to take great delight in belittling you, making you feel small. If we'd done something wrong, they'd line us up into two rows

The entrance to Singapore's Changi prison, where Lou spent the last year of the war. The pre-war jail housed 3500 civilian internees until mid-1944, when they were transferred to the Sime Road camp and replaced by up to 6000 military prisoners. Another 12,000 POWs were accommodated in barracks and camps surrounding the jail complex. Alexander Turnbull Library, War History Collection, G-7270-1/4-DA

facing one another, and you'd have to hit me and I'd have to hit you. They used to laugh. They used to take great satisfaction in doing this in front of the native population.

Did you have any contact with the local people?
Yeah, when we could. We found the Chinese were very good to us. We used to get food off them. When we went out on working parties we'd raid a bit of stuff: tapioca roots, bamboo shoots, snails, snakes, anything at all. I've eaten the lot: salamanders, lizards. As I said, at Loyang it wasn't too bad but then things started to whittle back a bit. They wanted volunteers for the Burma–Thailand railway, but I didn't go. Some of my mates did and they never came back, of course.

In mid-1944 Lou and thousands of other prisoners were moved into Changi prison.

That's when things really got tough, about the last 18 months of the war. We were building an aerodrome where the Changi airport is now—that was all swamp country. We worked on that for 14 hours a day, and it was pretty grim. There were a few beatings. We were in 'C' block, on floor three, and most of us were merchant seamen, navy and a few air force. In fact, we even had Italians in with us. When the Italians packed it in in 1943, two submarines came into Singapore. But the Japs banged them in the jail with us and took the submarines.

Inside the jail there were about 6000 of us. It was only built for 600. There were six to a cell when it was only built for one. Outside the jail was another camp, where most of the Australians were. There were about 12,000 in that area, around Changi. Sanitation was terrible. We were full of lice. Hygiene was just nil. There were some showers there, but you had to fight to get into them. When the monsoon struck we'd stand out in the rain. I got beriberi and I had dengue fever at one stage, but I was lucky. I got a few skin diseases, tropical ringworm, and my ears got infected, but otherwise I was reasonably fit. One of the worst skin diseases most of the POWs suffered was the cracking and drying of the scrotum caused through malnutrition. It was nicknamed 'Changi balls'. It was very painful at times. We had our own doctors but they had no medical supplies, only makeshift things. If you got a tooth pulled out you got no anaesthetic at all.

The comradeship in the camp was terrific. We'd play cards, we'd talk a lot—about food! We used to do a lot of walking. Inside the jail there was a double wall, and there was a road right round inside and we used to walk around it. We'd try to keep as fit as we could, but malnutrition took to us. We never got Red Cross parcels, we never got anything like that. We used to rely on what we could pinch or buy. There was a lot of black market activity. There were six of us off the same ship and whatever we could steal, coconuts or a pineapple, we used to pool together. If you got caught, you'd get punished.

One time three of us were on a working party and this Jap guard—he was only about 18, his rifle was bigger than he was—took us out to get some palm fronds to camouflage some trenches that we'd dug. We passed a Malay village and they had tapioca roots—we used to make chips and fry them—and I said to the guard, 'Tapioca, okay?' So we dug down, got some out, and next thing I heard this yelling and screaming, and there's a Malay running towards us with a big stick. We thought, oh well, the Jap will stop him. But the Jap had taken off. And we took off too.

We had radios in the camp, but only certain people knew where the radios were—I didn't. We used to get a lot of what we called borehole rumours (our toilets were boreholes dug into the ground in the courtyard), rumours that the Australians had landed in Malaya and all this. It was wishful thinking. We'd get one or two new prisoners come in, and they'd give us a bit of information.

The airport was not actually finished, but there was enough to land planes on it. The Americans strafed it one day with Lightning planes, then the B-29s came over and dropped a few bombs. That's when we knew there was something happening. Then they had us build fortifications. Every day we had to march out and salute the guards at the gate. Some of the guards were Koreans, and the Koreans were actually worse than the Japanese. They also had Indians. A lot of the Indians who were captured in Singapore went over to the Japs—they had what they called the Indian National Army—and they made us salute them too. But anyway, we used to go on working parties digging tunnels for the Japs into the hillside, and trenches, and that's the job we were on when the war packed in.

If it hadn't been for the atomic bomb, I don't think we would have lasted another six months. We were just right down. I was only six stone. It wasn't very pleasant, the last 12 months. All we got was rice and a bit of green stew. We used to eat snails or snakes. Then they dropped the atomic bombs, and then they told us the war was over. Prisoners were still dying when they liberated us; a lot of people were dying every day. They dropped 50 medical people by parachute first, and then 50 commandos—they were to keep us in the camp.

What happened to the guards?
A lot of them got belted up, of course, by some of our guys. I didn't see much of that. They herded them together and shoved them in a camp. Then the British navy came in off a cruiser called the *Sussex*, and we went aboard. I had a piece of bread with plum jam on it—the first piece of bread I'd seen for three-and-a-half years! We stayed aboard the ship that night, and then they took us back to the camp and started grading us. I was fortunate that I wasn't too bad. I'd lost a fair bit of weight, of course.

I was one of the first draft out, on a New Zealand ship called the *Monowai*. There were six merchant

Opposite: *Following the Japanese surrender, Lou was among 850 POWs evacuated from Singapore on the Union Company's* Monowai, *seen here in Wellington during earlier service as an armed merchant cruiser with the Royal New Zealand Navy. After reverting to the red ensign in 1943, the liner served as a landing ship during the D-Day invasion and later repatriated thousands of British and Soviet POWs and refugees.* Museum of Wellington City & Sea

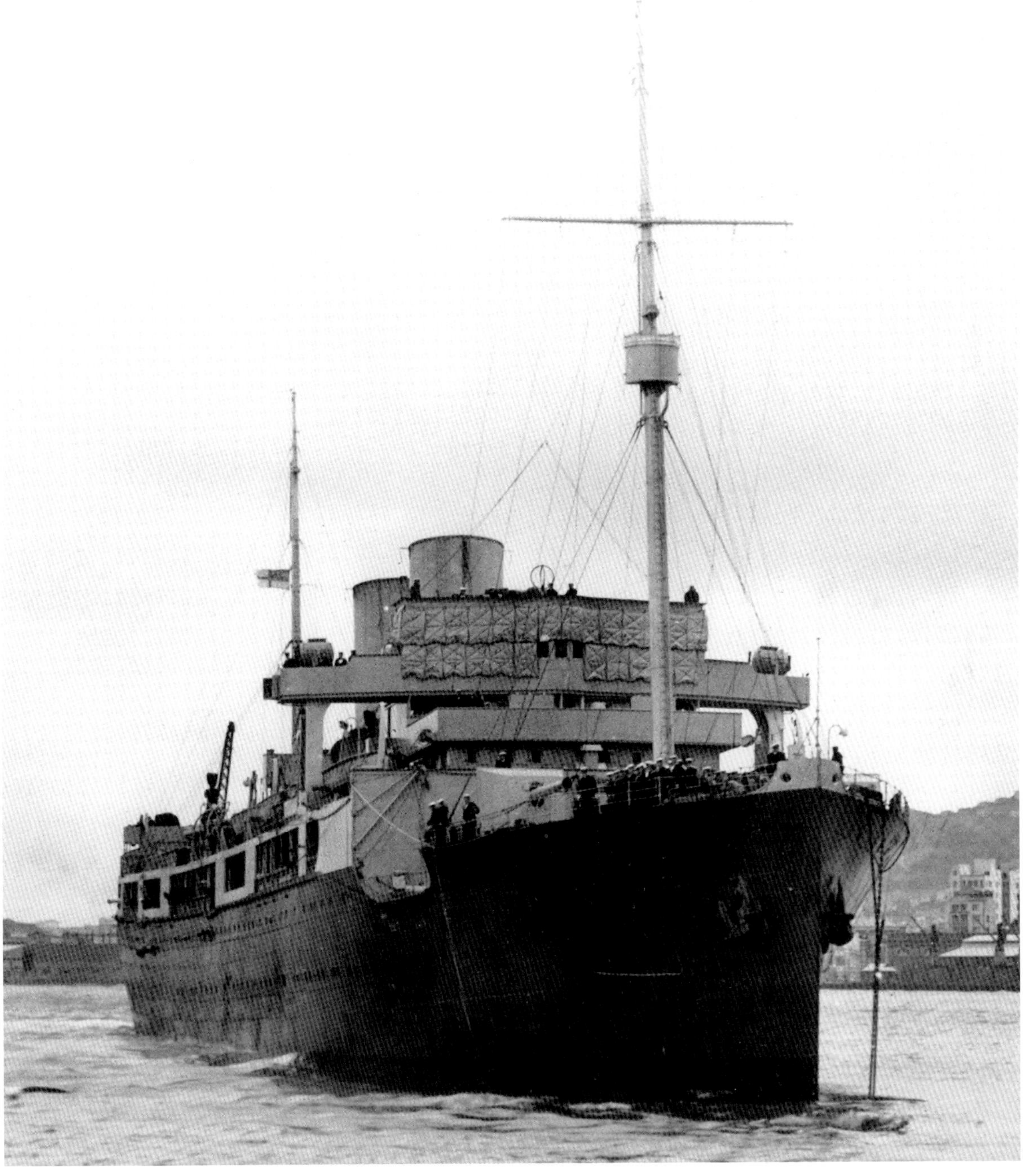

seamen on it; the rest were all British army and navy. We boarded that in Keppel Harbour in Singapore and they took us to Liverpool. We were the first ship to land in Liverpool from the Far East with prisoners of war on it, so they organised a big welcome.

Did your family know what had happened to you after the **Gloucester Castle** *disappeared?*
No, they didn't know. In fact, we were presumed dead. It was two years before they found out I was alive. I sent a prisoner-of-war card, the only one that was sent. They didn't know where we'd gone to.

I went back to sea again after I went home. I was home for Christmas 1945, but I couldn't settle down. I was scratchy. Things were pretty miserable in England then. Liverpool was still pretty damaged. I joined a ship called the *Empire Austen*. We went to America, through the Panama Canal to Vancouver, and back through the Canal. It was running for the UNRRA, United Nations Relief and Rehabilitation Administration, to occupied countries. We took wheat to Greece and all around the Greek islands.

I paid off that ship in Middlesbrough, then I joined the *Saminver*, run by the Blue Star Line. We went all round different places and then we went to Makatéa, an island about 70 miles from Tahiti. We loaded phosphate and came to New Plymouth—that was the first time I landed in New Zealand—in 1946. Then we came down here to Ravensbourne [in Dunedin]. In 1947 we came back again and I jumped ship in Lyttelton, then came down here. There were quite a lot of ship deserters at that time. I think eight jumped the ship I was on, the *Saminver*.

Then I joined another ship, after I'd been ashore for a while. Oh, I couldn't settle down. Me and a friend of mine joined a ship called the *Aldington Court* in dry dock in Port Chalmers with the idea of going back to England. She was a British ship under charter to the Union Company, running to Australia and bringing wheat to New Zealand. I did about three trips backwards and forwards, and when we came back to Auckland I jumped ship and came back down to Dunedin. And that was it—that was my seafaring days finished.

Did you do jail time for desertion?
Yes, for breaking the ship's articles. It was not for entering the country illegally because I was a British subject, but the shipping company sued you for breaking the ship's contract. I did a month in the jail down here. I worked in the cookhouse, so it was quite good. My old prisoner-of-war days taught me a few things!

I think one of the best things I ever did was jump ship here. I could never settle down in England. I used to enjoy my days at sea—not the wartime, the wartime was a bit different. When I was young I thought it was a big adventure. Yeah, I thought, this is it. During the war we never got much recognition for what we did. We lost a lot of men at sea. I was in convoys where five or six ships were hit—'Bang, bang, bang'—one after the other. But when we came home from the war we were treated as though we were a 'forgotten service'.

Lou married in 1948 and raised a family of five daughters and three sons in Dunedin. After trying his hand at various jobs, he joined the National Mortgage & Agency Company and worked in their seed store until his retirement. He was active in the New Zealand Ex-Prisoners of War Association and returned to Britain, via Singapore, for the 50th anniversary of VJ Day in 1995.

My friend Barry Lane off the *Gloucester Castle* was in Changi jail with me. We met again when I first went back to England in 1993. He has since died, but I was pleased to meet up with Barry again after all those years. When I went to England he took us out for a drive in his car; he had a brand new Vauxhall. He said, 'What kind of car have you got?' I said, 'I've got a Toyota Corolla.' He turned round and he went off! He was dead set against them: 'You'd buy a Japanese car!' I said, 'That's all we could buy, they're cheap, they're good cars too.' But I never thought I'd ever drive a Japanese car if you'd have asked me in 1945! I don't blame the Japanese now; there are some good Japanese now. There was just a certain type then. I'll tell you, I didn't meet any good Japanese, not in them days. It was an experience I wouldn't like to go through again. I was pretty lucky, I think.

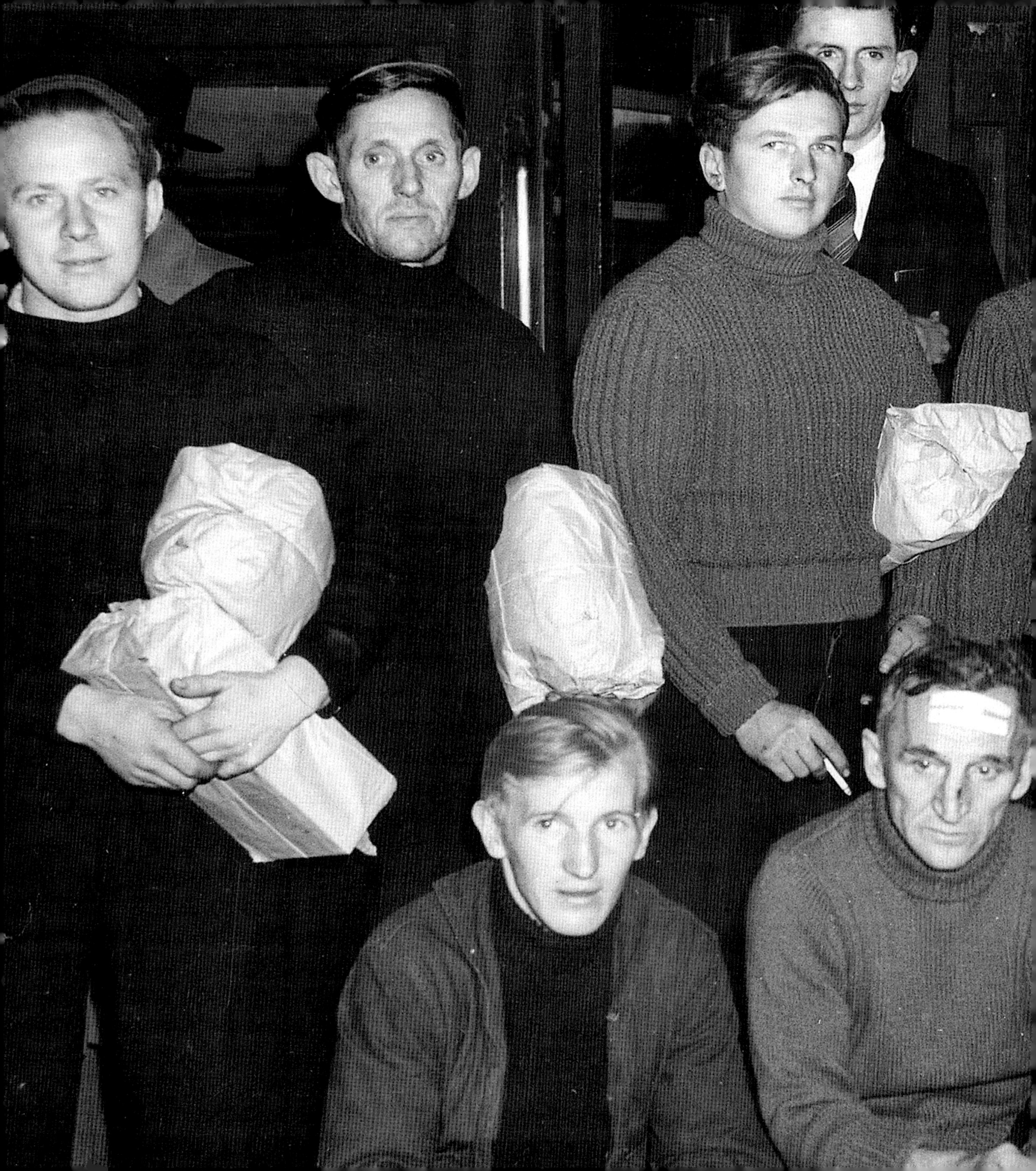

'A PIERHEAD JUMP'

THOR LARSEN, Boy, Seaman

The son of a Norwegian father and a New Zealand-born mother, Thor Einar Larsen was born in Napier in May 1927. His father, who came to New Zealand before the First World War, worked as a lighter master for Richardson & Company at Napier's Port Ahuriri.

I WENT TO NAPIER CENTRAL SCHOOL, but we left Napier in 1938, when I was just a wee fellow. We went to Auckland. Dad had been accused of pinching some wire, and it turned out to be a one-eyed guy called Fleetwood. Of course, Richardson's sacked Dad right away—bingo, you're gone. He wouldn't shop the other guy. He said, 'I'll take the kids to Auckland' (we were split up from our mother). When he heard the old man had lost his job, Fleetwood went and confessed. And when Richardson's said to Dad, 'You can come back, Larsen,' he said, 'You can stick it up your arse. You didn't believe me, so why should I?' So that's why he went to Auckland. Dad worked on the wharf up there.

Did you want to go to sea when you were young?
Oh, I never really thought about it. I just went with the flow, you know. I was always down the wharf, having a look around, fishing or looking at the boats. My father took me out on the lighters in school holidays. It was always interesting. After the war started my father still worked on the wharf, but he had something to do with the American stevedores up there. I used to go down and see the ships then.

Previous page: *Survivors from a Norwegian ship that was torpedoed by a Japanese submarine off New South Wales in May 1943. Norway's exiled merchant shipping fleet—the world's fourth-largest in 1939—played a vital role in the Allied war effort.* Australian War Memorial, 014820
Above: *Thor Larsen in Sydney during the 1940s.* Larsen collection
Opposite: *Thor's first ship was the Panamanian-flagged Norwegian tramp SS Carola (3842 tons), seen here in October 1944 at the Chelsea sugar refinery at Birkenhead, Auckland.* Alexander Turnbull Library, RNZAF Collection, 135667-1/2

'A Pierhead Jump'

When I finished school I was about 14. I was messing around on one or two farms, up in Te Kauwhata, and of course the war was on. I came back into town after a couple of years, just doing this and that, and then one day my father came up and he said, 'I've got a job for you.' That was 1944. I was 16. He said, 'Do you want to go to sea?' I said, 'Well, I could try it out.' The Manpower, or the [Labour Department's] Youth Centre, were getting after me. I don't know how it worked, but I think I was supposed to report to them. Dad said, 'No way. I'll get you on this ship and you'll be right. Once it leaves here they won't know where you are.'

So away we went, over to Australia on the sugar run. I didn't even sign any papers. I did what they call a 'pierhead jump'. Once you got on there, away you went and you didn't care about papers. Because it was a quick getaway, I just had more or less what I stood up in. This was the SS *Carola*. It was a Norwegian ship flying the Panamanian flag. It was a First World War boat, a real old-timer, did about four knots! It had all Norwegian officers on board it, officers and engineers. She had a Finnish bosun; she never had any other New Zealanders but me. Most of them were Aussies, because it was running over there. But it did other things, it was just like a tramp. If the cargo was there or if the government wanted them to carry something, they'd just say take this stuff away, and that's what they'd do.

belching and snoring and swearing. Terrible, bloody terrible! All bunks, two high. Port side was for the seamen, starboard side for the firemen. We just wore civilian clothes, mainly dungarees, dungaree jackets and shirts. I never had a suit, I couldn't afford one.

The food was quite good. On the *Carola* the cook was hard-case. The wharfies used to come into the galley and get in the way of the cook—he'd be trying to cook dinner and do this and that—and of course they had a coal-burning range and it was bloody near red-hot. All of a sudden he'd dip into a container, and he'd get this stuff and go 'whish' across the top of the heated range. You know what it was? Pepper! Jesus, everybody scarpered then, because the pepper, you couldn't stand it. The cook could—he was sweating away—but everybody else was out.

We also had big milk cans, and all the peelings and stuff used to go in the milk can, and they used to make what we called 'jungle juice'. That was good stuff, everything went into it and the cook put sugar in, then yeast, and slapped the lid on. I think it only took about ten days to brew. I thought I was clever. I got two empty whisky bottles, filled them up with this brew, put corks in and screwed the tops down. I thought that'll be good for Dad if I get back to Auckland. So we did a trip back and I said to the old man, 'Here's something for you, Dad.' 'What is it?' 'Jungle juice. You try it.' The old man would drink anything, so he tasted it and he said, 'Oh, that's okay.' But I lost the rest. I had it in my locker and with the movement of the ship the bottles burst, blew to pieces. And it stank—you got no idea, the smell of it—Jesus it stunk!

Then I signed off that ship over in Australia, and I joined a tanker. It was called the *Ohio*, but it was not the *Ohio* that went to Malta. It was another Norwegian ship under the Panamanian flag. We were on the American run. We went to San Pedro [Los Angeles] and San Francisco Bay and picked up our fuel, then we came down through the islands, zigzagging all the way through. We called into Noumea, New Caledonia, and we went to Fiji and Australia. That was good, it was good fun. After the *Carola*, [the crew's quarters] were really nice: two-berth cabins, you had a mirror and everything. Luxury!

On one trip when we left San Francisco we were steaming for about three hours, out of sight of land, and next thing, out came a big American aircraft. We were all waving and carrying on, you know. It had a speaker in the doorway in the side of the plane, a grille door. They said, 'Captain, you are now in an American naval target area.' We've got a gutsful of petrol, high-octane or something. This plane was circling, God knows what's going to happen. The captain didn't understand too much English. We were a mixed crew, mainly Australians and one or two Americans; I was the only Kiwi. Anyhow,

Thor's Norwegian seamen's union membership book. Larsen collection

they said, 'You are requested to stop your engines and await further orders.' One of the Aussies said to me, 'Do you think the captain understands what's going on?' I said, 'I don't know.' Everybody on the bridge, the captain, the mate, they were all waving. So this Aussie went up and he told the skipper. Next thing, stop.

We just stayed there, and the plane disappeared into the distance. We floated around for about three or four hours. Next thing the plane came out again, and of course everybody's on deck wondering what's going to happen now. He said, 'Captain, the United States Navy thank you for your cooperation. You may proceed on your way.' So the skipper said okay, and as soon as the engines started the plane started playing 'Anchors Aweigh'. It circled the ship and then away it went. It was quite touching, you know, all that Yankee bullshit.

Then we called into Noumea. We were dropping off oil there for the Americans. The American navy were guarding the oil installation, and generally we were only in there 24 hours if we were lucky, but we had a few hours off. We said to the mate, 'Would it be okay if we went up town and had a look-see?' He said, 'You be back at such-and-such a time or else.' 'Okay.' Well, we got to the gate and there's an American guy in a little white hat and blue naval uniform and he said to us, 'Where do you think you're going?' We said, 'Oh, we're going up town.' 'You can't walk through here.' We said, 'We're on the ship, we've got a pass.' 'No, no, you'll have to walk over them hills.' Crikey, these blinking hills full of bush. Anyhow, eventually he said, 'Go on, git.' So through we went, and the next thing he pulled out his .45 and shot it through the ceiling of the guardhouse. So away we went, of course, we were worried he was going shoot us. I think he flipped his lid, that joker.

What did you normally do when you arrived in port?
We went and drank, although they kept an eye on me when I was a boy. I'd go to the pub with them but they wouldn't let me drink, or they'd let me drink one or two. The bosun on the *Carola*, who was a Finn, was a bad-tempered bastard. I don't know if you've heard of Dolly Varden wine, but they used to sell it in bottles over in Australia, and it was good stuff, too. Anyhow, the second engineer said to me, 'Boy, you're the only one not drinking. You take care of that bottle for me.' Next thing the bosun said, 'Boy! Boys don't have bottles', and he took it off me. I said, 'Bosun, that belongs to the second engineer.' 'No, boys can't have drink like that.' So he buggered off with it. He went to walk back towards the ship, and of course the second engineer came up. 'Where's my bottle?' I said, 'The bosun's relieved me of it.' 'What! Where is he?' So he went outside and he gave the bosun a good hiding. But oh gee, he deserved it.

The funniest thing was, this Aussie joker, Bill Bailey, he'd been quartermaster on the *Queen Mary*. He was a good joker, and the bosun gave him a hiding. So anyhow, he seethed about this for months, and we got into port and were all down this pub as usual. There were columns at the counter and the bosun was on one side and Bill was on the other. After an hour or two Bill had filled himself with grog and he must have thought, I'm going to get even. So he stood up on the foot rail and looked around the column, saw the bosun was talking to these other guys, so he went 'Whack!'—hit him a beauty. The bosun turned around and all he could see was this column. Everybody else

Thor (left) with an Australian shipmate in Melbourne in 1944.
Larsen collection

was thinking he was going to tear the place down, but he must have thought, what the hell happened there? I never saw anything so funny.

The mate had a foxie [terrier]. That was a mad bugger too. He blamed me one day for kicking it. I never even touched it. He said, 'I'll fix you, Larsen, before you fix the dog.' I thought, Jesus, what's he going to do to me? It was this Aussie joker. As I came up to relieve him on the wheel, he kicked the dog on the way out, and of course the dog yelped.

Another time we did a trip with supplies for the troops to either New Guinea, Borneo or Bougainville, I can't remember which one, but there was some trading going on with the islanders and the crew. The islanders were discharging the ship. One of the boys traded a tin of bully beef for a human skull and trinkets, etcetera. Not far from the ship were a group of island women sitting in the shade, one or two of them were breastfeeding and had a baby on one breast and a small suckling pig on the other. I believe that this was a natural thing for them to do. I couldn't believe it.

The islanders working on board were eating mouthfuls of rock salt that they got out of the cargo, sacks of it. The cook went mad because the islanders had found his fresh veggie locker on deck and had cleaned it out and were sitting around munching the onions like apples. When we were about to sail the ship's cat went missing, so they got that also. Poor old cat. We soon learnt to lock up everything in all parts of the world.

What about when you were up in San Francisco, San Pedro?
Oh yeah, we got ashore there. We used to go to the bars and have a look around. But on the tankers you're not in long. We used to go to the same bars. It was good because they knew you and they'd say, 'Come on in!' They used to have a tin where you put any spare cash you had, and they'd say, 'Okay, that's for the party at Christmas' or whenever. So they'd decide to have a do in the bar, if a ship came in that'd be a reason for a party. They'd say, 'Come on, it's our shout.' That was good in America.

There were always troops around. There wasn't really much trouble with them because we used to stick to our own pubs. But they pissed us off, them in the uniforms, because they got all the sheilas, didn't they? The bastards! Jesus, I saw some fights amongst that lot too, American troops. God, they were fighting with Aussie servicemen and fighting with us, everybody. Of course, we loved it, it was good fun. Gave us a black eye or two, yeah. I wouldn't say I won too many, but I did all right, I held my own. Later on I got to know the ropes, I got a bit cheeky.

Did the seamen go off to the red-light districts?
Oh yes—not me, of course! That was always there. You went with the swim. [Your shipmates] looked after you like a long-lost brother, no matter who you were. There was real good camaraderie. The unwritten law was that no matter what happened, everyone stuck together. Nobody went anywhere by themselves, mainly because of safety in foreign countries.

I got in a few sticky ones, too. But that was after the war, up in the Persian Gulf, in Abadan, which was the main port for BP tankers. This was on a Norwegian tanker, the *Montana*. Around the seamen's mission they had a big fence, and nobody was supposed to get over that and go up to Abadan town. So of course we climbed on a shed and went over the fence. But one of the boys had been up there several times and done the same thing. He said, 'Don't jump over with nothing. Put two pairs of socks on, two pairs of trousers and two shirts, and you can flog that for money when you get into town.' So that's what we did. You could buy any known drink up there. I'd never seen rooms full of liquor, it surprised me. There were bottles of Aussie beer with quinine floating around in it.

Anyhow, because one or two of the boys had had enough to drink and wanted to find a girl, we went to a brothel. There must have been about six or seven of us. One of our jokers, he wanted the madam and she wouldn't have it. She said, 'If you don't leave I will make you leave.' We thought, oh yeah, how are you going to do that? Well, these buggers came in armed, with uniforms and rifles. We picked up chairs, we thought yeah, let them come, but as soon as we saw the rifles we put the chairs down. And we moved, don't worry. Yeah, he wanted the madam. We said, 'You bastard, you're getting us in trouble all the time.'

Do you remember hearing about the end of the war?
Oh yeah, it was a big moment. Everyone was happy, especially the Norwegians, who had been away from home for years. They must have been through a hell of a lot. They were overjoyed.

We were in Melbourne on VE Day. And boy, that was a shindig. God, you couldn't walk anywhere, it was so crowded. Everybody was so happy. Everybody was enjoying themselves, but maybe some were getting out of hand. They got a bit heavy-handed trying to control the crowds. My mate had his teeth smashed out. They came in with mounted police with big batons. Anybody who didn't get out of the way, they whacked them. Of course my mate, this Aussie guy, he happened to be in the way and he got the baton, knocked his teeth out.

The Norwegian freighter Anatina *was one of a number of ships commandeered by the Australian government to repatriate troops from South-east Asia in late 1945.* Larsen collection

In August 1945 Thor joined another Norwegian ship, the Anatina.

It was just an ordinary cargo vessel. This was at the end of the war, I think it must have been just finished. I joined this ship and she was empty, or they were discharging. And next thing the Australian government commandeered it to bring the troops back. We went up to Bougainville and Borneo. Of course, that was quite interesting. I think there were about 14 or 15 different vessels, cargo ships, passenger boats. They put bunks in the 'tween decks and down the holds. We took 600 troops back. We had cookhouses and showers and everything on deck for the troops.

I went over to Norway after the war, in early 1946. My father's two sisters and a brother were over there, and I was dead keen to go over and see them. I paid off a tanker in San Pedro, went through to San Francisco and joined a Swedish cargo-passenger ship, the *Argentina*. I went over there and paid off in Sweden and went over to Norway. It was good to see them. Boy, they made me welcome.

Thor signed off his last Norwegian ship, the Montana, *in Brisbane in 1948 and returned to New Zealand. He spent the next 15 years sailing on the coast as an AB with the Union, Canterbury, Anchor and Holm shipping companies; he also had a couple of years on the Shell Oil tanker* Tanea. *After getting married in 1963, he settled in Napier, and worked on the wharf until his retirement.*

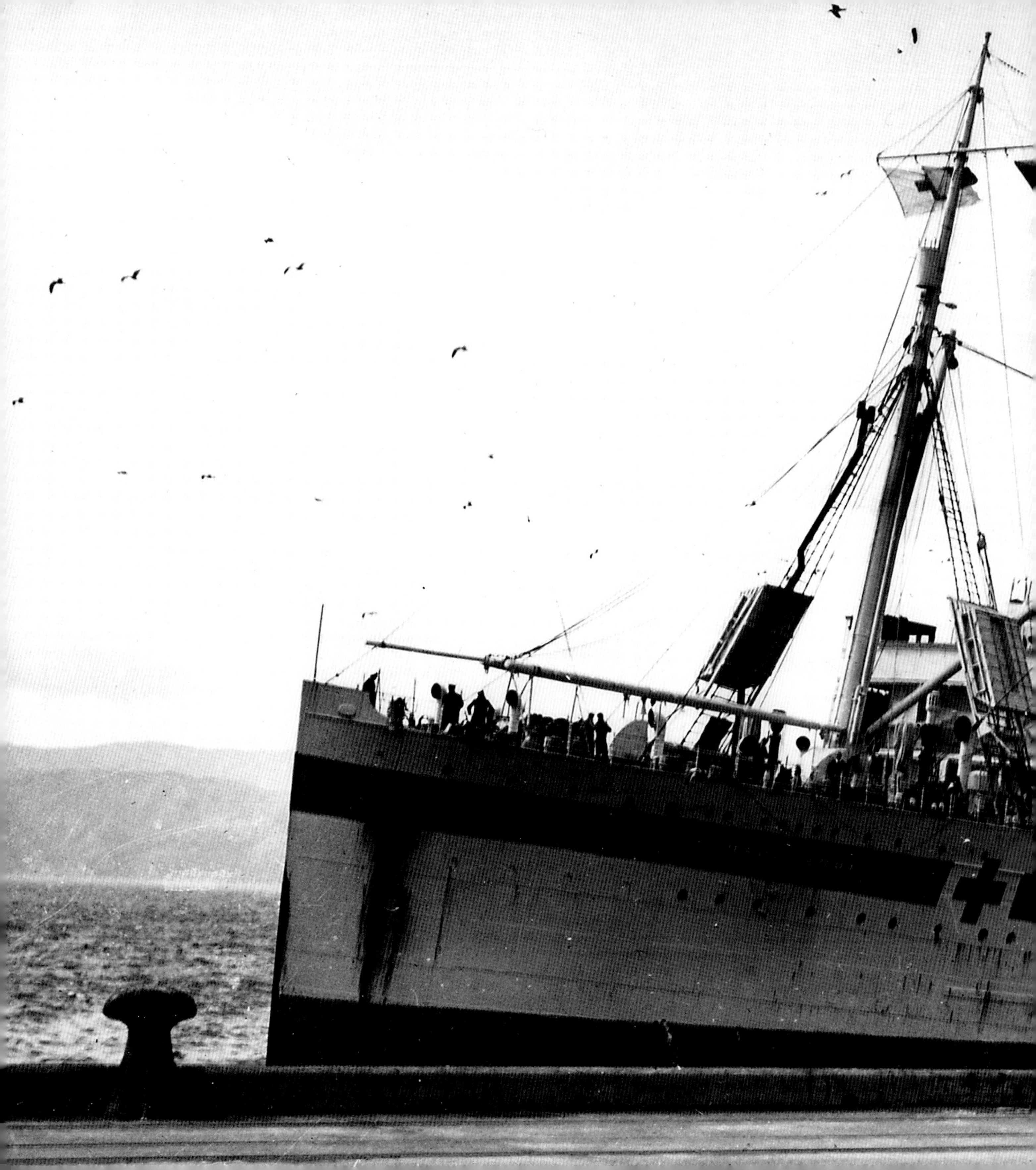

'UP THE RED SEA'

STEVE CAREY, Engineer Officer

Francis Lawrie Carey, who was always known as 'Steve', was born in Port Chalmers in 1921 to ship's carpenter Stephen Carey and his wife Daisy. His great-grandparents, David and Hannah Carey, had arrived in Otago in 1840 and later settled in a little bay on Otago Harbour that now bears the family name, Careys Bay.

I WAS NAMED AFTER MY MOTHER'S only brother, who got killed at Gallipoli. But when I was young my mother used to call me 'Francie' and I didn't like that. I'd be down the road with my father and he'd talk to his mates and they'd say, 'How's young Steve?' I thought, this is good, and I let this carry on—so, 70-odd years of 'Steve'.

I lived in Careys Bay till I was 21. I served an engineering apprenticeship at the Port Chalmers Marine Repair Works, which was a subsidiary of the Union Company. I went to King Edward Technical College in Dunedin for two or three years and then got an apprenticeship down here. And then I went to the night school. They had marine engineering classes there.

> *After further study by correspondence and private tutoring, Steve gained his third-class marine engineer's certificate.*

By this time the war was well under way, and we worked on various ships here in connection with the war. If you worked on a ship in the dock, working on the tailshaft, you'd work all night to get the shaft out and the stern bush out, and they'd get machining on it the next day, but if you carried on that day you got double time. As apprentices, my God, that was very valuable. I don't think they could make you work, but you did. So we carried on working. I can remember being down the dock, in the [shaft]

Previous page: *Arriving in Wellington in September 1945, the New Zealand Hospital Ship* Maunganui *looks somewhat the worse for wear after four years of constant voyaging.* Museum of Wellington City & Sea
Above: *Steve Carey in his Union Company engineer's uniform.* Carey collection

tunnel of the ships, and I'd be so tired I'd drop asleep, and later I'd wake up. It was appalling. It just shows how bloody dangerous it was. But there was no way we were going to miss out on paid work on double time.

When you became the senior apprentice down there, one of the great privileges was to go to Bluff. The Bluff dredge, the *Murihiku*, used to come up here and they had to have extra engineers. She was under tow—the *Awarua* was the tug. Anyway, away we went—my first 'deep-sea' trip. Oh, it was bloody good till we got to Cape Saunders, then we struck a bit of a southerly, and oh God, [seasickness set in]. After a while I didn't give a bugger. We put into shelter behind the Nuggets—it was too rough to carry on—and in the smooth water there I sort of came right a bit. Old Ken Braid (he was only a young fellow then) knew I'd been sick and he said, 'Go along and see the cook and ask if he's got any canned apricots. That's the thing for seasickness.' So I went along, and I got roared out of the galley: 'Bloody canned apricots, they'll want caviar and champagne next!' When I got back to the fo'c'sle I said, 'Why apricots, what's so special about them?' Ken said, 'They taste the same coming up as they do going down.'

They had a little ship running across to Stewart Island called the *Tamatea*, an old wooden ship. She'd been motorised, but she had a boiler for the anchor winch. She'd been taken over by the New Zealand government for the Yanks in the Pacific, so I got a job to go to Auckland in her. We were steaming down the harbour, and my mother came out to the end of the point there and gave me a wave, and I waved back. I was whistling along the deck, and the next thing there's this bloody roar. God, I bloody near jumped overboard. It was the old skipper, Hamilton. His wife, when the boat was being overhauled, just about used to run the show, and she was known as 'Tugboat Annie'. Anyway, I wondered what the hell I'd done wrong? It was whistling: 'Christ, don't ever whistle in a ship at sea!'

According to an old seafaring superstition, whistling at sea would bring on a gale.

We weren't far outside, and I was crook again. We struck northerlies. We finally put into Akaroa, and as we manoeuvred to go alongside the wharf—it was a four-cylinder, semi-diesel type of engine—one cylinder was blasting flames out. I didn't realise at the time how little the chief engineer knew. 'Oh,' he said, 'it's a fusible plug.' Well, I'd never heard of a fusible plug in a diesel before, but I thought, well, maybe this one's different. 'So what do we do?' 'Well, the last time it happened I got some hardwood plugs and we drove 'em in the holes.' Righto.

So we went up the street, and there was a garage there and they had a lathe. I said to the bloke, 'Have you got a bit of hardwood? I want to make some fusible plugs for a cylinder head.' He looked at me a bit, but he let me use the lathe and I turned up half a dozen of these, went back to the ship and drove one in the hole, and away we went. We get round Cape Campbell and God almighty, does it blow again. So we hightailed it into Port Underwood and got anchored in there. And the old skipper—by this time it was my fault we were getting all this weather!

However, luckily we got away. We got up the coast, and there was obviously something wrong with this cylinder that had been blowing. So we went into Hicks Bay and changed the cylinder head. It was cracked. We'd had a new cylinder head made in Invercargill. So, we got the new cylinder head out of the case and we went to fit it on, and the bloody spigot was too big. So what do we do? Well, we had a new file and an oilstone, so I sat down and oilstoned all the cutting edge off one face of that file. Then I was able to file the spigot down till it was the right diameter. What a job this was—in Hicks Bay. This took a day or more, and then we were ready to go. We went to get some steam up to lift the anchor, but by this time the journey had taken that long that we'd used up all the coal. So, out went the lifeboat and we rowed ashore and picked up driftwood and firewood around the beach, and we stoked up the boiler to pick up the anchor.

Eventually we made it into Auckland. I had a letter of introduction to the superintending engineer of the Union Company in Wellington, but some Yanks come down and they wanted anyone to go: 'Hey boy, you come up the Pacific with us, we'll pay you $500 [a month], and after you've proved yourself it'll be $600 and all the overtime you like.' This was bloody fantastic; by God I was tempted. But I thought, bugger it, so I turned that down.

I had a day or two there, then I came back to Wellington, and the first thing I did was go see the superintending engineer, Gillies. 'Where the hell have you been? We've been looking all over New Zealand for you. We want you to go on the bloody *Maunganui*.' Well, I remember the *Maunganui* coming through on the 'horseshoe' [trans-Tasman run]. God, I hightailed it home quick as I could, got my gear and away back.

> The Union Company's Maunganui *had been built in Scotland in 1911 and served as a troopship during the First World War. In January 1941 it was requisitioned by the New Zealand government for conversion to a hospital ship, primarily to serve the needs of 2NZEF in the Middle East.*

'Up the Red Sea'

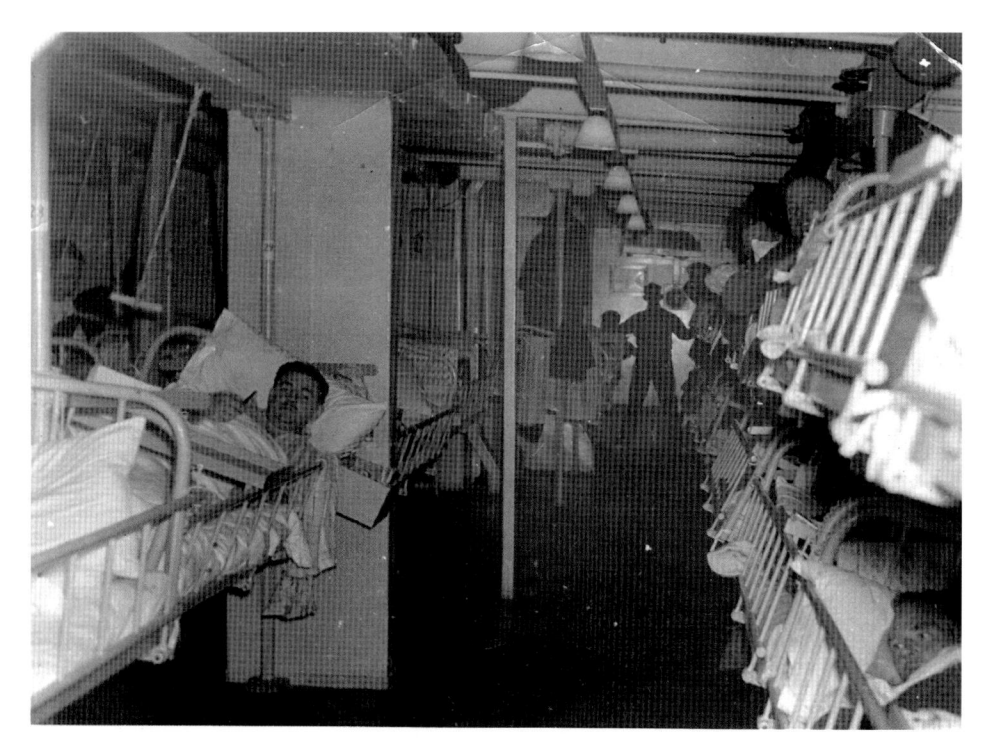

Inside one of the hospital wards on the Maunganui—*the patients' cots were gimballed to counteract the roll of the ship.* Kippenberger Military Archive, Army Museum, 1989.1064

So away I went. That was in early '42. She was a hospital ship by then and she'd done several trips. On the first trip I was sick all the way to Fremantle, but I stuck it out. By the time I got to Fremantle I could get a meal down, but I could only hold it for half an hour, so I wasn't getting much good out of it. I could hardly crawl, I was so weak. However, we left Fremantle and the whole world changed—the Great Southern Ocean's gone, and I was okay from there on. They used to be ten-day hops: ten days from Wellington to Fremantle, ten days Fremantle to Colombo, and ten days from Colombo to Port Tewfik.

Now, in Fremantle, they'd been blowing down a boiler for some reason or other, and someone had lit the furnace in the wrong boiler, the one that had been blown down. We didn't use that boiler till we got to Aden (we often went into Aden for orders) and they said they wanted the ship in a hell of a hurry. We get steam on this boiler going up the Red Sea and all the bloody tubes were leaking. I was ninth engineer, and the second engineer and the ninth were day-working and all the others were on watch. So we had to climb into the furnace. The boiler was still boiling. All the other fires were out, but it was hot as hell. We laid sacks and crawled in there with a tube expander, and it was black as the ace of spades. We worked away all one afternoon till we got the thing right. That was my first real experience, going up the Red Sea of all places. You couldn't have picked a hotter place, could you?

Anyway, we got to Port Tewfik and they loaded up with English patients. We went up to Port Said, picked up a few more there, then went to Mombasa. Now, that was a funny thing. When we went into Mombasa we got instructions to go over a mine-testing field outside the harbour. And next thing there were flags flying and Aldis lamps flashing and naval launches charging out to the ship. They said her degaussing gear wasn't working. In fact, we found out afterwards it was working, but because any major work had always been done in the southern hemisphere—she was 30-odd years old—her polarity had changed from the original. We were degaussing and making ourselves bloody dangerous.

We went from Mombasa to Durban. It was funny in Durban. There had been that many troops through, that if you went to a pub you didn't get a glass to drink out of, you got a can, a fruit can or something. If you had spirits you had a Bovril glass. And one of the things that always struck me as very touching was when the ships left—we weren't far from the end of a breakwater—there was a lady who came down and sang. I believe she was a famous opera singer and she did this to every ship. She did it to our ship too when we left, but we could hear her quite often.

This was Perla Siedle Gibson, Durban's famous 'Lady in White'.

Then away we went back up to Port Tewfik. We took up repatriated Italian prisoners of war. There was a swap going on, and these Italian guys—some of them could talk a bit of English—believed that Italy had won the war and they were being returned home to victorious Italy. We said, 'Look lads, it's not like that at all', and no way would they wear that. Every port we went into on the way up, they had to be all blindfolded and shutters put over the ports. That was a waste of time. They went ashore at Port Tewfik. The Red Cross took them from there.

I went away in the ship as a junior engineer, I had just turned 21. The New Zealand Army nursing staff—there were about 20 sisters and about ten other girls called VADs—they had to be 25 years of age before they could join the service. So, to a 21-year-old guy, a 25-plus woman looked pretty old. But after you'd done a couple of months up the Middle East and you were getting back, you know, they started to look a bit better! But I think the New Zealand nurses were pretty highly regarded.

On average, a trip used to take a month to Tewfik, and you were only in port overnight and then came back again. There were about 400 patients a trip. We would go from New Zealand practically empty, up to Tewfik, and then bring about 400 back. But then we would do special trips; we might go from Tewfik to Bombay or down to Durban or Mombasa. The Durban trip took a bit longer.

Of course, all this time you had that bloody heat. If you were on watch, by the time you went down to the first platform, second platform, up around the cylinders, and down to the plates, the sweat would be pouring over the top of your boots. We had an incident once in Colombo. We had the engine room proper, then there were deep [fuel oil] tanks, which were quite long, and there was a trunkway where all the pipes came through from the boiler room. The joint had blown right in the for'ard end on the bulkhead on the port side. There was steam screaming out of there. We'd come down the Red Sea to Colombo while this was going on. When we got into Colombo there was a beautiful breeze blowing and we got windsocks all rigged up blowing into this trunkway, which would be six to seven feet high and about eight feet wide. But by the time we'd finished bunkering there wasn't a breath of wind.

All hands had to turn to on this job, even the old chief engineer, a real old gentleman called Wattie Houghton. The only way you could get at this joint was to lie on top of one of the main steam pipes. The steam was shut off, of course, but it was still hot. Normally, when you went down on watch you had a woollen singlet and white trousers, but because you were going to be lying on this thing you had to put on more clothes or you'd have got burnt. It didn't make any difference anyway; it was so bloody hot it wouldn't have mattered if you had Antarctic gear on. Anyway, we all took turns. You got in on top, you lay on the pipe and undid these bolts, a great big flange, about 12 bolts around it. You'd get a couple of cants and you'd start to see stars and black out, and next thing you'd feel someone dragging you out. This went on all afternoon till we got that joint out and the new one in.

Then miracle of miracles—the old chief didn't drink, smoke or swear even, but he actually shouted us all a beer. Now that went down real well. We were sitting up on deck, and the mate came rushing down and said, 'When will you be ready to go to sea?' Someone else spoke for Wattie (he was deaf anyway): 'We're not going to sea till we've all had a beer.' On that ship the only thing we ever went anywhere to get fixed was when our main crankshaft broke and we had to go to Glasgow eventually to get that rebuilt. Apart from that everything was done on the ship.

Patients relax on the Maunganui's *boat deck during a voyage home to New Zealand.* J.B. McKinney, Wounded in Battle (1950)

We left Port Tewfik, and a couple of New Zealand wounded had symptoms that hadn't been diagnosed when they came aboard. A couple of days down the Red Sea someone twigged that it might be smallpox. So they dug out the vaccine and we all had to go and get inoculated. A lot of them didn't take, so when we got into Colombo there was a new lot of vaccine waiting. No one was allowed ashore, of course, and the water barges and oil barges came along and the hoses came on board, food and supplies all came on board. They even had an entertainment barge with conjurers and Indian snake charmers and all that, but they were about 20 feet out from the ship and the crowd had to look over and watch. Nothing was allowed ashore. The same thing happened in Fremantle. By this time there were five or six cases and two or three deaths from smallpox.

We carried on to New Zealand and anchored out in Wellington Harbour. You only had to look at someone and they'd snarl. There was Wellington. Half these guys hadn't been in New Zealand for two or three years. Well, [the authorities] finally came to their senses. After two or three days they cleared a little wharf called Miramar Wharf, put Red Cross stores, cigarettes and beer and fruit and everything down on the wharf, and we went alongside and took it all aboard the ship. And they sent us down the Marlborough Sounds. We were down there for the incubation period of the last case of smallpox, which is about ten days, I think, and if there were no more in between we were clear.

As the ninth engineer I was also the chief engineer of the launches, and the second mate was master of the launches. So we lowered the launch and all the lifeboats off one side, and the patients were allowed to go on fishing parties or land at isolated beaches, and of course there were hundreds of isolated beaches in the Marlborough Sounds in those days. We towed them away in the lifeboats and ran them up to the beach where they could go ashore for an hour or so. Another lot might say, 'We want to fish off that point over there.' It was a great thing for the second mate and I, we had a great time cruising around.

Eventually we got cleared. We went alongside Clyde Quay [in Wellington], and they had set up a small ward while we were down in the Sounds. You took all the gear that you were going to take ashore and it was all sprayed with formalin or something, and you stripped off all your clothes and walked through this. The formalin was sprayed all over the place and when you came out the other end you were clear. But there were no further outbreaks. I don't think they ever pinned down where it came from or how, although up in bloody Egypt anything could happen, couldn't it?

In March 1945 the Maunganui *was sent to join the British Pacific Fleet.*

We went into Melbourne and they did a few alterations on the ship, and we were told we were going up to the British Pacific Fleet Train. We went to Manus Island for a wee while, then up to the Gulf of Leyte. We lay there for a couple of months. There were about a thousand British naval ships there, all sorts: workshops, submarine depot ships, aircraft carriers.

I was the fourth engineer by that time. I was always a keen yachtie, and the chippie on the ship decided he'd build a little yacht. So I made up all the fittings. One of the occupational therapists had all sorts of stuff like calico, so she gave us enough calico to make sails and I drew them out and cut them. It was only a little thing, about ten foot long. So we went out in this little boat and we capsized the bloody thing, and there were sharks in the area. I'll never forget that chippie and I, we'd climb up and it would keep rolling over and we kept climbing onto the bugger.

While we were in the Gulf of Leyte there was great rivalry between the deck crowd and the engineers. They had two gigs, nice-shaped little boats, and they had lifeboat sails, but it wasn't enough sail area with the light airs you got up there. So we went to the mate and he let us take the sails out of one of the bigger lifeboats. We had them both rigged up and we had a floor plate bolted on for a keel. But the deck crowd had it over us because they were able to put all hands on and chipped all the paint off their

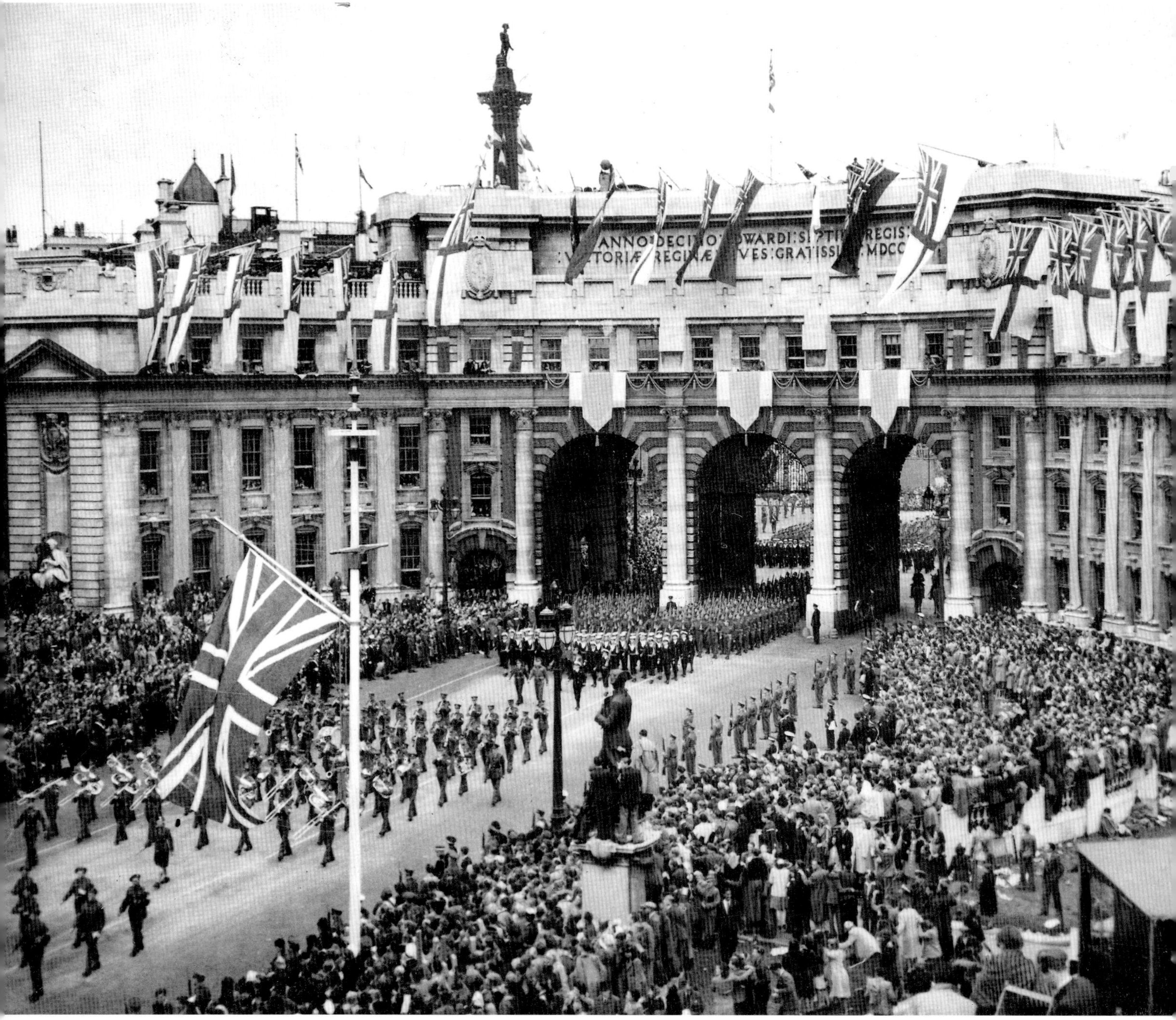

'Up the Red Sea'

gig. You see, there was 30-odd years of paint, and theirs was stripped right down—their boat was about four inches higher in the water than ours. We couldn't beat them.

> *Between August and November 1945 the* Maunganui *repatriated Allied prisoners of war and civilian internees from Hong Kong and Taiwan. In March 1946 the ship returned to New Zealand with the last 2NZEF invalids from Europe and the Middle East, bringing the total number of wartime patients it had carried to 5677.*

Well, she finished as a hospital ship. They repainted her in Union Company colours and rumours were rife that they were going to take occupation troops to Japan. Then finally it was decided that we were going to take a victory contingent to London, a whole shipload of them, army, navy, air force, WAACs, Wrens, all sorts of admirals and generals and Christ knows what. We had a very full complement on the ship, there weren't any bunks left. Anyway, we went to Tahiti and refuelled, and then to Panama. We were just scratching, too, getting there with fuel—the old girl burned 90 ton a day at 15 knots.

Out in the Atlantic, about halfway across, the penny dropped—they had no Merchant Navy representation on board. So they came down and got all the crew, and had a bit of a meeting in the saloon. They said, 'Well, look, this has been overlooked and we've decided that if any of you fellows would like to form a squad of 20 we'll enter the New Zealand Merchant Navy in this parade.' 'Yes, that'd be a great idea.' Then one of the blokes said, 'But wait a minute, we want the same conditions as armed services personnel—a month's leave with a travel pass to anywhere in the UK when it's all over.' 'Oh no, oh no no, we can't do that.' So that was that. Well, that's exactly what it was, wasn't it?—the forgotten service.

How long were you in London?
Six weeks at least. We went up and watched the parade. In fact, there was a whole crowd of us engineers up a tree in St James's Park. The band went past and one bloke, Jim Houston (he was an electrician,

Opposite: *British and Commonwealth service personnel, including the New Zealand contingent who sailed on the* Maunganui, *march in the 1946 Victory Parade in London—a celebration in which the New Zealand Merchant Navy was not represented.* Alexander Turnbull Library, Mrs Buckley Collection, PAColl-0813-11

Opposite: *Back in Union Company colours, the* Maunganui *undergoes survey in Wellington's floating dock after being sold to a Greek shipping company in 1946.* Alexander Turnbull Library, F-10362-1/1 (Archives New Zealand, AAQT 6403 4994)

a West Coast bloke), was sitting on a branch and it broke and he came down on top of hundreds of people underneath!

The Maunganui *arrived back in Wellington in August 1946 and was laid up.*

I went to a little coal-burning ship—I was second engineer—called the *Kartigi*, sailing out of Auckland down to Westport, Greymouth. We went into Wellington on one trip and there was a message that the superintending engineer wanted me. So I went up to see him and he said, 'I want you to go second engineer on the *Maunganui*, get her ready to hand over. We've sold her to the Greeks and I want you to hand her over.' So this suited me, I didn't like the *Kartigi* anyway—a bloody coal-burner, argumentative firemen, Christ, what an outfit! So that's what I did. It took about a month, I had to put all the boilers through survey, everything had to be surveyed.

Then I went up to head office in Wellington, and I was assistant to the superintending engineer for about a month. I hadn't long been married. Then I went to the *Waipiata*, *Waitaki*, *Waipori* on the trans-Tasman run, *Kauri*, *Waiana*. I got all the tickets [engineering certificates].

After returning to Port Chalmers, Steve worked on the National Mortgage & Agency Company's steam trawler Taiaroa *and the harbour dredge* Otakou. *He later ran a workshop for NMA's fishing fleet and supervised the construction of a fish factory and wharf on the Chatham Islands. He also became one of Otago's best-known yachtsmen, winning the Rudder Cup several times.*

Steve Carey died in Port Chalmers in 1997, survived by his wife and two children. I am grateful to his family and to Stan Kirkpatrick for allowing me to use the interview he recorded with Steve in 1994.

'Up the Red Sea'

JIM BLUNDELL, BOY, FIREMAN, REFRIGERATING ENGINEER

Richard James (Jim) Blundell, the eldest of three boys, was born in Napier in February 1924. His mother was a nurse and his father, a marine engineer, was tugmaster at Port Ahuriri in the early 1930s.

HE WAS AT SEA ALL HIS LIFE. He used to ply the lighters out to the overseas ships because at that time there was no port like the breakwater to tie up to. He used to take us out to the Home boats, as we called them in those days. He'd get us aboard and we'd end up in the galley getting a bloody good meal.

On the day of the [1931] earthquake he was approaching the port at Ahuriri when the quake occurred, and he saw the Napier hospital coming down. He was carting empty lighters behind him. They threw the hook over and he went round and got what labour was on them and brought them ashore. Unfortunately, my mother got smacked up in the earthquake and she was never the same.

Do you remember the quake yourself?

Yes, very much so. I was about seven. I was at St Mary's Convent School at Port Ahuriri. To me, remembering back, it was like a thousand steam trains, the noise and everything. Our school came down, bar the corridor. We had one victim who lost all his fingers; I can see them getting him out of the ruins. I remember coming up onto Hospital Hill and there were two nurses lying on the ground, and my father said, 'Oh lad, they're only having a sleep.' Quite a number of night nurses were caught in

Previous page: *Ships take evasive action during an air attack.* Alexander Turnbull Library, Ian Harper Collection, PAColl-8022-01-2
Above: *Jim Blundell, fireman.* Blundell collection

that nurses' home, which came down like a pack of cards. That was very vivid, plus the town burning and all that. And I still to this day fear earthquakes.

As a child Jim wanted to become a marine engineer like his father.

I used to be down on the ships when they were stripping them down. I wanted to be like my father because he was a hard bastard, you know, I admired him. But I'd lost the sight of my eye—I put a pair of scissors in it—and my father wouldn't condone me going into any foundries where I could lose the sight of the other one with steel or whatever flipping off the lathe. We went to boarding school because of my father being at sea; my mother couldn't handle three little shysters. So I went to St Pat's, Silverstream, and from there I went into the army.

My father, who had been in the First World War, wouldn't help me get away to war. If I went on with the conversation I'd have got a hiding. He'd been there, seen it all. So I put my age up, forged my father's signature and joined the Wellington East Coast Mounted Rifles—I thought I was going to be dashing on a horse and all this nonsense—but they disbanded and went into a mechanised unit or whatever. Eventually I went to Waiouru, in the winter: we lived in tents, slept on old straw palliasses and boots as your pillow; when you woke up in the morning you'd have icicles around the blanket. Then we came back to Napier, when the Japs were starting to move south. We were on guard with a .303. We couldn't have defended anything; it was all make-believe. At our young age we didn't appreciate how serious it was.

Then I was sent down to the prisoner-of-war camp at Featherston, as they were bringing the first lot in; there were only tents and things. And then I made out my eye was playing up and I was getting headaches, which was untrue. I wanted to get out, because I could see that I wasn't getting any opportunity to go overseas. So I got out and had problems with the Manpower, who to me were a proper bloody bunch of hicks among the sticks, men that would have been capable of going to the war but were dodging it in industry. So I thought, well, how I am going to get overseas?

After some time working as a clerk for the Hawke's Bay County Council, Jim got a job on a Port Line cargo ship, the Port Fairy, *which was loading at Napier in May 1943.*

My father was at sea when I pissed off. He never knew anything till he came home, then there was nothing he could do about it. I remember going up to the hospital to say goodbye to my mother, and the ward sister said, 'I want to have a word with you.' Christ, she took me down the corridor and stripped me down: what a selfish son I was, how my mother had lost her two brothers at the war, and now I was going away. And this woman knew what she was talking about because she'd just come back from the Middle East, she was nursing there. But I thought, I'm going.

I signed on the *Port Fairy* as engineer's boy. It was the only thing offering. You'd go down the engine room with coffee and be running around. To me it felt quite lowly, having been in the army and having had that education behind me, but okay, you had to accept what was offering. And the Poms didn't pay well, brother. Christ, you worked all sorts of hours. I worked it out one time, I reckon that job worked out about threepence an hour.

That was 11 May 1943. And two months to the day from when I left New Zealand, I was wishing

The 8337-ton Port Line freighter Port Fairy, *which Jim joined as a 19-year-old in May 1943.* Alexander Turnbull Library, F-18680-1/2

Operating from bases in France and Norway, the Luftwaffe's long-range Focke-Wulf Kondors searched out targets for U-boats as well as attacking Allied ships with their own bombs. This Kondor was shot down by a Coastal Command Hudson while shadowing an Atlantic convoy; several survivors can be seen clambering into an inflatable raft. Coastal Command (1944)

to God I'd never ever come to sea, because the shit hit the fan, as they say. We'd left Cardiff to go to South America and we got down to the south coast of Ireland and there was a U-boat outfit. We were ordered to go back to Gourock on the Clyde and wait until they got rid of this trouble south of Ireland. Next thing, we left with two troopships, the *Duchess of York* and the *California*. They were loaded with troops and servicemen, air force and that.

I think it was Sunday night, the 11th of July, and four Focke-Wulf Kondors come over. They came from four directions of the compass, coming right across, and they were expert at their occupation. My action station was in the ammunition party, down in the locker and bringing it up. I remember running, it was very vivid because you had to grab your tin hat and all that. I said to Harry Bryce, who was a Welsh guy with me, 'Christ Harry, look at the sunlight in the portholes.' But it wasn't sunlight—both

Opposite: *Officers and a seaman inspect bomb damage to their ship after an attack by enemy aircraft.* John Daysh-Davey, They Also Served (1946)

ships were raked from stem to stern with bombs. Of course they were on fire and they were drifting back from us, as we were going on.

Next thing, we turned about and lay off to bring some of these victims aboard. They were coming aboard up a net, and it was my first experience of seeing men with shit running down their legs, that's the condition they were in. The chief steward–purser opened the bond locker so you could get grog and everything to give to these guys. You'd light a cigarette and give it to them, and whisky or brandy, and they were that tense from the trauma they wouldn't touch much. But we were into it and it had no effect. That's from the stress you were under.

You heard men yelling out. They used to have a lifejacket with a red light, and they were all over the bloody place—it was getting dark. I remember one guy, we could hear him yelling out not to leave him, he had a wife and kids, you know. These were the distressing parts of that night. A lot of the guys who were on these ships jumped off the top. It's a bloody long way down. Apparently you're meant to hold onto your lifejacket, and some of them didn't and [when they hit the water] it went up and broke their necks. That's what I was told, I don't know how true it is.

We had the best of escorts, the navy, because of these troopers, and they played merry hell at these Kondors. Then we were told to get the hell out, apparently there was a submarine in the vicinity or whatever, so we buggered off.

The next night, Monday the 12th of July, we were having a funeral on the ship; one or two of the survivors had died. Next thing, away she goes again: 'Action Stations'. So I rushed down with Harry and Stan, two Welsh guys, and the captain's tiger was supposed to be with us. I said, 'Where the bloody hell is he?', because he was a big man and you had to haul this ammunition up on pulleys. 'Buggered if I know.' So we got what we needed up and I said, 'Let's go look for him.' I don't know what it was—a premonition, or an act of providence?—but I said, 'For Christ's sake, throw yourself!' We went flat on the deck and I don't even remember hearing any explosion, nothing. I said to Harry, 'Jesus, the bloody gun crew have copped it.' There was decking and crap flying everywhere, you know. But next thing they popped themselves up over the gun shield and Jesus, they were off like a bloody rocket.

The ship caught fire. The whole of the steering gear was blown out and the fire was all round the ammunition locker, so the captain gave the orders to abandon ship, or get up to the lifeboats. The only thing we had with us was a little corvette, but they were always in charge, the navy. He came alongside and said, 'No way.' He took all the survivors aboard and handed some hoses over. All the pumps were out; we were pouring buckets of water. Well, they fought the fire for several hours and eventually got it out.

Several other bombs fell close to the ship during the attack.

Te Awa, aged 22, was killed on 29 February 1944 when the MV Palma *was sunk by* U-183 *in the Indian Ocean.*

Then we set sail from there. We brought beef back. We arrived back in England, in Avonmouth, on the 8th of December 1943—cold as a frog's tit! The next day when we were signing off this guy stamped a 'V' on my card, and he was doing it to them all. I said, 'What the hell's that for?' 'Oh,' he said, 'you've volunteered for the invasion of France.' I said, 'Like bloody hell I have! You get it off.' He said, 'No, too late.'

Anyhow, we left there and went to New York. We went way up towards Reykjavik and then down. In New York we loaded up with ammunition, aviation spirit, planes strapped to the deck, and we set sail for Australia. We went to Sydney and unloaded there, and unloaded the rest in Melbourne. I went ashore one afternoon with a South African guy and a Bristolian guy, and got on the tiles. We got into a black-market restaurant, got into the booze, and these young sheilas said, 'Would you like a bottle of whisky?' 'Oh yes.' They ordered a taxi and we went out to St Kilda and bought a bottle of King George IV whisky for £5. Then we came back into Melbourne, and we were up in the park trying to drink this stuff out of the bottle. So I said to this Bristolian, 'Oh bugger, let's go down to a milk bar and get a glass.' We left these sheilas with the South African guy, and when we got back he's out the bloody monk [unconscious], the bottle of whisky's gone and his wallet's gone.

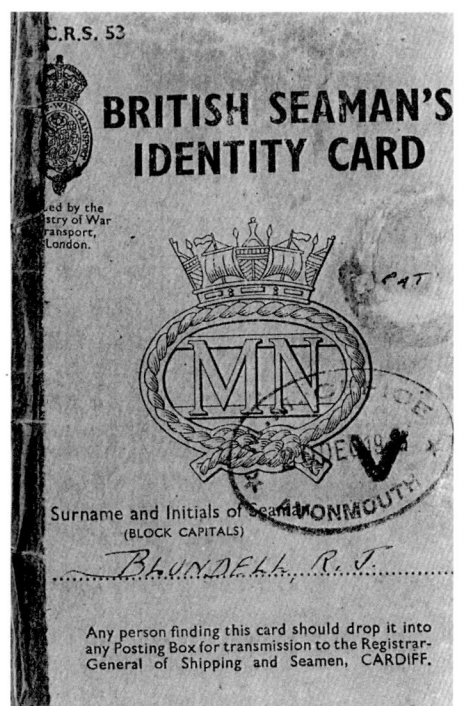

Then we came back to New Zealand. We arrived on St Patrick's Day [1944] in Wellington, and down at the wharf was the *Pamir*. So

Left: *The cover of Jim's British Seaman's Identity Card, with the red 'V' stamp added at Avonmouth in December 1943.* Blundell collection
Opposite: *Jim's brother John Blundell was one of over a hundred young New Zealanders who had the rare experience of working on a big square-rigged sailing ship during the war years. Seized in prize from its Finnish owners in Wellington in 1941, the four-masted barque* Pamir *made ten voyages under the New Zealand ensign between 1942 and 1948; this photograph was taken in Wellington in 1947.* Alexander Turnbull Library, Owen Collection, F-25572-1/2

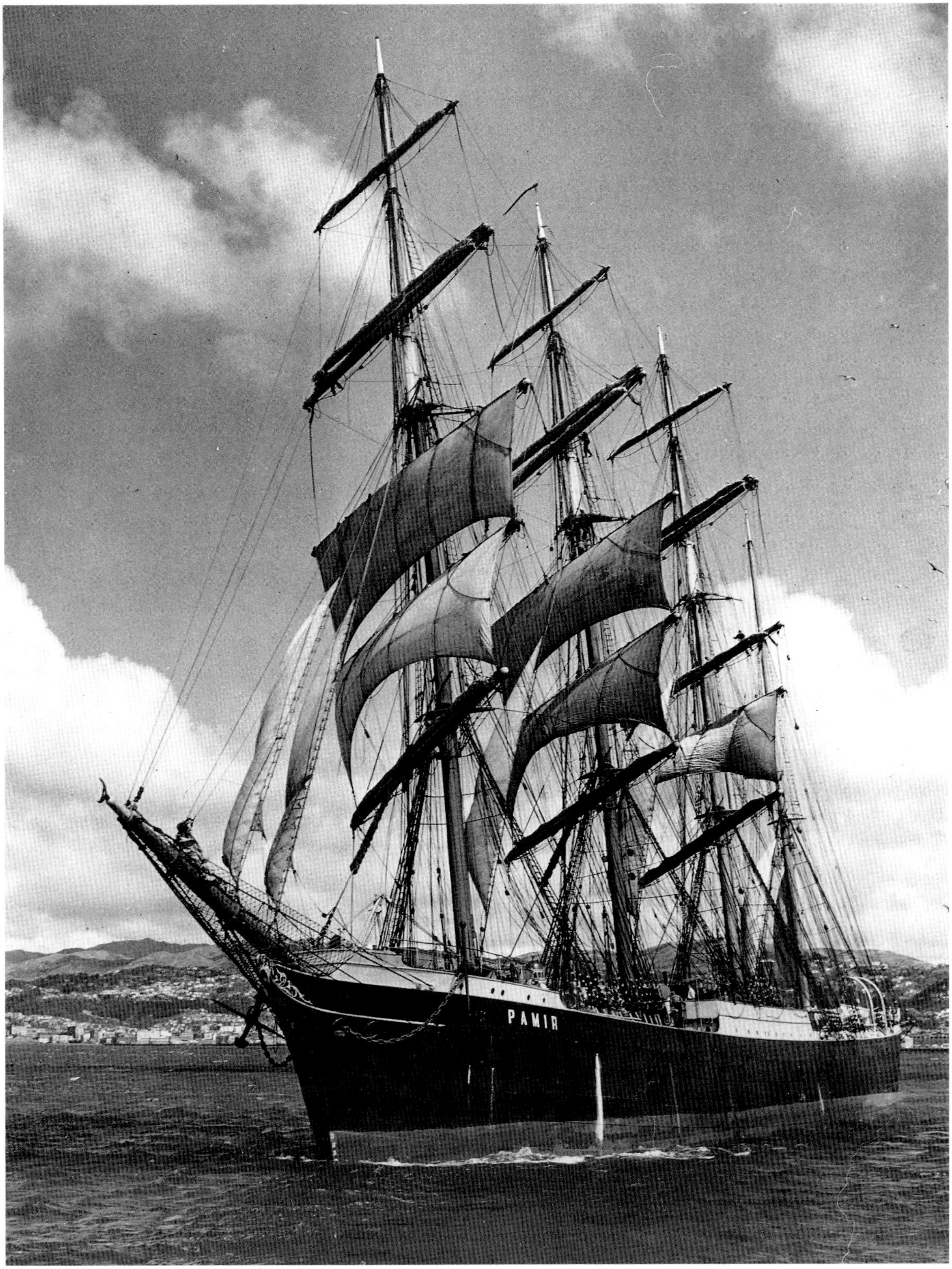
PAMIR

I went down there, and I could see my brother right up [the mast] in the royals. He spotted me and he was down before I had time to get my feet on the gangway. They were used to that, you see. When I saw the hands on him, and arms, that he had developed in that short time . . . He was only about 16. I think [he got on the *Pamir*] through my father; he had those connections, he knew all the old sea dogs.

> *Jim's brother John was a deck boy and later OS on the* Pamir*'s third and fourth voyages under the New Zealand ensign, to San Francisco in 1943–44.*

I went off back to England, and in the London docks these blasted customs officers came aboard. In your cabin you might have a whisky bottle or gin, and we used to let them help themselves, and then you'd say, 'Here's a packet of cigarettes', and they'd just mark your bag. But we had an engineer who was a miserable mean bastard, and he stuffed it up for the lot of us, and they went through the ship. I used to take a lot of cigarettes ashore. I never sold them, but I'd be in a pub and say, 'Here, here's a pack', you know. So they did the ship over, and my fine was either £19 17s 6d or £17 19s 6d, I forget, but it was a lot of money in those days. Well, that buggered me.

In London in those days, how would you say, it was an eye-opener to me. In the parks you'd be lying on the grass here and somebody would be [having sex] nearby—it was open slather. That was in the summer months. Oh, it left nothing to the imagination, you know? That was foreign to me.

Leave was great in England at that time. There was a great camaraderie amongst the public of Britain. All we had was a little Merchant Navy badge, but that opened the doors to everything. They'd do anything. We didn't need a uniform, just that little silver badge. But when I was on English ships, we'd arrive in a [foreign] port and they'd think I was a Pom—and they hated the English. I said, 'No way, me Nueva Zelandia', and I had a little map with me, 'I come from here, not up there.' And they'd open up—and that was in French West Africa, in South American countries. In America they were pretty good to us but they used to call us, 'You goddam cocksucking Limey'.

Anyhow, on this Saturday we came onto the London docks, and behind us the gates were closed. I was going to a ball with a sheila and they said, 'There's no going ashore. You're in here and you're staying in here.' This was the start of getting ready for D-Day. There were invasion barges along the docks and we went out with them, and then they went to holding paddocks or whatever and we went north. We came out to New Zealand light-ship and with enough sand to put on Oriental Bay as ballast.

Jim's United States fireman's certificate. Blundell collection

I decided then, well, enough's enough. So I came ashore and then went with the Yankee crowd in the Pacific, the United Fruit Company, which was under the Panamanian flag. I was on the *Platano*, which is supposed to mean 'big banana'. They were banana ships. We supplied the units of their 5th and 7th Fleets—you could be sent to the Philippines or anywhere—and also their Superfortress bases at Guam, which was very small, and Tinian, which was the big one. We used to dump off stuff there. I remember the gear was good, the food was good. I thought [the food] was pretty good on the English ship, but on the Yankee ships it was eggs sunny side up, maple syrup and pancakes, you know. You got bonuses with the Yanks, and they paid very freely. The American ships were dry ships, but you'd get cigarettes and all that.

What was your rank by this time?
On the American ship I was a wiper and then a fireman. Then I became third fridge engineer—that was good, you had your own cabin and all that. We had 13 nationalities on it: Hondurans, Nicaraguans,

An unidentified seaman celebrates VJ Day with a cigarette and beer in Wellington. While events in the capital were fairly orderly, VJ Day in Auckland was, as Jim recalls, marred by drunkenness and vandalism. Alexander Turnbull Library, John Pascoe Collection, F-1824-1/4

Guatemalans, Mexicanos, Americans, a German cook. The United Fruit Company had all their interests down in these countries. If I was on watch, they'd call me onto the earphones in the engine room, and they'd ring down and say so many revs and I'd have to tell the Spanish engineer. I spoke a bit of Spanish, enough for him to know what it was about.

Different ships, the Yanks. On English ships, the captain's word was law. There'd be a notice put up, say [ordering you to] wear or take your lifejacket for the next 48 hours. If you didn't have it, you were logged. No question. They never got up and spoke to the crew, that's all it was, a notice in the mess or wherever. So I went away with this American lot. I remember I'd come off duty, must have been eight o'clock in the morning, had my breakfast, and the next thing, 'Action Stations'. We were leaving the Philippines for America, and here's the captain: 'Now, we're going on our own. I don't know the chances . . . Now I'll hand you over to the gunnery officer.' 'Every guy's got to be prepared . . .' You know, all this bullshit, instead of on the Pommie ships, you do it or else. I was quite amazed when we got to Frisco, there were a couple of navy guys that'd been playing up and they came out to pick them up. I said to an American gunner, 'Oh shit, their discipline will be nothing to what the Poms get.' He said, 'Don't you believe it, they'll be broken within a few hours.'

But the chief engineer and the skipper hated Poms, and I actually blotted my copybook. I can remember in the dining room getting up from the table and saying, 'I'm sick to death of listening to this crap. You bastards never bothered to come in till it was all over in the first war and you only come in this one because you were forced into it.' That stuffed me!

Do you remember VE Day or VJ Day?
I was up in the Admiralty Islands at a place called Manus Island when VE Day arrived. I can't remember any celebrations. Well, there wouldn't have been because there was no grog on the ship. The hospital ship, the *Maunganui*, she was lying there.

As for VJ Day, we actually had arrived the night before in Auckland. Well, the whole city went bloody mad. The following morning it was reputed that they swept up five ton of broken bottles. They went nuts. I had a cousin who was in the navy—he fell off a tram and nearly killed himself, pissed. My wife, who was then my girlfriend, came up. We went ashore in the afternoon. Christ, they were rooting in the bloody house bar, they were rooting in . . . Oh, it was all on. They had the churches open in the afternoon for thanksgiving or whatever, and I believe a lot of people who came out, parents who had lost sons, they were disgusted, they were really upset over it.

Declining offers from the United Fruit Company to stay at sea or work on one of their plantations, Jim returned to Napier and married in January 1946, shortly before his 22nd birthday. The transition to peacetime life, however, would not be easy.

I came home and I thought I knew it all—been there, done that. And I ended up in Hanmer [Springs hospital] with post-traumatic stress. I was there five months, I think. I was only married a few weeks and I had one of these bouts. My mother, having been a trained nurse, called the doctor. He came up and said, 'He's had a bad heart attack.' You have all those symptoms. They tested me and said it was anxiety neurosis. I deteriorated and went down, down, down, and in the end I had to go [to Hanmer]. I was a cot case—by the time I got there I was down to seven stone—and all that stuff that goes with traumatic stress, you know, crying. I was like a bloody travelling pharmacy. I would never wish it on anyone. They were still treating guys from the First World War when I was there.

I still get the odd flashback, just something will trigger it and I've got to seek help, and that's what I would tell anybody to do. I was ashamed of myself, I really was. You can't do anything. You think, oh, I'll get up tomorrow, and you're still the bloody same. I would never wish anybody to go through it, because it's hell.

After recovering, Jim worked for many years for the Hawke's Bay County Council and was active in the Local Government Officers' Union and the Napier RSA. He and his wife Pat had seven children.

I always wanted to go back to sea. I kept up my union fees, but thank God in the end I never did, because I think I ended up better off working for the County Council. I had two brothers at sea: John stayed at sea most of his life and got his master mariner's tickets; the youngest one was an engineer at sea. I would love the young lads of today to be able to go down to the shipping office and sign on. But those days are gone.

I still love the sea. The rougher it is the more I love it. It's in you. That's what I can't understand: none of my boys wanted to go and none of my brothers' boys wanted to go. Strange. Yet we'd been brought up in that environment at home. To me, it builds character. You don't know the world until you've been in it. But they were happy days, the happiest days of my life. Yeah, they were. And let it be known, none of this was for God, King and Country. It was for sheer adventurism, nothing more than that. Those things were just adventures, real true adventures.

INDEX

Ships' names are given in italics; numbers in bold refer to illustrations

Abadan   82, 83, 84, 230
Absence without leave   49, 136, 139
Achilles, HMNZS   130, 184
Accommodation   **47**, 48-9, **61**, 103, 115, 134, 157, 161, 168, 209, 225-6
Aden   63, 158, 237
Admiral Graf Spee   35, 184, **185**, 196-7
Aikoku Maru   93
Albert Medal   122, 124
Aldington Court   218
Anatina   231, **231**
Anemone, HMS   148
Anzio landings   150
Aorangi   25, 28, **197**, 198
Aquitania   25, **70-1**, 72-6, **74**, 79, **136**
Archangel   36, 191
Athenia   34
Auckland   22, 29, 77, 80, 103, 104, 105, 222-4, 263-4
Awarua   235
Awatea   **24**, 25, 28, 33, 41, 45, 49, 67, 89-90, 103-11, **104**, **106**, 156-7

Battle of the Atlantic   24, 33-9, 78, 132-3, 147-8
Battle of Britain   197
Blackouts   30, 45, 84, 124, 134-5
Blue Star Line   25, 119, 144, 209
Bluff   144, 235
Bombay   75, 108, 135, 208

Boxing   149-50, 153
Bramham, HMS   **118**, 120
Brazil   138-9
British Promise   191
Brothels   50, 114, 138-9, 230
Buenos Aires   68, 139, 184, 201, 257

Canadian Star   38, 144-8, **145**
Canadian-Australasian Line   25, 28, 181, 196
Cape Town   108, 198, 209
Cardiff   62, 67, 133, 176, 197, 253
Carola   48, 223-6, **223**
Casablanca   175, 256
Centaur   **163**
Changi jail   42, 93, **214**, 215-16
Charlotte Schliemann   212
Chatham Is   30, 130, 246
Clothing   23, **59**, **61**, 69, 79, 94, 111, 213, 226, 239
Colombo   63, 73, 237, 239, 242
Conference Lines   25-6
Convoys   **20-1**, 22, 33, **34**, 36-8, 58, 78, 110, 115, 118, 124, 131-2, 147, 161, 169, 189-90, 191, 209
Cornish City   49, 182
Cunard White Star Line   74, 77
Customs   83, 260

D-Day   39, **178-9**, **186**, 187-9, 200, 260
Degaussing   31, 238
DEMS   31-2, 63, 83, 93, 105, 110, 119, 145, 158, 160, 169, 191, 198, 225, 254

Desertion   26, 49, 80, 130, 218
Deucalion   **118**, 118-20
Dolius   115
Dönitz, Admiral Karl   34, 36, 38
Dorset   **112-13**, 119, 121
Drinking   49-50, 75, 137, 160, 191, 226, 228, 239, 254, 256, 257, 258
Duchess of Bedford   **207**, 207-09
Dunedin   83, 130, 141, 218-19, 234
Dunkirk   197
Durban   22, 108, 198, 238, 239

Eagle, HMS   119-20
Emirau Is   30, 41
Empire Austen   218
Empire Beresford   135
Empire Bittern   168
Empire MacKendrick   152
Empire Trader   78

Falconer, Bill   **87**, 95
Federal Steam Navigation Co.   25, 56, 198
Fiji   85, 92, 105, 182, 226
First World War   23, 57, 74, 88, 102, 193, 209, 234, 236, 251, 264
Food   49, 76, 79, 115, 116, 134, 192, 213, 214, 226, 256, 261
Football   140, 141
Fort Louisbourg   149
Fort Mumford   45
Fort Richelieu   172-4
Freetown   57, 68, 124
Fremantle   63, 76, 192, 237, 242

Index

Gambia, HMNZS 84, 96, **97**
George Cross 124
Gibson, Perla Siedle 238
Glasgow 67, 68, 108, 110, 111, 114, 118, 183, 187, 240-1
Gloucester Castle 42, 209-10, 218, 219
Guam 261

Haifa 63, 158, 160-1
Halifax (Nova Scotia) 58, 64, 66-7, 110, 131, 197-8
Hamburg 56, 152
Hauraki 32, 42, **91**, 92-4, 96
Hawaii 76
Hokuku Maru 32, 93
Holmwood 30, 41
Homosexuals 137
Hong Kong 75, 106, 157
Hospital ships 28, 39, 98, 135, **163**, 172, 187-9, 198-200, **201**, **232-3**, 236-43, **241**
Houghton, Wattie 239

Île de France 135-7, **136**
Inanda 196

Kalingo 32, **44**, 45
Kamaishi 96-7
Kartigi 246
Kent 56, 57
Kiel **174**, 175-6
Kippenberger, Major-General H. K. 199, **200**, 201
Komata 30, 41
Komet 29, 35

Lady Connaught 187-9
Lech 206
Liberty ships 25, 26, 39, 135, 172, 189-90, 201
Lifesaving equipment **29**, 45, **59**, 65, 107, 111, 115, 116-17, **117**, **142-3**, 147-8, 161, 254

Limerick 32, 78, 157-62, **158**, **159**
Liverpool 62, 104, 107, 138, 145, 166, 190, 206-09, 218
Llandovery Castle 198-201, **201**
Lloyd's War Medal 122, 124
London 56, 58, 61, 127, 133, 139, 141, 197, 201-3, 245-6, 260
Luxford, Nola 137, **138**
Lyttelton 83, 98, 99, 166, 218

Maheno 88
Makura 103
Malta 36-7, 118-22, **121**
Manus Is. 243, 263
Maori 99
Marnix van St Aldegonde **109**, 111
Martin, Captain Bill 157
Mataroa 103, 104
Matson Line 89
Matua 28, **31**
Maui Pomare 111
Maunganui 25, 28, 50, 102, **232-3**, 236-43, **241**, 245-6, **247**, 263
Melbourne 78, 230, 243, 258
Mentor 116-17
Merchant Navy:
  age structure 22, 23, 41, 42-3, 72, 85, 206
  badge 23, **23**, 260
  casualties 23, 30, 34, 38, 40-2, 45, 127, 148, 209
  name 22-3
  propaganda **30**, 48
  reputation of 49-50, 139, 219, 245
Merchant Navy Reserve Pool 46-7, 76, 135, 141, 145, 183-4, 209
Michel 209-11
Middlesex 198
Molotovsk 36, 191
Mombasa 238
Monowai 28, 105, 216-18, **217**

Montana 230, 231
Montevideo 68, 184, 257
Montreal 46, 76, 152
Morgan, Captain George **109**, 111
Mozambique 38, 83, 184, 186
Murihiku 235
Murmansk 36-7, 135, 169-71

Napier 222, 231, 250-1, 257, 264
Naples 172, 199
Narbada 32, 99, 184
Nauru Is. 30, 105
New Caledonia 226, 227
New Guinea 75, 84, 224, 229
New Orleans 116
New York 46, 68, 78, 136, 137, 183, 201, 258
New Zealand Shipping Co. 25, 29, 56, 68, 78, 119, 196
Newcastle (NSW) 163, 180
Niagara 25, 29, 157, 180, **181**, 193
Norwegian merchant marine 36, 41, 223-31
Nurses 98, 189, 238-9

Ocean Faith 149-50, 152
Ocean Gypsy 169
Ohio (I) 121-2
Ohio (II) 226-7
Operation Pedestal 37, **112-13**, **118**, 118-22
Operation Torch 28, 36, 67, **100-01**, 110-11
Orari 67, 68, 69
Orion 29, 32, 35

Pamir 28, 258-60, **259**
Panama Canal 58, 64, 84, 130, 218
Pets 29, 63, 65-6, 67, 111, 149, 229
Philippines 98, 105, 157, 243, 245
Pitcairn Is. 58

Platano 261
Pool *see* Merchant Navy Reserve Pool
Port Chalmers 88, 99, 144, 184, 218, 234-5, 246
Port Fairy 251-60, **252**
Port Hunter 22, 41
Port Line 25, 89, 119, 252
Port Melbourne **183**, 184
Port Tewfik 63, 74, 75, 158, **160**, 208, 237-9, 242
Prince of Wales, HMS 75, 94, 213
Prisoners of war:
    Allied 28, 94-6, 213, 215, 245
    Axis 75, 208, 209, 238
    merchant seafarers 30, 32, 40-2, **86-7**, **92**, 93-9, 210-16
Puriri, HMS 32

Queen Elizabeth 135
Queen Mary 228

Rangatira (I) 28, 99, 182, 193
Rangatira (II) 99
Rangitane 25, 30, 41
Rangitata 25, 103, 177, 198
Rangitiki 25, 67-8, **68**, 69, 104
Raranga 49, 130-5, **131**
Rarotonga 102, 157
Red Sea 63, 74, 158, 160, 198, 238, 242
Remuera 57-60, 61, 102
Repulse, HMS 75, 94, 213
Rimutaka 62, 196, 198, 200
River Plate 68, 184, 197
Royal (NZ) Air Force 33, 85, 105
Royal (NZ) Navy 28, 32, 33, 34, 37, 72, 105, 106, 114, 162, 169, 216, 254-5

Ruahine 56, 78-80, 198

Salerno landings 199
Samavon 135
Saminver 218
San Francisco 28, 76, 102, 103, 157, 226, 229, 260
San Pedro (Los Angeles) 80, 84, 226, 229
Scharnhorst 37, 169
Schenectady 80-4
Seasickness 88, 133, 235, 237
Shaw Savill & Albion 25, 103, 104, 119
Sicily, invasion of 199
Singapore 42, 75, 76, 93, 106, 115, 198, 208, 212-18, 219
Smallpox 41, 108, 241-3
Southern France, invasion of 152, 173
Stewardesses 51 n.1
Submarines:
    Allied 83
    German 22, 24, 33-9, **38**, 45, 64-5, 83, 107, 116, 132, 147, 148, 190, 191, 258
    Japanese 32, 45, 161
Suez Canal 63, 158, 240
Sydney 75, 78, 90, 93, 103, **104**, 105, 163
Sydney, HMAS 75, 105

Tahiti 102, 157, 218, 245
Tamatea 235-6
Tanea 125, **126**, 231
Te Aroha 72, **73**, 78
Themistocles 48, 166-8, **167**
Tinian 261
Turakina 29-30, 32

U-boats *see* Submarines, German
Ulithi Atoll 84, **85**

ULTRA intelligence 33, 36, 38
Uniforms *see* Clothing
Union Steam Ship Co. 25, 28, 30, 32, 88, 99, 103, 111, 125, 127, 157, 163, 184, 218, 231, 234, 236
Unions 49, 72, 156, 264
United Fruit Co. 152, 261, 263
United States merchant marine 36, 46, 80-2, 261, 263
United States Navy 36, 84, **85**, 96, 226-7

Vancouver 28, 29, 92, 105, 106, 218
VE Day 139, 201, **202**, **203**, 230, 263
Victory Parade (1946) **244**, 245-6
VJ Day 139, 152, **262**, 263-4

Wages 46, 76, 82, 102, 103, 114, 144, 225, 236
Wahine 28, 90, 99, 111
Waikouaiti 90, **91**
Waimarama **37**, 119, 121
Waipawa 141
Waipori 163, 246
Wairangi 119, 121
Waiwera 140
Wellington **10-11**, 64, **70-1**, 72-3, 77, **77**, 80, 83, 102, 103, 105, 111, 125, 163, 182, 192, 242-3, 246
Westmoreland **62**, 63-6
Working conditions 46, **64**, 79, 82, 88-9, 103, 115, 133-4, 157, 166-7, **171**, 198, 238-40

Yachting 243, 245, 246
Yokohama 93, 94-6

'A Unique Sort of Battle'

Edited by Megan Hutching

Of all the Second World War battles in which New Zealand troops fought, the Battle of Crete was perhaps the most dramatic. For 12 days in May 1941, a mixed force of New Zealand, Australian, British and Greek soldiers tried desperately to prevent the island falling to the Germans, who invaded in spectacular fashion, parachuting in on the morning of 20 May. The defenders were hopelessly outnumbered and had little in the way of arms or munitions, having abandoned most of their weapons during the retreat from Greece. When the authorities finally realised the island was going to fall, they ordered the evacuation of thousands of soldiers. For many, this was the beginning of another battle — for survival.

'*A Unique Sort of Battle*' contains the stories of 15 New Zealanders, who describe in their own words their experiences on Crete. Many recall the chilling sight of German paratroopers dropping from the sky, the scream of the dive-bombing Stukas, and the loss of life on both sides. The soldiers recount the treacherous trek through the mountains once orders to abandon the island were issued, a gruelling journey with little food, water or shelter. Those fortunate enough to be evacuated recall the relief of getting on to a ship, while a seaman involved in the rescue operation tells of the nerve-wracking run through Bomb Alley. The men who remained on the island recount their struggle to stay hidden in the hills, the support of the Cretan people and their experiences as prisoners of war.

Together with Ian McGibbon's insightful overview of the battle, these personal stories offer a unique perspective. They stand testament to the bravery and sacrifice of all New Zealanders who have fought for their country.

HarperCollinsPublishers

Inside Stories

Edited by Megan Hutching

The Second World War saw over 8000 New Zealand military personnel — one in 200 of the country's population at the time — incarcerated by enemy forces. The prisoners were captured mainly by the Germans and Italians, though some were held by the Japanese. Far from being safe, prisoners of war had to endure privations nearly as demanding as those they faced when engaged in active fighting.

In *Inside Stories* 16 POWs recall their experiences behind the barbed wire of enemy compounds. Many tell of their shock and disbelief at being taken prisoner, and their fear of violent action by their captors. Once interned, thoughts generally turned to the possibility of escape, and a number of men featured describe their bids for freedom. For most POWs, the days would drag interminably. Concert parties, lectures, card games and sports all helped pass the time, and in some cases diverted the guards' attention from escape activities. As the war drew to a close, the challenges facing POWs increased, and several soldiers tell of forced marches under the charge of jittery guards, as prisoners were moved away from approaching Allied troops. Lack of food and bitterly cold conditions pressed many POWs to the limits of their resolve.

Together with Ian McGibbon's astute overview of the POW's role in the Second World War, these personal stories preserve a sometimes forgotten aspect of this global conflict. They stand testament to the courage of all who faced the war from behind enemy lines.

**HarperCollins*Publishers*

A Fair Sort of Battering

Edited by Megan Hutching

In *A Fair Sort of Battering*, 13 New Zealanders tell of their experiences and reactions in the Italian campaign of World War Two. Day-to-day life and major historical events are described from the perspective of members of the army, including the Maori Battalion, engineers, artillery, nurses and Tuis, as well as pilots and sailors. Roberto Rabel's introduction provides a fascinating overview of New Zealand's participation in this hard-fought campaign.

In October 1943 the New Zealand Division landed in Italy, and by 14 November the troops had entered the line and engaged the enemy at the Sangro River. They had come straight from the harsh deserts and searing heat of North Africa, only to find themselves fighting a very different war. Beset by snow, sleet and mountainous terrain, the Division fought its way up the east coast of Italy before crossing the Apennines, where the advance came to a halt at Cassino. Three hard-fought battles then took place. Over the next few months the New Zealanders suffered heavy casualties in vicious street fighting amongst the ruins of the town. After Cassino, they continued up Italy to reach Trieste in April 1945. *A Fair Sort of Battering* tells the story of this campaign in the words of those who experienced the battles, the cold of winter and the heat of summer, the loss of friends, and the warmth of the Italian people.

**HarperCollins*Publishers*

The Desert Road

Edited by Megan Hutching

Neutral Egypt was never meant to be a New Zealand battlefield. Kiwi troops arrived expecting a short stay before continuing to France. Mussolini had other ideas.

For the New Zealanders, the campaign became their longest and most important land engagement of the war.

Fought amidst swirling sandstorms, torrid temperatures and debilitating diseases, the North African campaign tested the resolve of soldiers and medics alike. The Kiwis were in a foreign landscape — whether sheltering in a slit trench or perching on a rocky outcrop scanning the horizon. Rommel's bold tactics and British incompetence made life even more difficult.

Nearly 3000 New Zealanders who helped defeat Axis troops did not survive to tell the tale. *The Desert Road* features 16 men and women who did return. Their words reflect the fear and bravery, courage and compassion, humour and sadness that characterised the Second World War.

HarperCollinsPublishers